11.05

Teddy's - pickup for Sean
Online

Gavrick 011-61-7-40...2

IS IT YOU OR IS IT ME?

SCOTT WETZLER, PH.D., WITH DIANE COLE

Is it you *or* is it me?

How We Turn Our
Emotions Inside Out and
Blame Each Other

HarperCollins*Publishers*

HarperCollins books may be purchased for educational, business, or sales promotional use. For information please write: Special Markets Department, HarperCollins Publishers, Inc., 10 East 53rd Street, New York, NY 10022.

FIRST EDITION

Designed by Elina Nudelman

Library of Congress Cataloging-in-Publication Data

Wetzler, Scott, 1955–
  Is it you or is it me : how we turn our emotions inside out and blame each other / by Scott Wetzler, Ph.D., with Diane Cole. — 1st ed.
    p. cm.
  Includes index.
  ISBN 0-06-018743-3
  1. Emotions. 2. Blame. 3. Man-woman relationships. I. Cole, Diane.
 II. Title.
  BF561.W48 1998
  152.4—dc21   98-11875

98 99 00 01 02 ❖/RRD 10 9 8 7 6 5 4 3 2 1

Contents

Contents

Acknowledgments

What started as random observations noted during therapy sessions has culminated in this book. It's been a thrilling process for me, and I've had much assistance and guidance along the way. I want particularly to acknowledge the efforts of Diane Cole, a talented writer, who has helped me to express many sophisticated psychological ideas with clarity, eloquence, and energy that I hope make this book accessible to all readers. I also want to thank Gail Winston, the editor who shaped the manuscript, and Joelle Delbourgo, a publisher who "got it" from the outset. As always, Pam Bernstein represents me with great professionalism, but, more important, she is one of my most fervent cheerleaders. I appreciate all she's done.

The individuals whose stories are told here also made an important contribution. I've been in practice for nearly fifteen years, and over that time I have seen many patients. I want this book to be as authentic as possible, but in the interests of confidentiality, I alter many details in order to disguise their identities.

The Department of Psychiatry at Montefiore Medical Center and the Albert Einstein College of Medicine has been my home base for my entire professional career. I cannot imagine a more supportive or enriching environment, and I have benefited enormously from the interaction with my colleagues there.

Acknowledgments

The two people who are most deserving of acknowledgment are my wife, Graciela, and my son, Joshua. My love for you is boundless. This book is dedicated to you both.

—Scott Wetzler, Ph.D.

Thanks to Scott Wetzler, a gifted psychologist who generously gave me what I came to think of as an honorary Ph.D. in psychology in the course of writing this book. Thanks to my hard-working agent, Lynn Seligman; to editors Gail Winston and Joelle Delbourgo; to Sandee Brawarsky, who introduced me to Scott, and to my good friends Roberta Israeloff and Jean Mizutani. Most of all, thanks to my husband, Peter Baida, and our son, Edward, whose love and understanding make everything worthwhile.

—Diane Cole

Introduction
Is It You or Is It Me?
Why We Blame Each Other

As a psychologist, I see many patients troubled by love and confused about what they feel. I'm struck by how frequently I hear several key questions: Why isn't my spouse or partner giving me the validation or support I expect and need? Why does it seem that my partner is not on my side? Why do we fight so much about who's right and who's wrong? Why do we see things so differently? Why do I feel hurt, frustrated, and embattled so much of the time?

An increasingly wary, secretive, and combative atmosphere has come to cloud too many romantic relationships today. The individuals and couples I treat feel so bruised and vulnerable that they are oversensitive to the normal pulls and pushes of relationships, especially intimate ones. They blame their partners that they feel bad; then, leery of being hurt further, they lash out or close themselves off. Their thin skin becomes ever thinner, their edges ever sharper.

The deeper I delve into my patients' emotions, the clearer it becomes that these conflicts go beyond what we think of as commonplace fears of intimacy or commitment. The disagreements that consume these couples are over more than priorities (he wants this and she wants that). Nor can the differences in how men and women communicate wholly explain what I'm seeing in my consulting room.

No, after listening intently to many patients, I believe that what I've been seeing is the emergence of a special pathology in which romantic conflicts stem from a fundamental disagreement and confusion over who's doing what to whom. It's not merely that my patients have different emotional reactions or attitudes; it's that they can't even agree on what's going on between them.

I call the dynamic whereby we attribute our internal psychological frailties to the external world and see others as the cause of our pain an *inside-out dynamic*. Unable to tolerate uncomfortable emotions—whether anger, anxiety, frustration, disappointment, or self-doubt—we hold others responsible for them. We look outward rather than inward for an explanation of why we feel the way we do. We disown our feelings; at the very least, we fail to acknowledge the role our own personalities and behaviors play in generating and perpetuating those feelings.

This is the reason so many of us are perplexed by what goes on in relationships. We can't agree about who and what are responsible for our emotional reactions. We accuse our partners of making us feel bad (angry, anxious, insecure, whatever). We tell them that *they're* angry, not us. They in turn tell us: It's just the opposite; *you're* the one who is angry, not me. No wonder that when we fight, each person feels that his or her partner started it. Even worse, we can't even agree on what the fight is about.

Without any consensus about these basic issues, we begin to ask, in genuine confusion: *Is it you or is it me? Is it your problem, or is it my problem? Whose fault is it? Which one of us is crazy (or lying)?*

I'm not a believer in the collective unconscious or in psychoanalyzing an entire era. Nevertheless, I feel that it is no accident that certain psychological issues come to the fore at certain times in history. For example, Freud's description of hysteria among women emerged at a time when Victorian culture decreed that female sexuality should be denied and repressed, a condition that led to the hysterical symptoms Freud noted. Similarly, the term *passive-aggressive* (the subject of my previous book) was coined by military psychiatrists during World War II to refer to soldiers who were unable to assert themselves within the command structure, and as a result asserted themselves indirectly by failing to carry out orders (this explains why passive-aggressive behavior is pervasive in large bureaucracies and among men who perceive the women in their lives as authority figures).

More recently, in the countercultural 1960s, Erik Erikson introduced the concept of the *identity crisis* to refer to adolescents of the baby boom generation who were trying to figure out who they were. And in the hedonistic 1980s, Christopher Lasch captured the egotism of the era by coining the phrase "the culture of narcissism."

That brings us to the 1990s, and the emergence of the inside-out dynamic.

Why are we more reluctant than ever to take responsibility for our emotions? Why has externalizing blame become so prevalent today? Why have we turned our lovers into adversaries, our romantic partners into enemies? Why do we seem to be more confused than ever?

To clarify: I don't believe that my patients are any more raw and vulnerable than people of any other generation. Nor do they have any greater difficulty with intimacy. Romantic relationships always have and always will entail opening ourselves up. When we get involved, we become vulnerable, sensitive, dependent. As others begin to matter to us, they elicit and arouse in us a whole host of emotional reactions. There is sure to be anger, anxiety, and insecurity, just as surely as there is love, elation, and fulfillment. Disappointment, uncertainty, and ambivalence will also be a part of the equation, because that too is human nature. These reactions are as inevitable today as they always were.

What distinguishes the 1990s is a change in attitude about these emotional reactions. We seem to believe that we should not allow ourselves to feel vulnerable. We are cynical, hard-edged, skeptical of the possibility that romantic relationships can and will cater to our needs. Popular culture tells us to be self-reliant and autonomous: Don't depend on anyone; it's too risky. We seem to expect to be disappointed. By lowering our expectations, we try to prepare for the worst so as never to be caught off guard.

Our emotional rawness is a natural by-product of developing intimacy, but if we fail to understand this, we become confused when our feelings of vulnerability emerge. Not understanding these feelings, we feel threatened by them. And when we feel threatened, we become defensive. We become angry. But who should be the focus of our anger? Still confused and not understanding how and why we're responding this way, we blame others for the fact that we feel as we do.

As a therapist I ask the question "How and why is it our partner's fault that we feel afraid of rejection, disappointment, or ambivalence?" As I see it, this attitude reflects a basic misunderstanding about the uncomfortable emotions that inevitably accompany falling and being in love.

Many of us think that something must be wrong with the relationship (and, more specifically, our partner) when we start feeling vulnerable. Others come to view these confusing feelings as an avoidable feature of romantic entanglements, minor obstacles that we can easily step around. But that's not so.

With the advent of the sexual revolution, we mistakenly came to believe that greater sexual freedom would make building a relationship easier. But postrevolution, after we jump into bed with someone we are left with the same uncomfortable emotions as before: How much does the person care for me, and how much do I care for him? Should we go forward or should we pull back? We are just as needy, self-conscious, disappointed, and angry as ever. Sex doesn't make it any easier to create a meaningful intimate relationship; it may even make it harder.

Further contributing to our cynicism is the sky-high divorce rate. Too many of us witnessed our parents' divorce, an experience that made us understandably wary. We think, "Love can sour and turn ugly tomorrow. Why let ourselves go into a relationship that statistics tell us is likely to run aground?" Because virtually no stigma is associated with divorce now, we may prefer the easy exit of divorce, rather than take on the hard task of owning up to and working through the inevitable feelings of doubt, ambivalence, and disappointment that any serious relationship brings to the fore. It's much easier in the short run to blame others and walk away. But, as I'll show you, it is not a good long-term solution.

In business, of course, we've come to believe that lean-and-mean is the key to success. Unfortunately, this philosophy has come to be applied to many other aspects of life—such as romance—for which just the opposite approach is needed. According to the business model, our primary focus should be our own needs and looking out for number one. Catering to other people's needs is seen as a negative: we are "enabling" or being "codependent." The message is that we should not take care of others nor expect them to take care of us. Self-sufficiency is the order of the day.

Of course, economic advances for women as well as for men have given us a freedom we never had before, and we can all be self-sufficient in ways not previously possible. Economic autonomy is something to be proud of. But as a psychologist I believe we need to exercise that freedom by taking emotional risks, not guarding against them. The lesson to carry over from our work-world accomplishments should be a certain self-confidence in our ability to handle difficult situations, in whatever arena. The message we should absorb is: *We're more resilient than we give ourselves credit for, and better able to handle uncomfortable emotions than we think.*

Instead, our cynicism about love and overemphasis on self-reliance have contributed to a confusion about the very nature of mutuality in relationships. We struggle with our uncertainty: Are we partners on the same team? Or are we individuals competing over who's right and who's wrong, who's winning and who's losing, whose needs are being met and whose are not?

This is the lens through which many of my patients see their romantic relationships. Given this perspective, we may find it difficult, if not impossible, to tolerate the anxiety, vulnerability, anger, misgivings, and other uncomfortable feelings engendered by relationships. We mistakenly come to believe that if only our partners would change or would treat us differently, we would feel better, less vulnerable. Feeling bruised and blaming others for it, we may choose to lash out, make a futile and frustrating attempt to change our partners, or merely close ourselves off only to become locked in the prison of our own mistrust.

But the solution to our psychological problems can be found within us, not outside, in attempts to change those around us. We need to take ownership of our own psychological frailties. If we're too tender to the touch, that's our problem, not our partners'. *Just because we feel hurt doesn't mean that someone is out to hurt us. And just because we have suspicions does not mean that people are not trustworthy.*

When patients ask "Is it you or is it me?" they may truly be confused over their role as opposed to their partner's in the relationship's derailment. They recognize that something is "wrong," but they are not yet ready to acknowledge how their own vulnerability predisposes them to feel hurt. Casting blame is far easier.

This is the quandary so many of us find ourselves in: We're uncomfortable where we are and uncertain and fearful that another way will be any better. We may want to open ourselves up and connect with others, but we are petrified of the emotions that will be evoked.

We turn to the inside-out dynamic as a way to fend off hurt, but it does not protect us in the least. Instead, it actually perpetuates our sense of vulnerability and all the other uncomfortable emotions we're trying to deflect. We become mistrustful, combative, and defensive and damage the very relationships we seek to salvage and enjoy.

To allow love to flourish, we must acknowledge our bruises, our fragility, our disappointments and insecurities. Avoiding intimate relationships and the concomitant emotions is not the solution. Nor is venting our emotions. We must come to terms with them.

It's not easy. Learning to live with ourselves and love another is an achievement. But I have helped countless individuals and couples to make these connections, and I can help you, too.

For me, the key is threefold: Insight. Mastery. Tolerance. Gain *insight* into the attitudes, mind-sets, and preconceptions through which we see our partners. *Master* our emotions. And learn to *tolerate* (in ourselves, as well as in our partners) the frustrations, fears, and anxieties that intimacy arouses.

Personal growth means having enough insight to accept weaknesses, fears, and frustrations as our own, without blaming others for them. It means learning to tolerate the uncomfortable feelings that intimacy and romance arouse, whether these emotions are anxiety and anger, or ambivalence and disappointment; these emotions characterize every human relationship, and we must expect them. Finally, we need to become more resilient in the face of life's ups and downs, and thicker-skinned regarding everyday slights. As we learn to master our own emotions, we will also learn how to cope more effectively with the same emotions in our partners. And we'll discover that the better emotional self-control we can exercise, the less threatened we will be by other people's emotionality.

It is my deep belief that the only way to reconnect, repair, and

achieve love is to understand the major psychological mecha-
nisms that underlie love and the ways in which we unwittingly
fight against love. That is why the focus of this book will be how
and why we turn our emotions inside out. The more insight we
have into our emotional game playing, the better equipped we
will be to begin to change and heal our relationships, and the
deeper emotional maturity we will win for ourselves as individuals. It is not enough to follow some simple, albeit useful and
important, rules on how to talk with each other or how to resolve
arguments. We must first understand some basic psychological
principles.

In the chapters that follow I will help you understand that *our
relationships are reflections of our inner lives.* How we feel about
others, along with what we expect from them and what we are
willing to do for them, is a reflection of how we feel about ourselves, including what we need from others and what we have to
give them. Our anger and anxiety represent attitudes we have
about our own inner strength and self-esteem. If we feel weak
and emotionally fragile, we'll think that others are dangerous;
and if we're convinced we're unlovable, then we won't believe
that anyone could possibly love us. Once we achieve greater clarity about what we're doing and what our partner is doing, we'll be
able to answer the question "Is it you or is it me?"

In the chapters ahead, I explain how and why we fight, provoke, and prolong battles with our partners that, in reality, are
ongoing arguments with ourselves, arising from our own doubts,
fears, anxieties, discomforts, and frustrations. I describe how we
blame others for our own disappointments, and how uncomfortable we can be with dependency. I explore the differences
between men and women that all too often lead us into competitive, hostile relationships. I also delve into the shared fears
(including those related to sex) that make both men and women
feel vulnerable in relationships, and how these fears get twisted

around. I help you see the terrible, hurtful costs of blame and mis-trust—the bitter fights, broken relationships, and mutual recrimi-nations that make some marriages and divorces bloodier and more prolonged than a war.

To help you to heal and forgive, I give you the insight to go beyond past traumas and hurts and see your current relation-ships, not through the filter of the past, but as they really are. Most important of all, *I distinguish between the blame that really does exist "out there" and the causes that reside within.*

Ultimately, my goal is to help you to move forward to a new openness toward romance and toward life itself: to sort through the confusion, to let go of anger, to tolerate feelings of vulnerabil-ity, to forgive and perhaps even to forget. Once you have done that, you will be able to begin to trust and to love another. More than that, you will have learned how to love and to trust yourself. My hope is to inspire you to take the leap of faith that trust requires—but to do so in an open-eyed, realistic fashion.

The great writer E. M. Forster took as his motto "Only connect." My goal is to help you clarify your own emotions and relation-ships so that you will be able to connect, or reconnect, with a trustworthy and loving person in your life.

IS IT YOU OR IS IT ME?

1
How Did We Get So Confused?

The Psychological Dynamic That Turns Our
Emotions Inside Out

How does this inside-out dynamic work? How does it change our view of relationships? And why does it lead to so much confusion between people? The case of Nina, a woman who blamed others for her own vulnerability, provides a dramatic example. Nina saw herself as threatened by those closest to her. To defend herself she would attack them, but in attacking them, she was attacking a mirage, a projection of an enemy who actually existed within.

Imprisoned by Mistrust: Nina

From the moment Nina stepped into my office, I was struck by her intensity. Everything about her, from the dark, stylishly tailored suit she wore to the sharp, angular movements she used to punctuate her sentences, gave off an aura of edginess. She spoke quickly, without mincing words: She had just celebrated her fortieth birthday—alone—and with no romantic possibility on the horizon, she was convinced that she would always be alone.

"Why is that?" I asked, surprised. She was tall, trim, and attractive, and her long black hair was neatly pulled back to reveal a sculpted face with high cheekbones. Raising her dark eyebrows for emphasis as she spoke, she came across as a formidable woman with a highly competent professional presence. In her direct fashion, Nina told me she was uncomfortable revealing the personal concerns that had brought her to therapy. Indeed, as she sat tensely perched on the edge of my couch, unwilling to sit back, it was evident that she was extremely uncomfortable.

"I don't mean I'll never get another date," she stated matter-of-factly. "I meet guys all the time. Even if I do work long hours, I'm only one of a handful of women lawyers who negotiate the kind of deals I do. Getting a boyfriend isn't the problem. It's just that things never seem to work out." She paused, then added abruptly, "What else do you want to know?"

Her increasingly edgy tone, I thought, was less proud than defensive. But what was she defending herself against?

"Tell me about some of these relationships," I said.

Nina pursed her lips. In what I would learn was her typically analytical fashion, she reviewed the history of at least six different relationships, including her most recent affair, with Jack, which had ended in the last few weeks. Although the men were quite different in their personalities and eagerness to be involved with her and she had had varying levels of interest in them, I began to detect what I thought was a recurrent pattern. Just as she had not yet found a way to sit comfortably on the couch in my office, she had never found a level of comfort with any of these men.

In some cases, not "feeling right" in the relationship led her to keep things at an emotionally distant and superficial level. In other cases, she ignored her instincts and tried to "dive in," as she put it—with equally unsuccessful results. Regardless of her approach, she didn't know how to get "in sync" with the men in her life.

She continued, "Going to bed with someone doesn't make things any better. I feel just as self-conscious once we've had sex as I did before. I haven't found a man yet who can give me what I need or want in a relationship, and it makes me mad. If I keep my expectations low, at least I won't be disappointed."

It seemed odd that someone so attractive and so in command of her professional life would feel so hopeless about her personal life. The more Nina talked, the clearer the contrast became: Though she was outwardly strong and self-assured, she was inwardly vulnerable and oversensitive.

It struck me that when it came to romance, Nina viewed relationships through a glass darkly. By her own admission, she brought to the realm of romance a skeptical, cynical outlook. She was mistrustful, a mistrust that colored everything she saw. For instance, if someone she had just met asked her out, she jumped to the conclusion that all he wanted was to go to bed with her; but if someone showed sincere interest in her, she felt he was only trying to hook her in and set her up for disappointment. I wondered whether her mistrust was justified or whether she was blaming her partners for her own feelings of vulnerability. Were these men as malevolent and threatening as she portrayed them, or was she misreading the relationships? Was she truly just unlucky in her choice of men, or was she herself contributing to her romantic failures?

I asked her to describe her recently ended relationship with Jack in more detail.

Without hesitation Nina told me they had dated for several months, seeing each other primarily on Saturday nights because her work schedule prevented their getting together more frequently. Jack was a courtly man who enjoyed sending her flowers and liked to call her at her office just to say hello, even when she told him she was too busy to take personal calls. Although there were many clear indications of Jack's deepening interest, Nina seemed to prefer a slow pace.

Six months into the relationship, Nina was still not comfortable opening herself to Jack. She could not shake her awkward self-consciousness, fearing that showing certain sides of her personality would reveal too much. But Jack was clearly smitten, and when he broached the possibility of their moving in together, Nina became even more frightened. She liked Jack, but if he moved in, she was concerned that she would lose her sanctuary, the one place where she could escape from her self-consciousness.

I asked what specifically frightened her about the prospect of Jack's moving in.

"Well, you know, I can get pretty irritable," she said, "especially when things don't go well at work. I need my own space to decompress."

Yet when Jack first made his suggestion, she had answered him without mentioning at all her fears or her need for privacy. She did not tell him she felt self-conscious or discuss her desire to keep the pace slower. Instead, she accused Jack of trying to use her. She told him point-blank, "You're just a freeloader." As Nina saw it, all Jack wanted was a rent-free living arrangement; the flowers and phone calls merely had been ploys to make her fall for him. Jack couldn't be trusted.

In fact, Jack *had* been struggling financially to open his own consulting business and was having serious cash-flow problems. Putting two and two together, Nina deduced that his suggestion was a means for him to save thousands of dollars in rent. In her view, Jack was an exploitative, uncaring man, looking to take advantage of her. But this view didn't jibe with other things she had told me about Jack: that he was a sensitive, emotionally expressive person who truly seemed to be head over heels in love with her.

What accounts for this discrepancy? Instead of owning up to her own fears and self-consciousness, Nina had turned her feelings inside out and misread Jack's intentions. Feeling threatened and frightened, she had immediately assumed that Jack was dangerous and couldn't be trusted. Rather than examining the assumptions on which she based this conclusion, she blamed *him* for how *she* felt. If she had been able to take responsibility for how uncomfortable she felt, she would not have needed to turn the tables on him, lashing out with what I believe was an unfair accusation.

But Nina did not yet have the insight to realize what she had done.

Although her suspicions stung, Jack tried to be rational. "Sure I would save a few dollars. And if we split costs, as I assumed we would, so would you. But that's not the point," he said. "It's *you* I want to live with, not the four walls of your apartment."

Blinded by her fears, Nina could not be convinced. Jack had admitted he would save money, hadn't he? The seed of doubt had taken root. Her mother had always warned her about men who live off their women. And even though Nina had long since discounted much of what her mother told her, she could not shake the nagging echo of her mother's voice: "Men only want sex and money."

The more I listened, the more it seemed to me that Nina gave this relationship the same spin as she gave every other one: Jack would have taken advantage of her generosity if she let him; like all the others, he didn't really care about her.

But as I saw it, Nina's preconception that no man can be trusted had determined her perception of Jack far more than had Jack himself. Nina had discounted all the evidence that pointed to Jack's love for her. She ignored the fact that he could have found a smaller apartment on his own, or moved in with his sister, whose apartment was far larger than Nina's. When Jack tried to reassure her, all she heard was further evidence to bolster her preconception. She focused solely on one possible ulterior motive to explain all of Jack's loving behavior. Nina started with the "evidence" that she felt frightened, then proceeded to find a reason for it and judged Jack as untrustworthy. By filtering Jack's behavior through this predetermined conclusion—her mind-set of mistrust—she twisted the facts and distorted the larger picture. Her view couldn't lead to any conclusion other than the one she came to. Nothing Jack said or did would have made a difference.

But I came to a different conclusion: that Jack really did care, and that Nina's reasoning, confused by her overwhelming sense of vulnerability, had misled her. Nina was afraid that when he got to know her better, he would not like what he found. She felt small and ugly inside, uncomfortable in her own skin, she told me. From the moment Jack had suggested moving in with her, Nina had felt she would be exposed.

Nina and Jack's argument had taken place four weeks prior to our first session. She hadn't heard from him since: further evidence, as she saw it, that he didn't love her. More likely, her insult had done its damage and soured him on the relationship. In lashing out, Nina had irrevocably broken a relationship which seemed to have some potential. Although she wouldn't admit it, I think Nina herself had some doubts about the way she had handled that situation, which was why she decided to enter therapy at this time.

Taking all this into consideration, I told Nina that, yes, there was a grain of truth to her perception. Jack was hard up for money for his business, and moving in with her would have benefited him financially. But, I asked rhetorically, what's wrong with that? What's wrong with relying on someone you care about when you need help? Why did that necessarily mean he was going to take advantage of her? Why did that discount all his loving behavior? Most important, wasn't Jack's supposed exploitation of her a convenient excuse to blame Jack for her own feelings of vulnerability?

Nina needed to explore the underlying fears, as well as the psychological dynamic, that had led her to see Jack as she did. She needed to gain insight into how she had distorted her perception of Jack and his motives. For Nina's therapy to work, she had to begin to ask the question "Is it you or is it me?"

We Create Our Psychological Reality

Let's begin by trying to see the world through Nina's eyes—or, as I prefer to think of it, through her psychological mind-set.

In my training to become a psychologist, I studied many different personality theories, explanations of how we become who we are. Although these theories differ in many ways, there is one unifying premise: *Each one of us makes his or her own psychological life.* Our perceptions, reactions, and experiences are filtered through a particular set of lenses that we call a personality, or a *mind-set,* and this determines how we experience the world, achieve happiness in relationships, and find fulfillment in work. Given the fact that each of us has his or her own personal mind-set, we can never escape our personal view—or our personal blind spots—and be completely objective. Making sense of other people's behavior and intentions can be particularly difficult. We're all complicated beings, our thoughts and motivations are rarely simple, and words or actions may be misleading, ambiguous, contradictory, and just plain confusing. No wonder there's so much fertile ground for misinterpretation.

The concept of a mind-set is very useful in understanding how we view ourselves and the world we create for ourselves. The mind-set we bring to a situation is a complex brew, but its essential components are our temperament, sensibility, and the varied assumptions, preconceptions, expectations, and attitudes we hold about ourselves and about the world in general. Childhood upbringing seems to be a major determining factor in the development of these mind-sets. If we were deeply loved and happy as children, brought up to feel that the world was an open, happy place, chances are we bring some of that optimistic expectation with us when we meet a potential romantic partner. Because we felt loved, lovable, and worthy of love, we don't doubt that someone can love us and will. By the same token, we are also inclined to bestow our love on others.

But what if our childhood was troubled? What if we came from a family that was critical, cold, or dysfunctional? What if our parents' love was difficult, or perhaps even impossible, to earn? Going even further, what if we were abused? If we felt deeply unloved or unappreciated as children, there's a good chance that we reached adulthood not only with low self-esteem, but also with a basic feeling that we are not lovable, not worthy of love or entitled to be loved. We might feel that the only way to be loved is to suffer. And we might think that we don't have the emotional resources to love others.

Because early childhood experiences so powerfully influence the development of these mind-sets, and because they become so deeply ingrained as our life experiences build on earlier experiences, mind-sets are extraordinarily difficult to change. That is why therapy is such hard work and the gains achieved can be so gradual.

Our mind-sets determine our perception of events and relationships through a psychological mechanism called *projection*. Projection is the technical term for the inside-out dynamic. It refers to the assumptions, preconceptions, expectations, and attributions we automatically make about others. It's like a personal slide show in which we ourselves are the slide projector. We project onto the blank screen of another person's actions or character our own psychological photograph and interpretation of it. We project what's going on inside us onto people in the outside world. When we project our personal mind-set onto a relationship, we are employing the inside-out dynamic.

In its healthier aspects, projection accounts for much of what's wonderful about human nature: compassion, empathy, connectedness, romantic fusion, altruism, a sense of community, vicarious experiences. We learn to understand other people's feelings as our own. But in its unhealthy form, if, like Nina, we are predisposed toward being mistrustful, we see enemies all around us and live in a world filled with danger and malevolence.

To put it another way, we create our own narratives, highlight certain themes that speak to us, identify those who will fill the roles of the protagonists and the supporting players, and imbue it all with dramatic force. If we create stories of beauty and romance, then that is who we are. If we create stories of demons and dragons, then that, too, is who we are.

I don't mean to suggest that all reality is subjective. Of course there are objective facts that span the whole range of human experience (from loving gestures to abusive experiences, from winning the lottery to living in poverty, and so on). But we make of these facts what we want. It's not *all* in our heads—but much more of it is than many people acknowledge. It's my job as a psychologist to help people see how they have become the authors of their own stories; to understand the mind-sets and filters through which they see and define their worlds; and to keep those personal slide shows from interfering with their happiness.

In Nina's case, it was clear that her particular mind-set, one I would characterize as both suspicious and oversensitive, had distorted her perception of Jack and his motives. If she had bothered to remove the darkly tinted lens of her mind-set—that is, rethink what she was projecting—she would have perceived Jack's intentions in quite a different light. It was clear to me that she would not be able to break free of her pattern of romantic failures until she gained the insight that would allow her to see things differently. I was hopeful about the outcome of Nina's therapy, because on some level she already had a dim awareness that she had misread Jack.

Nina's Childhood

Over the next months, Nina revealed a childhood history that I came to understand as the source of her mind-set of mistrust. Nina's mother had suffered from a degenerative illness that required Nina, the only daughter, to be constantly on call to care for her. No matter what Nina did, though, her mother did not feel better and was not appreciative of her daughter's efforts. Nor was the mother any more gracious to Nina's father, whom she called an irresponsible drunk.

Nina's father kept his distance from the increasingly debilitated and embittered mother by working long hours, and then staying out most evenings and weekends, drinking at the neighborhood bar. Like many alcoholics, he had his charming moments, but he was an unavailable and erratic parent. As a result, the burden of maintaining the household fell on Nina.

Nina took away from this childhood a number of long-lasting assumptions about relationships: Don't depend on anyone. Don't expect to be treated gently and kindly. Men will let you down (as her father had her mother).

In my analysis, Nina identified with her mother's view that men are untrustworthy—an attitude apparent in her relationship with Jack and numerous other men. But deeper analysis revealed that Nina also felt that her father was justified in distancing himself from his angry, rejecting wife. Thus, Nina saw herself as an angry, unlovable woman, just like her mother. This was the part of her psyche that she would not allow anyone to touch, that she wanted to keep hidden from Jack and other men.

No wonder Nina felt so anxious when Jack suggested they live together. She feared she would be "found out" at last, as the childishly angry and emotionally needy person she felt her "true" self to be. This was the Nina no one in the business world ever saw. This side only became apparent in romantic relationships that touched her at her core. But any man who saw this core, she was convinced, would surely reject her and distance himself as her father had done.

In this way, Nina's childhood experience had led her to believe that men might court her, but they wouldn't come through for her. When Jack wooed her, he reminded her of those moments when her father was charming. Rather than reexperience the disappointment her father had so often caused when he resumed his distant attitude, she preemptively rejected Jack before he could reject her. And so Nina's mind-set persisted into adulthood and continued to color the way she experienced romantic relationships, long after she was fully grown and her parents had passed away.

The Mistrustful Personality

For Nina, as for all of us, trust is a central psychological issue. Our sense of trust reflects a basic belief and attitude about the world: Do we expect to be nurtured or deprived? Do we feel our surroundings to be safe or do we feel constantly in danger? These attitudes define the conditions under which we are willing to trust another person and allow ourselves to be vulnerable with him or her. As I see it, *trust derives from the comfort we feel within ourselves*. That comfort and trust in ourselves allows us to trust others.

Nina's personality may be characterized as mistrustful. Let's look more closely at the characteristics of a mistrustful personality:

· Edgy suspiciousness: Feeling overly sensitive, we read provocations into everyday interactions, even imagining them when they don't exist. Evidence of malevolent intent is sought and easily found.

· Antagonistic behavior: Bitter arguments develop amid a constant feeling of embattlement. Discussions quickly turn into acrimonious confrontations in which neither party is willing to compromise. There is a constant grating on each other's nerves and sense of being at odds with each other.

· Catalogue of personal hurts: Ancient offenses, real or imagined, never fade, so the anger is always fresh. Accusations old and new abound.

· Rivalry: Instead of a sense of mutuality, feelings of envy and competition predominate. Instead of acting in partnership, the two people are taken over by an adversarial tone.

· Quick-trigger anger: Because anger is not modulated or moderated, explosive outbursts are only a hair trigger away. (For example, the patient who told me, "She says 'Good morning' and I want to rip her head off.")

· Lashing out: With no restraints or inhibitions, the relationship takes on an incendiary quality. What feels unsafe to each party may in fact be quite dangerous.

· Feeling invalidated: Because each partner perceives the other as having an opposite view of reality, there's a sense of being unsupported and undermined. "One of us must be lying or crazy."

■

For those of us on the lower end of the mistrust scale—whose mistrustful feelings are rare and manageable—mistrust may temporarily derail interactions or put us at odds with our partner for a short while. Before long, though, the healthier couple is able to right itself and straighten things out. It's like a singing duo who may play some off-key notes but are able quickly to regain their harmony.

But for some of us mistrust is pervasive, characterizing our personalities and the majority of our relationships and interactions. When the mistrust level is very high, psychologists call it a personality disorder. Studies suggest that 3 to 5 percent of us have this personality disorder, in which deep-seated mistrust can significantly damage relationships and leave behind toxic fallout.

At its most extreme, mistrust becomes paranoia. Those who are clinically paranoid have gone beyond mere suspiciousness and feeling threatened; they are absolutely certain that people are out to get them. Psychotic paranoids don't just see things slightly differently; they are delusional. Their projections are so off base that they've lost contact with reality.

But please don't misunderstand me: The mistrust I am talking about here is not paranoia—it's well within the realm of normalcy. Most of us aren't out of touch with reality by any means; like Nina, we merely misinterpret the significance of interpersonal events, especially when it comes to a romantic partner's intentions. The lens through which we see the world puts a distinctive tinge on how *we* see and interpret what others do and say, and when we're feeling mistrustful, our mind-sets convince us that our partners are uncaring or cruel.

We may not like to admit it, but occasionally we all have some traits of the mistrustful personality. We've all acted in antagonistic ways, been oversensitive, and have inappropriately lashed out in anger. Some of us may act and feel this way more intensely, more often than others; others of us, less so. These traits are part of all of us. And even the most subtle manifestations of these traits can tear at the fabric of our relationships.

Circular Reasoning and Self-fulfilling Prophecies

Because mind-sets determine the way we view and experience the world, we are predisposed to make certain judgments and assumptions. We use circular reasoning in that we view information selectively, allowing through the filter only those facts that fit our preconceived notions.

Once we're primed to see something, that's all we can see. For instance, when I bought a new car a few years ago, I didn't know anybody else who owned a Saab. The next thing I knew, the only cars I saw—on the highway, in the parking lot, on the street— were Saabs. Either they had had a huge increase in sales or, more likely, I was just noticing something I had not noticed previously: that many Saabs were already on the road.

Once a preconception is securely in place, only confirming evidence tends to get through the filter. Because we process information selectively, anything contradictory that would refute our preconception is filtered out (or at least viewed with skepticism). For example, if we're suspicious and predisposed to look for danger, we see everything as a potential threat. When we feel vulnerable, we don't give people the benefit of the doubt because we feel we don't have the luxury to be open-minded.

The mind-set of mistrust is thus based on a hermetic or autistic logic. Even though we may stick to the "facts," in making sense of those facts, we may ignore the context, lose perspective, and miss the obvious. As the spouse of one of my patients told me, "She twists my words in order to hear things I'm not saying."

Similarly, Nina selectively filtered the facts in a way that led her to conclude Jack was trying to use her. Even though there had been some basis for doubt—he was short of cash—that in itself was not a reason to insult him. But Nina disregarded the many ways in which he was also tender and loving and saw him solely as exploitative.

Nina's case further shows that preconceptions can be particularly damaging in that they tend to become self-fulfilling prophecies. Since we act on our perceptions (as Nina did in pushing Jack away), a mistrustful mind-set can lead us to provoke situations, pick fights, and elicit behavior that further confirms our preconception. For example, although Nina was the one who had rejected and insulted Jack, she viewed the fact that he didn't call again as proof that he didn't love her and had only wanted to save money. This was yet another relationship in a long line that confirmed Nina's belief that she wasn't loved, and that relationships don't work out. According to this reasoning, her cynicism was fully justified.

In a sense, our mind-sets and preconceptions do serve to justify our feelings and behavior. Unfortunately, if we're misinterpreting others, then our behavior is based on a fallacy and we undermine relationships that might otherwise thrive. For instance, if we think we're being attacked, we feel justified in retaliating, and sometimes act preemptively to avoid being attacked. If we think we're going to be rejected, it makes sense to protect ourselves by pretending we're not interested. And if we think, "He's only out for himself," then we too feel entitled to be out for ourselves. When, in response to our actions, others then do attack us, reject us, or act in selfish ways, we will have created the outcome we claim we hoped to avoid. Around and around we go, never escaping our preconceptions.

Sifting Projections from Reality

Since a mind-set of mistrust distorts our perceptions and thinking, trying to sort objective reality from our own projections can be confusing. Sometimes in relationships, our partner really is the source of our discomfort. Sometimes our partner really does mean to hurt us or is indifferent to our feelings. And sometimes we really should be wary and skeptical. Sometimes, in short, mistrust is warranted.

But there are also times, as I believed was the case with Nina, when our fears are all in our heads, when the mistrust resides within. Our mind-set may tell us someone is out to hurt us, but no one is. We project onto our partner a hurtful motive, but we're misinterpreting his or her intention on the basis of our own fearfulness. We blame our lover or spouse for our feeling the way we do; in fact, our own emotional vulnerability is leading us to feel bad.

And therein lies the confusion. We don't know which dangers really do lie "out there" and which fears we are projecting. Whom should we trust, and of whom should we be suspicious? Was Nina right not to trust Jack, or was she turning her emotions inside out? How could she learn to sort through which was which? This book is intended to help explain the complexities that underlie these questions.

The psychological dilemma of trust vs. mistrust is never wholly resolved, but is, rather, one we confront every day in new and varied manifestations: Should we trust? Whom do we trust? How do we show that trust? What must others do to deserve our trust? Our predisposition to trust or to mistrust will characterize our personality and determine the likelihood of when, why, what, where, and how we'll trust, or not trust, someone or something. But each situation and experience we face is new, and so we continually face this same psychological challenge, always in different forms: Should I trust this car salesman? This investment adviser? The cute guy at work who asked me out for a date? What signals do I follow about who is really trustworthy? What warnings should I look out for, to guard and protect myself against being sold a lemon, swindled out of my savings, having my heart broken?

Because we do need to sort through these different signals, some degree of mistrust characterizes all people and relationships. No one is, or should be, completely trusting. But we all have the capacity to react suspiciously and take things too personally, especially when we feel sensitive or hurt. And it is admittedly difficult to demonstrate to others that their trust is warranted and has been earned.

So should Nina have trusted Jack? Obviously, it depends on Jack's personal qualities and behavior. Could we say definitively that Jack deserved Nina's trust? I don't know. Since everything I knew about Jack had been filtered through Nina's mind-set, I can't be certain. But I did know that Nina had a mistrustful personality, which made it difficult if not impossible for her to trust any man. She lacked that comfort within herself which forms the basis for all romantic relationships.

Love cannot exist in a context of suspicion and doubt. We all need to relax, turn off our radar detectors, and rely on others to take care of us. At some point, we need to trust those we're involved with. By contrast, perceiving a lover as an enemy or rival can devastate relationships and preclude the possibility of new ones. Mistrust creates a gulf between people, a chasm of doubt and danger. The only way to bridge that gulf is to feel that there is a realistic foundation for trust.

Obviously, naive trust is not an answer. We need good intuition, judgment, and a certain amount of healthy skepticism. But when we suspect, rage, and blame first, and ask questions later, the balance is out of kilter. The key is knowing when our suspicions are well founded and when they are off base—when they are projections. We need to differentiate between when we feel vulnerable because people have acted harmfully toward us, and when we only imagined it. It's crucial to be able to trust our judgments and instincts about people and situations. But we must also keep in mind that our mind-sets can mislead us terribly. We must learn to be more objective.

Admittedly, distinguishing between rational and irrational mistrust can be tricky. When I question patients about their cynicism, they point to numerous types of evidence to justify their position. They say they're not paranoid—their romantic partner really did intend to provoke them—and in fact there usually is a grain of truth to their suspicions. For instance, Jack's suggestion to move in with Nina was in part financially motivated, but this did not mean that saving money was his sole purpose nor that he was taking advantage of her.

In therapy, I try to stop people from being misled by their mind-sets. But it's hard work relearning and reestablishing instinctively whom to trust and whom to avoid. As one patient told me, he needed to take a remedial course, Life 101, to learn the basic principles of how to read people and respond appropriately. Doubting our perceptions is like questioning the floor beneath our feet: Will it hold us? This kind of self-questioning may be uncomfortable and cause us to become somewhat tentative. But sifting our projections from reality is the first step toward making psychological change.

Moving Toward Insight

As therapy progressed, Nina began to see how her childhood had formed her worldview and had led her to defend herself against rejection. She came to understand the complex inside-out dynamic of the way she projected her vulnerability onto her potential romantic partners, and how that resulted in her viewing them as dangerous and unreliable. She learned to set aside her mind-set of mistrust, and gained the insight she needed to move forward with her life. Although initially Nina felt that I would be critical, like her mother, eventually she came to trust that I would treat her gently and sympathetically. She even learned to sit back in my couch. What accounts for this remarkable change?

Beyond therapy, there are few ways to change an ingrained mind-set—and love is one of them. But there is a Catch–22. When our mind-set interferes with our ability to achieve love (as it did in Nina's case), how can love begin to change that mind-set? Love may be transformative, but only if we give it a chance. That's why, as I work with patients in treatment, I often wonder which comes first: the personality change (a change in our mind-set and the expectations we bring to relationships) or the advent of a loving relationship?

This last question came increasingly to mind as, in the course of our sessions, I saw Nina progress from being imprisoned by her mistrust to being able to build a solid relationship with a loving and beloved partner.

After spending many months identifying and acknowledging her recurrent pattern of mistrust and oversensitivity, Nina was determined not to allow these reactions to interfere with her next relationship. Then, as is so often the case with therapy, Nina became involved with the right man just when she was ready. This was Warren, a widowed businessman who, unlike previous men in her life, was unflappable and endlessly patient.

An anecdote gives an idea of the strides Nina made. When Warren gave her a food processor for her birthday, Nina's disappointment was at first acute. Her gut reaction, she told me later, was the thought "If he really loved me, he would have given me something more personal. Anyway, he's the one who loves to cook, not me." But whereas before, her disappointment would have led to a sarcastic comment and argument that could have derailed the relationship (as it had with Jack), she now was able to restrain her gut reaction. Instead of lashing out, she was able to focus on and respond to the extremely romantic card he had composed to accompany the present.

Still, Nina was bothered by this incident. True, I said at our next session, a food processor isn't the most romantic birthday present, but did that mean that Warren didn't love her? As she had done with other men, Nina was looking for evidence that Warren wasn't right for her and had invented tests to prove his coldheartedness. The food processor provided her with sufficient evidence.

Because of the insight she had gained, however, Nina was able to hear me when I suggested that this was another example of how her mind-set of mistrust misled her. In fact, she acknowledged, Warren gave ample evidence of his love by doting on her in many ways, such as bringing her hot coffee in bed every morning and listening to her sympathetically as she described the pressure she was under at work. Ultimately, Nina even came to appreciate the birthday gift when she discovered, much to her surprise, how much she enjoyed cooking with Warren. What better way for two people to unwind and share a pleasurable activity than in preparing a sumptuous feast for each other? "Maybe it was the right gift after all," she admitted.

In the early months of Nina and Warren's relationship, there were many similar incidents that could have set off Nina's temper. And sometimes she did explode. But she also softened and let herself be vulnerable with Warren. She marveled that he was still there, tolerant of her outbursts, reassuring when she became anxious, not revolted by her emotional neediness. Eight months into the relationship, she felt comfortable and unself-conscious enough to agree to move in with Warren. And though she still felt some trepidation, she gave up the spacious apartment that she had been unwilling to share with Jack.

Nina's transformation was difficult and gradual but was remarkable nonetheless. Through the insight she gained in therapy, Nina had been able to set aside the mind-set of mistrust that had undermined her prior relationships. It's not that she made a radical change in the way she thought; she was still oversensitive and prone to mistrust. What allowed her to build a solid relationship with Warren, whom she eventually married, was making slight changes in her perceptions, combined with her trying to not act on her preconceptions immediately. These small psychological changes, such as giving Warren the benefit of the doubt, made an enormous difference in Nina's life and happiness.

This brings us back to the question of which came first, the change in Nina's mind-set and personality or the transformative power of her relationship with Warren. The answer is that they occurred together. Because of the insight she had gained in therapy, when she met Warren, Nina made every effort not to allow her mistrust to derail their budding relationship. This gave Warren the opportunity to prove that he was in fact trustworthy—something she had never given Jack the opportunity to do. A less patient or understanding man would not have meshed well with Nina's personality. But had she met him earlier, even though he was patient, she still might have put him off. Nina was lucky enough to meet the right man at the right time. With the help of therapy, she made her own opportunity.

The Lessons of Insight

By *insight* I mean the identification of a pattern of distortion. Nina gained insight by becoming aware of her mind-set and how it skewed her perceptions of men. She learned to distrust her initial perceptions and reactions, and she taught herself to compensate for her inner biases. Instead of buying in to her mistrust, she began to question it and reevaluate the situations and relationships which evoked it. She learned to evaluate objective evidence of men's motivations based on their behavior, not just on her subjective reactions.

Nina's journey toward insight shows that we can change our mind-sets and learn to set aside our mistrustful projections. Moreover, not all of us are wholly committed to our particular preconceptions and mind-sets. We may have enough insight to recognize that we ourselves contribute to the problems we encounter in relationships. For instance, one patient dreamed that he inadvertently broke his glasses and could no longer see clearly. This reflected his growing realization in therapy that he couldn't trust his initial impressions and perceptions of people. He was sincerely confused about the degree to which the difficulties in his marriage were a function of his mistrust or of his wife's actual behavior. He was genuinely asking the question: Is it my problem, or hers?

How do we disentangle the perceptions and preconceptions that can cause confusion, whether in long-term relationships or in short-term squabbles?

Because behavior follows from the way we see things, we need to change the way we perceive events and people's intentions. This is why insight is so important, and why the first step in therapy is to call attention to the deeply ingrained patterns and mind-sets that stem from mistrust. Unless we learn to recognize our tendency to distort or misinterpret people's motives, we'll never control our behavior; instead, our mind-sets will control us.

My job is to help tease apart the unrealistic distortions and develop a more realistic view of others' intentions. I try to serve as a reality check by helping, and then teaching, my patients to compensate for their internal biases. I encourage them to see that people's motives are complex, and the world is far from black and white. Any mind-set that merely confirms our preconceptions is by definition an overly simplistic view of the nuanced and ambiguous meanings that characterize human interactions. Similarly, because people are multifaceted, the mistrustful solution is too simplistic, leading one to respond to only a single aspect of another person's behavior or personality.

By contrast, as we change the kind of lenses through which we see the world, we not only see things more realistically but also see more colors and textures. We become capable of a full range of emotions and perceptions. (If only the world were as organized and coherent as the paranoids among us believe! Someone who has a suspicious, conspiratorial viewpoint attributes an artificial, malevolent meaning to innocuous situations. When we're feeling mistrustful, we perceive antipathy when apathy is a more probable reality. We like to think of ourselves as being people of importance, worthy of having an adversary. But more often than not, we're irrelevant, and what we experience as being intentionally meant to harm us is usually not directed at us at all. The reason we choose to react suspiciously is that it is too much of a narcissistic blow to our ego to realize the world is indifferent to us.)

But setting aside one's preconceptions and facing reality is easier said than done. Not only are these patterns deeply ingrained and familiar, they also serve a function. Venting our emotions and acting on our angry impulses is easier than changing the way we see things. It's difficult to stifle an impulse (just as it is difficult to resist the temptation of food when we're on a diet), and in the short run, it may appear to be more satisfying to act on our anger. But in the long run, it is more beneficial and gratifying to resist our impulses and transform the way we see things.

We need to stop and think before reacting: Did this person really intend to hurt me, or am I being oversensitive? And even if we conclude that there was malevolent intent, we must still ask the question, Is retaliation the most constructive response?

Of course, it takes two people to make a couple, and ideally both partners will be asking these questions. In the next chapter we'll explore what happens when both partners' conflicting projections land them in the most confusing place imaginable: the Land of He Said/She Said.

2
The Land of He Said/She Said
Are We Struggling with Our Partners or Ourselves?

More than any other psychological defense mechanism, projection can lead to enormous confusion over who's angry at whom and why. As we saw in the last chapter, it can be a perplexing challenge to sort through just one person's projections and distortions. Imagine how much more complex the equation becomes when you introduce the personality and mind-set of the other partner within the couple.

Even a psychologist can find it difficult to disentangle the mutual projections and recriminations that result. To illustrate: One of my patients wanted to leave his wife, but he feared that if he did, she would kill herself and he would be unable to live with the ensuing guilt. Although he chose to remain in the marriage, he blamed her for his decision. If we look at the husband's psyche in isolation, it's clear that he has projected his own fragility (his belief that *he* could not handle such a rejection) onto his wife. But when we examine the wife's behavior, the situation becomes far more complex. Sensing his desire to leave, the wife had played on his guilt by threatening to kill herself. Not only did she use this as leverage to keep him in the marriage, but her threats confirmed his preconception of her fragility, despite the fact that she was not as fragile as she pretended to be. Who's responsible for this confusion? Is it he or is it she? We need to analyze this relationship in the dual context of the husband's projections and the wife's contribution to his view of her.

Although psychologists think of personality in terms of an individual's projections and mind-set, these dynamics are played out in two-person interactions (or, in the case of family relationships, multiple-person interactions). To put it another way, each of us projects our emotions and attitudes onto our partner, and he or she does the same to us. What ensues maybe a clash of projections.

I'm convinced that the level of anger and suspicion I find in relationships today derives from this clash of projections. Our hostility reflects a fundamental disagreement about how we see things. The conflict lies in the discrepancy between how I (with my preconceived notions) see a situation and how you (with your preconceived notions) see it. No wonder partners look at each other in angry bewilderment and ask, "Is it me, or is it you?"

To give you a better idea of how this works, imagine how you would respond if someone tried to project her uncomfortable feelings onto you, blaming you for how she feels. You'd probably say something like "Not so fast. I didn't do what you accuse me of doing. I'm not responsible for your unhappiness. I'm not the way you see me at all." And then what? Inevitably, your partner would deny your contention, disowning what you had projected onto him, and challenging your view of the event. And so the stage is set for conflict.

To give another example, a patient felt justified in her prickly temper because her husband was not to be trusted: He undermined her at the slightest sign of weakness with insults and put-downs. But from his standpoint, she was the aggressive and hostile one; he was simply protecting himself. In this circle of blame, who was right and who was wrong?

In fact, there is no right or wrong. Each of us lives in a separate psychological reality, and we literally do not perceive events the same way. It is no wonder that these versions of reality come into conflict, and that we feel like adversaries.

Different perceptions over who's doing what to whom constitute as fundamental a disagreement as we can have. When couples can't reach a consensus about what's going on, they fight. Sometimes these misunderstandings can be affectionate and humorous. At other times, they can undermine basic trust: Are you crazy, or am I? Are you lying to me, or is this just a misunderstanding?

Welcome to the Land of He Said/She Said.

We've all been there: A wife tells me how awful her spouse was at their dinner party last week. "He wouldn't let me talk. All the conversation was about him and his job." Then the husband pipes up, "That's not what happened at all! Let me tell you my version. She spent hours preparing dinner in the kitchen, and somebody had to entertain the guests." Even the most mundane events have multiple versions, depending on who's doing the talking.

In the Land of He Said/She Said, couples make no effort to listen to each other. They may appear to be listening, but they're thinking to themselves that they've heard it all before and quickly discount what's said. ("He doesn't understand." "She's just being stubborn.") How can they truly listen and hear what the other is saying when, in their mind's eyes, they see everything in completely different terms? There is an unwillingness to tolerate—or even entertain the possibility of taking seriously—the partner's alternative viewpoint. ("She's just twisting the facts to suit her case.")

In relationships characterized by these reality wars, both parties feel that the partner refuses to validate their way of seeing things. It goes beyond a difference of opinion; the withholding of validation is perceived as a form of persecution. We feel that our partner is depriving us of the confirmation we require, and so we fight that much harder to prove and defend our view.

It's a fight that can be, and may be, fought forever, for the following reason: To allow an alternative view to filter through would threaten the very nature of our established worldview. If we need to see a relationship in certain terms in order to explain how we feel, then to see it any other way brings that explanation into question. For example, if we're convinced that we're angry, anxious, sad, or whatever because our partner doesn't take good care of us, then everything he or she does must be understood within that framework. If we were to discover that our partner is not out to hurt us, then we must consider the possibility that we're overreacting and being oversensitive—that we are anxious and sad for our own reasons. This insight can be so overwhelming and threatening that we return instead to our familiar, preconceived notion that it's not my problem, it's yours. How much easier it is to say "It's not me; it's you" than to acknowledge my own responsibility.

Just because others see things differently is no reason to feel threatened by them. We need to learn to accept that others, even the romantic partner we love, will necessarily see things differently from the way we do. One of my goals in therapy is to help people develop the psychological capacity to accept others' separateness.

Boundary Problems

When we ask the question "Is it me or is it you?" we're asking who's responsible for what's going on between us: the problems, the conflicts, the misunderstandings. The more we turn our feelings inside out, the more confusing it becomes to figure out who's doing what to whom. The more mutual projections there are, the greater the confusion and the greater the level of strife. In psychological terms, this interpersonal confusion is a boundary issue and refers to the ambiguity over where "I" ends and "you" begins.

Psychological boundaries between people—that is, where my psychological self ends and your psychological self begins—can be blurry and permeable, not nearly as clear-cut as the physical boundaries that define and separate our bodies. In part this is because psychological boundaries are defined by our ever-changing interests and personal involvements. As we become romantically involved with someone, our sense of self becomes absorbed by him. We experience ourselves through the relationship. This is a healthy, normal process of romantic fusion, a kind of self-transcendence that embodies the magic of love.

But those of us who have weaker, more permeable boundaries are threatened by this fusion. They feel as though they're losing their selves, as though they're about to be swallowed up by the beloved, and are made anxious by the confusion over where "I" ends and "you" begins. The more permeable our psychological boundaries are (or the more threatened we feel by the natural permeability that develops with intimacy), the more likely we are to use the inside-out maneuver: "I'm uncomfortable, so you must be making me feel this way." "I feel unlovable, so you must not love me." "I can't imagine giving anybody anything myself, so I have to assume you're not going to give me what I want." "I'm angry, so I have to believe this relationship is not safe."

Unclear and permeable boundaries lead to our projecting our thoughts, feelings, and assumptions onto those around us. Only by establishing and delineating better boundaries (what's me and what's you, what's inside and what's outside) and reclaiming our projections can we escape conflicts and confusion. And when we succeed in doing that, we will be able to apportion responsibility (what's my fault and what's your fault) and ultimately to answer the question "Is it me or is it you?"

Looking Outside Rather Than Within

The tendency to look outside rather than within is actually quite understandable. Remember for a moment when you were a kid. Maybe you accidentally knocked over and broke your mom's favorite vase, or you came home fifteen minutes after curfew. What would be the first words out of your (or just about any kid's) mouth? Set the emotional scene: You feel terrible already, guilty, ashamed, fearful of what your mom or dad will say and do. So you find an excuse, a way to deflect responsibility. You even believe it yourself when you insist, "It's not my fault! Jimmy dared me to jump over that vase!" Or "Don't blame me! The other kids made me stay out late!" Or you may turn the tables by trying to take the high ground: "Curfews are stupid. Who gave you the right? You just don't get anything." Or "How can you give me such a hard time about a vase? You're so materialistic!" *You* break something, but your parents are the ones with the problem.

Age makes no difference. When we're scared, or if our psyches have been scarred, our anxiety, discomfort, guilt, or shame can be so overwhelming that we cannot face these feelings, not to mention the negative consequences of our own behavior. (The child's "He made me do it" becomes the adult's "He made me feel this way.") Unable to control or tolerate the discomfort, we vent our feelings, act out, place the blame *outside* ourselves. Sometimes we even lie. Anything to disown our feelings.

Feeling threatened and having lashed out, we then claim we're merely innocent bystanders. The distorted logic (which seems quite logical to us at the time) goes like this: "You're the one who attacked me; I'm just defending myself or reacting in kind. It's your fault; I'm blameless. You're the perpetrator, I'm the victim." I call it Teflon reasoning, because nothing sticks. We justify our own anger and aggressiveness by projecting it onto another.

The only way to sort through the complex psychology of mutual projection is for each person to understand what he or she is doing and what the partner is doing. Let's examine this process in detail in one couple who blamed each other for a host of unresolved feelings and whose bitter, never-ending fights would continue until they learned to reach consensus over what was going on between them.

Loving and Fighting: Vic and Nella

It was Nella who first called me for an appointment, ostensibly to set up a consultation for her husband, Vic. In our telephone conversation, she voiced a mixture of loving concern and blunt anger, explaining that Vic had become so withdrawn that she was losing patience with him. Nella's tone was tinged with equal parts tenderness and frustration. Although Nella emphasized that it was Vic's appointment (and Vic's problem), she worried that he would not come without her, or that if he did, "I'm not sure how much he'll tell you."

"Whatever feels comfortable," I said out loud. But I wondered to myself whether Nella's decision to join her husband might hint at an underlying awareness that she too played a part in their marital drama and that she was struggling with questions of her own. We arranged a time and hung up.

When Vic and Nella arrived at our first meeting, I was struck by their remarkable physical symmetry. Both were in their late thirties, tall, lean, and athletic, with strong jaws and thin lips. At the same time they made an interesting study in contrasts. Redheaded Nella was dressed in a flamboyant array of floral colors, whereas pale-haired Vic wore a nondescript faded blue work shirt and jeans. When I motioned them to sit, they automatically settled at opposite ends of my office sofa, like prizefighters claiming their own corners. Their body language further dramatized these differences. While Nella sat completely upright and erect as in a position of command, Vic slouched down as if trying to fade into the recesses of the leather upholstery.

Nella began speaking almost immediately. "Our marriage isn't working. All we do is fight," she said. Beneath her outwardly straightforward words, however, lay an imploring undercurrent. She glanced at Vic, as if asking for his validation, but his face remained impassive, noncommittal.

She took in a deep breath and plowed ahead. She told me she had married Vic seven years ago after a long courtship. When they met, Vic had owned his own small contracting business. Proud of Nella's aspirations to become a dentist, Vic had footed the bill for her studies. Now that she was successful, with a practice of her own, she was returning the favor by putting Vic through a graduate course in architecture. She wanted to be proud of him, too. But he just wasn't pulling his weight.

"How so?" I asked.

Nella paused and turned to Vic once more, as if waiting for a cue or comment that still hadn't come. His studied silence seemed to push a button for Nella, who tensely pursed her lips with visible irritation. Her growing agitation was further reflected in the quickness with which her complaints suddenly began to spill out. She felt let down, disappointed, she told me, leaning closer and closer toward me, as if to convince me of her view. She was as needy for my validation as for Vic's.

She continued, "When I was in school, I did everything for him. I was so grateful. But now that the roles are reversed, I feel like Rodney Dangerfield. He shows no appreciation, no respect. Every time I pay a semester's tuition, it's like money down the drain." She let out a deep sigh. "He isn't getting good grades. He doesn't try. He just doesn't care."

I thought, does she mean he doesn't care about his grades—or about her? I turned to Vic, who, somewhat curiously, had still said nothing. "What's your take on all this?" I asked. "Why did you come here today?"

Now we both glanced at Vic, who merely shrugged. "Well, it was her idea," he drawled softly.

Abruptly Nella threw up her hands in exasperation as if to say,

"You see?" Her gestures, it seemed, were as flamboyant as her clothes. Out loud she said, "Getting him to talk is like pulling teeth."

Nella's sarcasm succeeded at last in getting a rise out of Vic. "I guess I'm lucky you're a dentist."

With the abruptness of an igniting fire, Nella's cheeks turned nearly as red as her hair. "That does it," she exploded. A torrent of invective followed. "You don't care, Vic. You're making a mockery of my concerns. It's a waste of my money to come here today. I'm fed up to here."

"Right, right," he repeated, nodding as if to say, "I've heard it all a million times before." But his silent gesture only egged her on more, to increasingly global and less rational complaints and criticism.

As I watched and listened, it struck me that without realizing it, Vic and Nella were acting out their difficulties with as much clarity as if they had written a dramatic script just for me. Within minutes of entering, my office had become the metaphorical boxing ring for their entire relationship. Each had managed to provoke the other to a familiar pattern of angry and bitter recriminations. Although Vic's posture, huddled defensively in his corner of the sofa, seemed to say that he wished the fight would stop, he did nothing to allay his wife's concerns. He didn't even tell her that he understood what she was saying. He would sit there forever, his body language said; whatever she flung at him he could take. For her part, Nella seemed equally entrenched, poised to attack with one accusation after another.

Now she turned to me as if to a referee mediating a dispute. She asked, "Why should I give him money to go to school when he's so unappreciative?"

Vic shook his head in disgust. "You're the one who told me to close my business and go to school full time," he said, in a tone that suggested Nella deserved what she got. Their eyes met, locked in battle.

Although they were looking straight at each other, neither one really saw the other. Each one viewed the other as adversary, opponent, enemy, in a conflict neither one would (or could) leave. The question was, why?

Instead of coming here to the neutral corner of my office to seek help, they could have called it quits, gotten a divorce. But they hadn't. Further, even though it had been Nella's idea to come today, Vic was here, too, apparently willing to work out their problems. And even as she complained about Vic, Nella was constantly looking toward him, yearning for some sort of loving word or reassuring gesture.

But the more she looked, the more Vic held his silence. Indeed, when I asked for his response to one of Nella's assertions, he said, "Does it matter what I say? She's going to attack me, regardless."

Clearly, something was tying them together. Theirs was an intimacy grounded as much in anger as in love. As antagonistic as they appeared, they were totally involved with each other. The intensity of their connection was palpable; if anything, their connection was *too* raw. They believed, and I guess it was true, that their destinies were inexorably linked. Despite their hostility, they clung to each another like tired boxers in a clinch. They were holding each other up, even as they fought.

His and Hers Emotional Baggage

All of us lug around our past, like huge steamer trunks on our backs. Some pieces of baggage weigh more heavily—and therefore are more painful to carry—than others. But even when our backs ache, it's hard to unload those battered suitcases. We're used to them. They're familiar and well worn, and we cling to them like security blankets.

And as I came to find out, both Vic and Nella carried into the marriage their own emotional baggage, psychological scars that long predated their relationship.

As take-charge as Nella appeared to be, she confided that inside she felt like "a big nothing." Somehow, she had not benefited psychologically from her professional achievements, and she had built an aggressive exterior to compensate for a vulnerable interior. Even though she was financially independent and self-sufficient, she still felt emotionally dependent. Perhaps that's why she was deathly afraid of allowing herself to depend on anyone—whether financially, professionally, or emotionally. And she further feared that her husband, who was now financially dependent on her, would, as she said, "take me for a ride."

Like many people with a mistrustful mind-set, her suspicion didn't jibe with the fact that she was the one who had urged Vic to quit work and go to school. She had fostered the very thing she now claimed to resent. This is not as paradoxical as it first appears. As long as Vic was financially dependent on her, Nella felt, he would not leave. So she enticed him with her generosity. On the other hand, if Vic were to succeed in his new career and became *less* financially dependent on her, she feared that a man as handsome as Vic would find somebody else. It was this dilemma that aroused Nella's fears and anger.

From where I sat, though, Nella's suspicions appeared to be unfounded. Vic loved Nella dearly. He had supported her when she needed money and had stayed with her through thick and thin, despite her temper. But, feeling unworthy of Vic's love, Nella devalued it and lashed out at him for providing it. In this way, Nella found her adversary: However much she hated it, if she could engage Vic in battle, it meant he was still there.

Vic, of course, brought his own baggage to the marriage. Having grown up in a contentious household, he hated fighting and conflict in general—thus, his tendency to withdraw from open battle with Nella. At times he became paralyzed, unable to respond to her insults. Feeling so dependent on and afraid of Nella, Vic didn't know if there was a place for his anger in such an important relationship. So he tried to keep his anger under wraps.

Despite his silence, Vic was every bit as multilayered as Nella. He was ambitious but afraid that he did not have what it took to be a success. On the one hand, he felt the need to rely on Nella for help and took great pride in her achievements; on the other, he was intimidated by her and the very strength upon which he relied. Vic's hopes were at odds with his fears.

After taking all this in I realized: *They are not fighting with each other. They're each battling with their own personal demons.* Although at first glance they (like many couples who come to see me) appear to be two people caught in a struggle with each other, they were proving to be two individuals with quite separate personalities, each battling, in parallel fashion, with something within. The more I listened, the more convinced I became that the marital partner and "enemy" whom Nella saw was not really Vic; nor was Vic's real opponent Nella. Rather, the enemy had been determined by the baggage and projections each one brought to the relationship. They were shadow-boxing with their own fears in the boxing arena of their marriage.

Nella, it seemed to me, was fighting a battle less with her husband than with her own insecurities. She battled to control her over-the-top temper and overwhelming sense of fragility. Vic, for his part, was struggling to overcome his fear of conflict and his own sense of inadequacy. Nella had found a husband who provoked her temper, and Vic a wife who reinforced his feelings of ineptitude. Was this a coincidence? I'll come back to that question a little later.

Shadow-boxing

When the first session ended, Vic and Nella seemed destined to carry their baggage, and their boxing ring, with them wherever they went. As they rose to leave Nella tried to make up by inviting

Vic to lunch at an expensive restaurant down the street. "Remember the time we went there for Valentine's Day?" she purred softly. But even this sweet gesture was fraught with conflict. Although the enticing offer appealed to Vic—he momentarily put his arm around her in a gesture of reconciliation—the smile that had flickered across his face disappeared just as quickly as it had emerged. After a moment he said, "Does that mean I'm off probation?" (Vic's sarcasm, I later discovered, reflected his resentment at Nella's extravagance when it suited her, but not when it suited him. He viewed her gesture as arbitrary, not generous.)

In response, Nella angrily shook off his arm and stormed out alone. As I closed the door, I glimpsed Vic ambling behind, while Nella glanced back at him over her shoulder, as if waiting for him to catch up. This image dramatized perfectly what I had seen in my office: Each partner viewed the other as the enemy, yet each also needed the other to continue the fight.

It also vividly captured how rife their arguments were with projections and the distortions that resulted from them. For instance, Vic interpreted Nella's conciliatory invitation to lunch as a provocative and hurtful reminder of his poor grades and financial dependence. He felt she was twisting the knife, but was she? Similarly, Nella read into Vic's defensive silence a deliberate withholding of the love she desperately desired. No wonder Vic deflected Nella's invitation to lunch. Having projected his own interpretation ("Nella is arbitrarily lording it over me by means of her money"), he felt justifiably provoked. Vic thus missed the fact that Nella was genuinely offering to make up and was indirectly apologizing for the insults she had hurled at him earlier in the session.

By turning their emotions inside out and blaming each other, they caused something curious to happen: They actually induced the other to behave according to their preconceptions.

Thus, Vic transformed Nella's rapprochement into the taunt he expected, while Nella converted Vic's slight into the coldness she had come to dread. This maneuver is a more complex version of the self-fulfilling prophecy, discussed in the last chapter. By getting our partners to confirm our preconceptions, we close the circle of our projection; our spouses truly become the enemies we imagine.

To give another example, if I expect you to disappoint me and then angrily make it difficult for you to do what I want, who is ultimately responsible for my disappointment? Having thus induced you to behave in a certain way, am I then entitled to blame you for it? Vic and Nella's story dramatizes the fact that relationships are composed of so many layers of mutual projections that it becomes easy to disown responsibility for our own contributions to what goes on.

Our projected assumptions and expectations confuse the issue of who's doing what to whom. We can see this in couples like Vic and Nella with their constant second-guessing of each other. They anticipate certain reactions and patterns of behavior from their spouse; they then gauge their own behavior according to that expectation. For example, because Vic expects Nella to overreact, he will underreact. Nella then predictably overreacts because she believes that Vic isn't taking the issue seriously enough. Who's responsible for this interaction?

And so, is it Vic's problem (as Nella contends) that brings them to see me, or hers (as Vic's silence suggests he believes)? Or do they both bring difficulties to the relationship? In the Land of He Said/She Said, projections fly back and forth: "You started it." "No, you did." "It's your fault." "You must be kidding. Let me tell you my version." Vic and Nella were caught up in this blame game, and it was my job to tease it apart.

I often wonder why so many of my patients need to see in their partners enemies or adversaries. And why, feeling as they do, do they remain in such antagonistic relationships? The answer has to do with projection. By transforming our partners into enemies, we create what we want: someone to do battle with, someone to explain our uncomfortable emotions and failures.

A part of us needs and enjoys this struggle. When we transform our lover into an enemy, we are projecting onto our partner negative yet nonetheless crucial aspects of *ourselves* that we may wish to reject, but that also complete us as complex human beings. Our enemies thus confirm and reinforce attitudes we hold about ourselves.

Having enemies helps us make sense of ourselves. They provide a narrative and a way of dealing with frustration, anger, and failure. If something didn't work out, then it must be because someone was trying to thwart us. Unable to face our own imperfections, we blame others for them. (I'm reminded of the patient who showed up late for an appointment and told me that my clocks were wrong.)

But the enemy is not out there. It is our own insecurities, fragility, and lack of self-mastery. We may feel ourselves to be at the mercy of powerful forces outside us when in fact those powerful forces consist of our own emotional turbulence, our own doubts and fears, our own sense of inadequacy.

When we see enemies and adversaries instead of partners or colleagues, we are taking a simplistic response to life's admittedly complex, ambiguous, and difficult challenges: How do we make our way in life, find love, achieve our goals, create meaning, and master varied emotional conflicts, stresses, and frustrations? There are no easy answers. By blaming and turning our feelings inside out, we deny responsibility. It's a psychological cop-out, and it will not in any way help us to achieve those goals.

There are rarely clear-cut solutions to our problems. However much we may like to tell stories with heroes and villains, people are rarely all good or all bad. The real world is less clear and much grayer than we imagine. The people we're involved with are more multifaceted than we appreciate. The challenge we face is to accept the truth that when we meet with failures, limitations, and frustration in our lives, it doesn't mean that we have an enemy. In most real-life stories, there are no enemies, no powerful forces out to control us. This is what Vic and Nella needed to learn about themselves.

Reclaiming Projections, Defining Boundaries

When patients tell me about important people in their lives, they may think they're talking about someone else, but I automatically assume they are talking about themselves. This is because of projection. Similarly, when I hear them complain and rail against their partners, I wonder what it is in themselves that they are running from, what enemy they fear within.

The challenge to delineating what's me and what's you lies in learning to break free of our preconceptions; in ceasing to blame others for feelings and attitudes that come from within; and in starting to see our partners not as adversaries but as people who are on our side. This means reclaiming projections and undoing distortions. We must clear the air of the dense fog that pollutes relationships. We can do so by defining boundaries: by owning our own individual baggage, sensitivities, and personal history. We need to apportion psychological responsibility—I did this and am responsible for it; you did that and are responsible for it—until there is a consensus over who did what to whom.

Let's see how Vic and Nella began this process: At the outset of therapy Nella told me, "I'm fine; Vic's the one who has to change." In my view, though, the only way for them to make progress was to change this basic assumption. Only when each partner took responsibility for both the good and bad aspects of their marriage would they be able to see that they were on the same, not opposite, sides. To begin painting a more complex, nuanced picture of their marriage, I made two points:

- Vic was not solely responsible for their problems; Nella's own insecurities had contributed as well.

- Vic had much of great value to contribute to the marriage.

I was able to bring home both these points when Nella announced at a session early on in the therapy that Vic had proved to her once and for all that he didn't love her. At the movie theater the night before they had happened to sit beneath an exposed ceiling beam. As soon as she noticed it, Nella became terrified, convinced plaster would fall on them. Agitated, she urged Vic to complain to the manager, get a refund, or at the very least to move their seats. But Vic said it was nothing, she was just working herself up, and refused to budge.

Maybe Vic was right. But Nella was as convinced that she was in mortal danger as Vic was that no problem existed. When they asked me who was right, I sighed. Who knew for sure whether Nella's fears were reasonable?

I replied, "In a way it doesn't matter how real the threat was. What matters is that Nella *thought* it was a threat. Clearly, this is something that Nella felt strongly about, Vic. It would have been easy just to move your seats and let the issue end there. Why not give her the added security she needs, the validation for her feelings, by moving to the other side of the theater?"

But that wasn't the whole story. I then turned to Nella and said, "Like Chicken Little, you think the sky is falling, and if Vic doesn't see things the same way, you're convinced he must not love you. Why do you frame everything as a test of his love? What would happen if you started from the assumption that Vic does love you, which he clearly does, and that even if he doesn't see things the way you do, he still loves you? Whether he was right or wrong, Vic did not believe the danger was real. Why must you feel so invalidated by that?"

When I framed their dispute this way they both had to agree: On the one hand, Vic could have and should have "supported" her. On the other, Nella should not make him constantly jump through hoops to prove his love. Nella had her own insecurities that contributed to their conflicts. Like many people who are flooded with emotions, she needed to own up to her anxiety, control it, modulate it, and find effective solutions for dealing with it. Blaming Vic or making him jump through hoops didn't make her any safer. The only way she would feel better was by exercising better emotional control and seeing that she wasn't in the danger she imagined.

To both of them I said, "All this fighting distracts you from what I see as the main message in this marriage—you love each other very much. When you see each other as the enemy, you forget that important fact."

The therapy began to take hold as I showed Nella that by providing Vic with the financial backing he needed during this transitional period in his life, she was fortifying their marriage, not destabilizing it. I asked her, "What's the worst thing that could happen if you let go of the purse strings?" She replied, "He'll take advantage of my generosity." "So what?" I said. "How does that put you in any danger? Even if Vic never completes his degree, the worst thing that would happen is that you'd lose one semester's tuition." At that point in her life, Nella was financially secure, and even as I spoke I could see the tension disappear from her face. We had defined and delimited the danger. The more deeply it sank in that there truly was nothing to fear, the less controlling and stormy she became.

My second objective was to help Vic, who felt he was inarticulate, to speak up for himself. Both Vic and Nella needed to see that Vic could also fortify the marriage. As I worked to assuage Nella's fears, I made sure to ask Vic what he thought about each and every issue that arose. However much he tried to avoid answering, I refused to accept his shrugs and sighs as a response. When Nella tried to put words in his mouth, I stopped her; and when she tried to interrupt him, I still wouldn't let him off the hook. Vic needed to speak up, not only so Nella would not be able to twist his words to suit her needs but also because when he did talk, he proved to have very sensible ideas.

I focused on the positive attributes he brought to the marriage. Beside his abiding love for Nella, Vic had remarkably good judgment. They both described how he had soothed Nella when her mother died; how he had helped her navigate various thorny business negotiations when she started her dental practice; and how romantic he had been when he proposed to her, on her birthday, and how his love was still there today.

This dual approach allowed Nella to be satisfied that I had taken her concerns and emotions seriously, while Vic felt better understood because he had been given the chance to air his own views. As our sessions continued, I tried to help her tolerate more anxiety and doubt. At the same time, I encouraged Vic not to be afraid of Nella's temper tantrums, and helped him see that he had resources to deal with and respond rationally to Nella's hyperbolic assertions. Most important of all, rather than withdraw from or provoke more fighting, I urged him to take on the role of the person who calms and restores reason.

As they came to see, the solution to their difficulties did not lie in fighting with each other, but in gaining insight into their own psyches. Vic had to overcome his sense of inadequacy and assert himself with Nella, however intimidating she might appear to be. Vic had hoped that I might have the strength to calm his wife. But had I done so, or had Nella calmed down on her own (owing to better self-control, medication, whatever), it would not have changed Vic's sense of inadequacy, for Vic's low self-esteem was not to due to Nella's hysteria. Only by confronting his fear of her hysteria would Vic's self-esteem improve.

As the insight dawned on them that they both had their own fears and sensitivities, they were humbled. At the outset, remember, Nella straightforwardly said she wanted me to change her husband, and although he never said so out loud, Vic clearly wanted me to rein in his wife. Now Vic and Nella were learning the truth of what I told them early on: Therapy was not about their changing another person, but about each changing oneself. Similarly, it's a fundamental mistake to believe that in changing others, we can change ourselves.

They now knew that the only change that mattered was what occurred inside, not outside. If we feel vulnerable, no amount of defensiveness can protect us from potential hurts, and if we feel unlovable, no amount of success or flattery will change this. What others do to us has very little to do with how we feel and think about ourselves. *We need to feel better about ourselves in order to feel better about others.*

So many of us believe that change can come from outside: from other people, professional success, or material possessions. But unless these outside events touch our inner core—and when I speak of personal change, I mean what goes on in that inner core, with all its raw emotions, vulnerability, and insecurity—the way we feel remains untouched. Among my patients are popular politicians, multimillionaires, and beautiful models who, despite their success, still feel unlovable inside. Buying a fancier home, winning a popularity contest, or getting somebody to go to bed with us doesn't give us respite from uncomfortable emotions and ideas about ourselves. Our emotional baggage, which determines so many of these deeper feelings, is not easily lightened or tossed off. The only way to change these patterns is from within, not without.

Our spouses and romantic partners are not obstacles to our own self-mastery and psychological maturation. Our spouses may be threatened by our changing—they may even try to resist it—but that does not matter. Personal growth takes place *within*, and whether or not others support it is irrelevant. "This is not about someone else's acceptance; it's about your own motivation to change," I tell my patients. "You're avoiding facing your anxiety not because your spouse can't handle it, but because you are afraid."

Trying to untangle our fears from our projections leads me to return to the question I asked earlier: Was it a coincidence that Vic and Nella's insecurities, mistrust, and projected anger matched so neatly? Is it mere chance that these two personalities fit together so snugly, confirming each other's preconceptions and expectations?

As a therapist, my answer is that "coincidences" like these speak to the nature of self-fulfilling prophecies. In marriage, we all have certain ideas about who our spouses are and what we expect of them. The preconceptions, projections, expectations, and emotional baggage each of us brings to a relationship have very little to do with the person we actually become involved with. In a sense, then, it's beside the point that we may have married someone who fit our own emotional template right off the bat—or who, through projection, eventually came to seem to conform to that emotional template. Viewed in this broader context, the painful, angry distortions couples like Vic and Nella project onto one another become far more understandable, perhaps even predictable. Thus, Nella felt that Vic's behavior confirmed her worst suspicions, and Vic found in Nella the angry, controlling shrew he always feared. It was no coincidence at all.

The Importance of Boundaries

What Vic and Nella learned applies to all of us. When our boundaries become blurred, we must take steps to clarify them. Apportioning responsibility is the only way out of the Land of He Said/She Said. To impose our problems on others, or take theirs on as our own, leads only to confusion and conflict.

This is easier said than done. Initially, patients often dispute my apportionment of responsibility. They rationalize their tried-and-true patterns, pointing to past experience to explain and excuse their behavior. For example, Nella tended to overinvolve herself in Vic's schoolwork. She habitually overstepped bounds by criticizing and revising his term papers, making Vic feel both intruded upon and infantilized. In an attempt to establish boundaries, I asked Nella, "If Vic got a failing grade on a term paper, or didn't complete his degree, how would that personally harm you?" Nella pointed to the importance of Vic's career to their marriage and their financial situation, and to the difficulty of standing around and watching Vic fail.

I told Nella that these statements were rationalizations for the fact that she had different ambitions for Vic than he did for himself. She might feel that she would be personally harmed if he did not achieve these goals, but in fact she herself was not hurt by Vic's academic problems, and therefore did not need to rescue him. Although Vic might have been desperate enough to accept her assistance, he resented it. These were his problems, not hers. Moreover, her overinvolvement had led to a pattern that actually encouraged Vic to *not* to do his homework as a way of acting out against her. She was controlling him while he indirectly fought her control. Similarly, in the same way that she expected him to disappoint her and he did, he expected her to become angry with him and she did.

To help them delineate better boundaries, I suggested that Nella could be supportive of Vic's career, sometimes even help him (if requested), without taking on his problems as her own. Such a stance would respect the boundaries between them. At the same time, I tried to show Vic that his achievements were for his own benefit, not his wife's, and that he did not need her to rescue him. In fact, he didn't like it when she did.

Boundary setting entails not only allocating responsibility (yours and mine), but also gauging and respecting gradations of involvement in each other's lives. We can be head over heels in love with someone, but still not completely immersed in the person's life; we all retain a separate sense of self, with our own separate needs, interests, and goals. In this vein, Nella needed to realize that what happened to Vic did not necessarily affect her and her safety, and that what happened to her didn't have to affect Vic. Just as Vic must face some of his problems on his own, so did she—a sobering thought for a woman who, despite her resourcefulness, cried for help at the slightest danger.

The complexities of sorting through these issues can be enormous. One final example: When Nella's father had a benign tumor removed from his gastrointestinal system, despite his excellent prognosis Nella remained concerned about his health and insisted he consult his doctor whenever he felt the least discomfort. One day, the minute Vic arrived home from a long study session at the library, Nella began an anxious monologue about the most recent tests her father had gone through. Vic, bleary-eyed from his schoolwork, merely said, "The test results were okay. Why don't you relax?" Nella exploded, accusing Vic of "not giving a damn" about her father. In response, Vic got defensive, saying, "What do you mean? I visited him in the hospital every day." He also deflected Nella's anger: "Hell, I spent more time with him than your brother did." By redirecting Nella's anger to her brother, Vic succeeded in establishing marital peace.

When we discussed this incident in therapy, it struck me that although Vic's initial response was tactless, he had tried to reassure Nella, and as far as I could tell she was overreacting. Nella had displaced her anxiety about her father and transformed it into anger at Vic. This may have defused the emotion, I said, but Vic wasn't to blame. Vic's tactic of redirecting Nella's anger toward her brother also missed the point. Although Vic no longer had to bear the brunt of Nella's temper, that did not help her focus on the real source of the problem, which was her anxiety over her father's condition.

Nella needed to learn that however uncomfortable we may be, someone else is not necessarily responsible for how we feel. Was Vic responsible for Nella's anxiety? Clearly not. But under stress, it looked that way to Nella.

What Nella did was convert her internal emotion, anxiety, into an external interpersonal conflict. But in order to find an effective solution, she needed to recognize her emotion as anxiety, not anger. Similarly, the only way she would feel better was by dealing with her anxiety, not by discharging it as anger.

Had Nella recognized her anxiety as such, she could have found more effective solutions to deal with it. She could have gathered more information about her father's illness, which would have given her more confidence in the doctor's hopeful prognosis. She could have approached Vic in a more engaging way, which would have made him more interested in consoling her. Finally, Nella could have just sat with her feelings, learning to live with uncertainty. After all, there are no guarantees in life. In externalizing and defusing her emotion, she short-circuited these solutions.

Unfortunately, when we vent our anger—in other words, act on it and express it in unproductive ways—it's next to impossible to retain perspective. That is why, in the next chapter, I will focus specifically on anger and how to modulate it.

3
Confronting Anger
Getting from Mutual Rage to Mutual Respect

What makes the inside-out dynamic so dangerous is that it's not just a way of thinking—suspecting others, blaming them for our problems, confusing what's me and what's you—but it also predisposes us to take action. Unfortunately, the actions we then take or words we choose are usually aggressive, angry, and destructive. We end up tearing apart the relationships we value the most.

In its typically circular way, the inside-out dynamic serves to justify our anger. If we feel threatened, we have no choice but to protect ourselves. But because we think we're just protecting ourselves, *we* may actually act in quite provocative ways. It never crosses our minds that we're escalating the conflict, or that our anger is based on a misinterpretation. All we know is we hurt, and we feel entitled to lash out. Sometimes we go even further: In anticipation of being attacked, we decide to make a preemptive strike ("I'm going to get you before you get me"). But what if our expectations are wrong? What if no attack was coming our way? What if the vulnerability comes from within? Then we, not the others, are at fault.

More often than not, when I see couples like Vic and Nella embroiled in bitter fighting, not just one but both partners are itching to put up their dukes. Each sees provocation coming from the other, and each feels entitled to retaliate. They're caught in a vicious cycle of conflict that threatens to spiral out of control with each ensuing escalation. These relationships have an incendiary quality; they can ignite at the slightest angry spark. At best, they merely *feel* unsafe; at worst, they *are* unsafe.

Only when we have gained control and mastered our emotions can we establish the sense of safety necessary to make romantic relationships flourish.

The Psychology of Anger

My patients are often surprised when I tell them that everybody fights. Not only that, people are most likely to fight with those they love the most. The more we care, the higher the emotional stakes, and the more likely we are to get angry. It's a truism that the opposite of love is not anger but indifference.

Please don't misunderstand. I'm not saying that it's healthy to be involved in a contentious relationship. You don't need a Ph.D. to know that pervasive, destructive anger is a clear signal that problems exist, or to understand that anger can corrode the most loving of relationships. What I am saying is that aggression is as much a part of human nature as love, sex, fear, and dependency. As a result, it's inevitable that some degree of anger will be present in even the healthiest relationships.

That's why, however intimate we are with our lover, we won't know him or her completely until we've also felt our lover's anger—and of course the same goes for our lover's knowing us. Fighting can be one of our most intimate experiences precisely because we no longer are on our best behavior. Our moments of anger are about as raw and powerful as any we can experience.

Given the intensity of the emotions invoked, it's no wonder that many of my patients struggle with anger, often finding themselves caught between venting and stifling their feelings. On the one hand, they feel that their anger stems from a legitimate slight or hurt and they want to express their emotions. On the other, they know from past experience that doing so with the full force of their feelings will serve no constructive purpose but instead will set off a downward, destructive spiral. With no good solution to their dilemma, couples engaged in these chronic battles often descend into despair, believing that no amount of talking will help them solve their disagreements. That's when they come to see me.

My approach has two parts. First, I help them examine whether their response was in fact justified or an overreaction. Frequently, there is a real foundation for their feelings, but their anger was too intense or vehement. Just because our anger is justifiable doesn't mean we are entitled to lash out.

Second, I help them modulate their anger, thus allowing them to express themselves in the most effective manner possible. For the real challenge lies in learning *how* to fight—respectfully and constructively. And to do that, we need to explore the psychological principles that underlie this powerful emotion.

We often think of anger as an impulse: "I feel angry," or "I have anger inside me that I need to let out." Many of us believe (like my patients) that we must either vent anger or stifle it, yet neither option is any good. It's hardly productive to deal with work stress by yelling at the boss and maybe getting fired. Neither is it a solution to stifle anger and risk hypertension or an ulcer. But like many "irresistible" impulses, anger is not easily repressed or muffled. Even when it is not expressed directly, it comes out indirectly, often insidiously.

I prefer to think of anger not as an impulse that must be dealt with but as an emotion that emerges from relationships and the way we think about them. More specifically, anger frequently arises from our mistrustful mind-set. If we are thin-skinned, we feel more easily threatened and are more likely to lash out.

Because our anger is meant to compensate for our inner fragility, if we feel vulnerable we think that the only way to stand up for ourselves is to be supremely vigilant and hard-edged. The only way we believe we will be heard is to yell and get angry. Otherwise, we fear, our partner will lull us into old patterns and take advantage of our vulnerability.

When anger is viewed this way, it becomes clear that the best way to dissipate and manage this volatile emotion is to change the way we think. For in changing the way we think, we change what we feel and how we behave. We begin to reinterpret our distorted perception of others as enemies and to reconsider what function our anger serves. We see that threats and escalation may intimidate others, but they aren't truly effective to produce the basic changes we want. Once we understand that in fighting others, we are actually fighting ourselves, we'll be much more likely to tame our anger, perhaps even let go of it.

Venting and the Vicious Cycle of Retaliation

From their first session in my office, Vic and Nella, whom we met in the previous chapter, demonstrated the danger of chronic, volatile fighting. The smallest issue, even a look taken the wrong way, had the power to provoke a major battle. But eventually, through the hard work of therapy, Vic and Nella learned to control their anger. They discovered how to voice their differences openly, in ways that did not deteriorate into ugly squabbles that left them both feeling bruised and hurt.

To help us modulate our anger, we need first to explore why we often find anger so pleasurable, and why we find it so tempting to give in to the most obvious manifestation of anger: venting.

When we vent, we do what most people do when scared or faced with feelings that make them unbearably uncomfortable: We get angry. We lash out. We blame. We rage. We scapegoat. We battle endlessly with an outside target, the enemy out there, our partner. We say, in effect, "You're the reason I feel so bad." In short, venting anger is the action component of turning emotions inside out.

Like Nella, many of us feel venting our anger as a cathartic experience. We believe venting will get the anger out of our system and somehow cleanse us. But as a psychologist, I disagree. Although such acting out can momentarily defuse the pressure cooker of our emotions and therefore temporarily lessen our discomfort, venting is ultimately both self-defeating and misguided. In the heat of the moment, we may feel justified in letting our anger spill out, and we may even feel a momentary pleasure as we curse and rage. But there are consequences. If you are convinced by the premise of this book—that how we think and behave toward others reflects how we think and feel about ourselves—then you'll understand that our anger harms us every bit as much as it does our partner.

When our anger goes out of control, we destroy the sense of safety and trust necessary to make a relationship thrive. The danger is not merely that our partner may retaliate. The greater danger is that by venting anger we create a feeling of unsafety within ourselves, for we ourselves feel safe and secure only when our *own* inner emotional turbulence is under control. Indeed, when we feel strong inside, we also feel safe and can exert better control over our emotions. It's not just that when we are afraid, we are more likely to get angry; it's also that when we are angry, we are more likely to be afraid. That's why we make a mistake in saying that others are responsible for our anger ("You provoked me"). We ourselves must take responsibility for our own lack of control.

Aside from the damage it does, to the self and to the relationship, venting anger is not an effective means of self-expression or problem solving. Rather than achieve what we want, typically our anger causes the opposite response. Furthermore, venting tends to harden and reinforce our preconceptions and projections, perpetuating the illusion that our partner is the enemy.

Venting is not the answer. However raw our emotions may be, we are better served by learning to hold our temper, understand what we're feeling, and *then* express ourselves—when we can do so constructively and appropriately. Even when we can't do that, at least we can learn to sit on our hands and tolerate the uncomfortable feelings without acting on them. Self-control, modulation, and mastery are the keys to dealing with anger.

Another way venting backfires is that it initiates a cycle of tit-for-tat retaliation. Edward Albee captured this most memorably in his play *Who's Afraid of Virginia Woolf?*, with his angry, embattled couples caught in an unending sequence of provocation, retaliation, and self-vindication. Although Vic and Nella were not as nasty as Albee's characters, the pattern was the same: For instance, when Nella rationalized her reluctance to pay Vic's tuition by saying he did not appreciate what she was doing for him, Vic retaliated by withholding his affection. As a result, when Nella tried to make up, Vic felt justified in rejecting her, which in turn led Nella to feel justified in lashing out at Vic in a temper tantrum that left them both feeling sour and bruised.

When I treat patients who are caught in this type of embattled cycle, probably the most confusing part of my job is teasing apart who's angry at whom and why. Like Vic and Nella, these couples are full of mutual accusations, hurts, and recriminations: "You're the one who's angry." "No, you are." "I'm justified in my anger because you [fill in your own blank, it could be anything]." Everything has been turned inside out and all around so many times by both partners that complete confusion reigns over who actually did what, and who's projecting what onto whom. Who started the fight? Who's responding to which provocation? Who's initiating a new round of hostilities? Who's feeding whose anger?

In this complicated game, both partners are responding to their projections rather than objective reality; each anticipates the other's moves and preemptively strikes out or defensively positions him- or herself against the expected attack. Because this cycle is based entirely on preconceptions, expectations, and misunderstandings—even when the provocation is a real one—the fight must be understood in the context of the whole pattern of the relationship and not as an isolated incident.

Of course, as so often happens when we turn our feelings inside out, neither partner takes responsibility for his or her anger. Nor does either partner own up to the deeper feelings, problems, conflicts, or inadequacies that led to the initial outburst (whoever "started" it is immaterial and impossible to figure out, in any case). Both partners become ever more angry and entrenched, looking for and finding provocation anywhere and everywhere.

Such was the case with Vic and Nella, each one egging the other on in an increasingly bitter cycle. The more withdrawn Vic became in response to Nella's temper outbursts, the more justified Nella felt in complaining that Vic was withholding and uncaring. The more they fought, the less they trusted each other; and the more mistrustful they became, the more they fought.

Even when hostilities ceased momentarily, a residual wariness remained, as if they were merely standing on guard waiting for the next showdown.

Their fights had become so automatic that they had stopped listening to each other. As Vic said, "I've heard it all before." But when we stop listening, all we hear are our preconceptions, all we see in our "enemy" is a projection of ourselves, and the only thing that can happen is a self-fulfilling prophecy.

As I pointed out to Vic and Nella, refusing to listen is a fundamental error. It reflects the fact that underlying the fighting is a basic disregard for each other's point of view. (In this case, Vic felt that Nella wasn't entitled to her anxiety, while Nella had no respect for Vic's independent thinking.) When couples reach this point, fights serve no constructive purpose whatsoever; arguments become battles intended to tear each other down and pierce each other's defenses. And, as Vic and Nella further demonstrate, unconstructive fighting often turns into destructive fighting.

An example of this is the following interchange. Nella began a session one day by turning to Vic and saying, in a scolding tone, "Tell him what you did."

Following his pattern of withdrawal from the conflict, Vic remained silent. True to her pattern, Nella then charged right in: Vic had intentionally left the birdcage open, allowing their parrot to fly free and damage some of the living-room furniture. Vic didn't dispute his responsibility; in fact, he apologized. But Nella continued her tirade: "I do all the work in this relationship. He's not even trying."

Finally, Vic said wearily, "She doesn't even listen. I told her I was sorry. What more does she want?" As he and Nella often did, he put me in the role of judge, addressing his comments to me rather than to his wife. Continuing to direct his comments toward me, Vic said that his wife was overreacting; he hadn't "intentionally" let the parrot damage the furniture.

Now it was Nella's turn to address me in my perceived role of referee, instead of her husband. Clearly, regardless of what Vic said, Nella could not let the issue go. She cited incidents that had taken place back when they were first dating, over ten years before: Vic didn't care then, and he doesn't care now, she declared. The louder and more emotional Nella became, the less focused and rational her points became, going off the topic completely. She wasn't problem-solving; she was spinning her wheels. Her argument had degenerated into global accusations, what I call "kitchen sink" accusations—she was throwing everything at him but the kitchen sink. But how could Vic respond to such generalities? And what did incidents that happened so far in the past have to do with the present?

Nella then went on to make yet another mistake commonly made by couples caught in this kind of fighting: She bolstered her complaint with an unrelated threat. She told Vic that if he did "something like this one more time," she would refuse to pay his tuition. It was an empty, imprecise threat—it was unclear what exactly Vic would have to do to deserve the punishment—and anyhow, the threat was unlikely to be carried out. And it backfired because Vic now felt entitled to retaliate by ignoring what she was saying. He rolled his eyes in my direction as if to say, "You see how hysterical she is, doc. That's what I have to deal with all the time." Instead of responding, he just let her rant and rave, and the argument continued to go nowhere.

As this fight showed, Vic and Nella had long since ceased to talk or listen to each other. At most, they were addressing me, and at worst they were merely venting. They did not view their disagreement as a problem to be solved, a manageable dispute in which each of them was entitled to his or her position. It was a fight to be won or lost. And that is why it went off track.

Even worse, their fights had become ever escalating in their intensity, dangerously so. It's as if they couldn't let go of the issue until they reached a climactic denouement characterized by ultimatums, threats, yelling, cursing, malicious words, and sometimes even pushing and shoving. They were out of control; their anger knew no bounds. This is why their relationship felt so unsafe to them.

For relationships to feel safe, we must feel strong enough to handle our partner's anger, and we need to feel that our own anger is not so dangerous that our partner can't handle it. Successful relationships establish a natural safety net that protects both partners. When we have such a safety net, we both feel much more comfortable and secure. We know that should either of us have a precipitous fall, in the form of a flare-up, our anger will not destroy either of us, or the relationship itself. Learning to fight fairly and constructively means learning to create a safe environment that can tolerate both partners' anger. When we lack that security, our fights can be much more easily ignited and, once started, will cause that much more damage. Like many couples, Vic and Nella needed to learn how to fight fairly and, in doing so, how to create this safe environment.

To work toward this goal, Nella had to learn to control her venting. For his part, Vic needed to understand that anger (his or someone else's) does not have to be so all-consuming and destructive that we dare not risk expressing it.

One of Vic's dreams showed just how dangerous he perceived his anger to be. In the dream, Vic became enraged by the taunts of a female classmate, lost control, and beat her up. Only when he saw her lying bruised and battered on the ground did he realize what he had done. Filled with remorse, he desperately tried to care for her wounds.

The revulsion Vic felt in retelling this dream explained why, even when provoked to his limit, he preferred to remain silent rather than show his anger. It vividly demonstrated the bloody casualties he feared would result if he joined the brutal verbal warfare Nella regularly engaged in.

To me, though, it wasn't only that Vic believed his anger was dangerous to others (specifically Nella). He also identified with the victim, the classmate lying bruised and beaten on the ground. He imagined that another person's anger (again, Nella's) could also devastate him.

Vic's dream also demonstrates that our own sense of vulnerability derives far less from what we perceive to be our partner's aggression than it does from a projection of our lack of control over our own aggression. When we believe that anger (whether our own or the anger we project onto our partner) can be this dangerous, we undercut our own sense of safety, which is necessary for a relationship to develop. We begin to feel as though we have to walk on eggshells with each other—or else come out with guns blazing.

It is interesting to note that just as Vic and Nella perceived their anger to be toxic to their marriage, they thought it dangerous to expose me to their hostility. When patients transfer their feelings about each other onto me, it provides an opportunity to analyze their projections in a context that is new and different from their familiar relationships. Being part of a new, therapeutic relationship allows people to develop insight when they cannot do so in ongoing, more complicated, relationships (where it's less clear who's doing what to whom).

For example, when I needed to reschedule our appointment one week, Vic quickly agreed to the time I proposed even though he had told me many times that he had a tight schedule. When the actual day arrived, though, he never showed up. Only at our next appointment did he reveal that he had been angry at me because the change had inconvenienced him. "Why didn't you let me know at the time?" I asked. "You seemed stressed out," he replied. "So what," I said, "what would have happened?" "You would have been irritated with me and have paid me back one way or another," he said.

Thus, Vic's thinking about our relationship in therapy mirrored the fears he projected onto Nella. That is, in addition to fearing that I couldn't deal with his anger, Vic believed I'd retaliate and he'd be in jeopardy.

With me as with Nella, Vic's solution was to disengage until he was no longer angry. Had he come to the session, he feared he would have been provoked to anger. It was better, he believed, not to show up at all; in the same way, with Nella he felt that it was better to keep his mouth shut than to respond.

I told Vic that disengagement may indeed be better than becoming violent, but it is an ineffective strategy because it perpetuates the sense that he and others are so fragile. Instead, Vic needed to learn that his marriage (as well as other relationships, such as ours in therapy) could tolerate anger. I didn't mean this as a license to vent or act out. Rather, he needed to find his way toward effective self-expression. I told Vic, "Your anger is not as destructive as you imagine, and Nella is more resilient than you know. See what the relationship can handle."

For her part, Nella did not hesitate to let me have it when she thought I made a stupid comment, when she felt I was siding with Vic, or when she believed I wasn't being sufficiently sympathetic to her. She vented as openly with me as with Vic, but after each outburst, she tried to smooth over the rough spot with flattery. After one session in which her temper had led her to use particularly harsh words against me, Nella offered to prepay her bill. This was her way of apologizing, but Nella didn't see the connection between her explosiveness and her desire to repair the relationship. When I pointed this out to her, she told me that if she were in my shoes, she couldn't deal with someone with such an intimidating temper. She assumed I was as intimidated as her husband was and believed I resented having to cater to her neediness.

Nella also told me she had come to believe that escalating a fight actually worked. After all, her experience had taught her that tears, threats, and hysteria often got her what she wanted. But I showed her that it only worked in the short run to silence the disagreement—and, more literally, to silence Vic. Her intimidation only drove the disagreement temporarily underground: It always resurfaced later.

Nella needed to learn that it's possible to demonstrate steely determination without making outrageous threats. "We can get people to do something they don't want if we have enough leverage; but it's at a tremendous cost to the relationship," I told her. I pointed out that just as with her parents' threats when they bullied her, her threats only served to undermine her credibility, and make Vic feel justified in his withdrawal. Nella in turn felt her hysteria was justified by his stonewalling. Too many of us feel that unless we communicate in a dramatic way, we won't be heard. Not true. We'll be heard much better if we speak in a calm voice, use reason, and act appropriately.

Contain the Fight

Being able to lower our voices and calm down is essential. In the heat of battle, we lose control and do and say things without concern for the damage we might wreak, and this loss of control devastates our built-up store of trust and security. However loving and in control we may be the majority of the time, even a few instances of being out of control can be enough to unravel the relationship's safety net. This is why it is crucial to contain fights and to prevent them from escalating. The nature of the disagreement is not the problem, nor the fact that there is a disagreement; emotional damage is always due to the fight's destructive escalation.

Most of the couples I see in therapy are concerned about their fighting. They recognize the harm they do to themselves, to their partners, and to the relationship itself. If in retrospect—no matter how explosive their anger was, how little control they may have exercised at the time of the fight, and even if they felt justified in their anger—they are able to express sadness, regret, or guilt and acknowledge the fight's destructive consequences, I hold a positive prognosis for their ability to change. Only when patients do not exhibit guilt or concern about their anger am I pessimistic. I can't instill a conscience in my patients, but when they do have one, I can help them develop better emotional control.

I begin by helping them to anticipate the destructive consequences of their anger, rather than recognizing them only belatedly. I remind them of prior arguments and the patterns that are likely to recur should they act in a certain way. By suggesting different responses that could lead to better outcomes, I help them see that they have a much wider range of choices in handling difficult situations than they currently realize. When they see they have a choice, they feel that much more in control.

I emphasize to them the importance of taking and keeping track of our emotional temperature when we're caught in the midst of a fight. Maintaining emotional control is not an automatic function; it is a conscious and deliberate decision. Just as we must monitor our speed and not go too fast when we learn to drive a car, we need to consciously decide to take our foot off the accelerator, perhaps even put on the brakes, when we fight. If we're not aware that we're driving too fast, we won't ever make the decision to slow down.

Taking our emotional temperature is essential because emotional thinking clouds our rationality. That's why I advise taking a step back as soon as we feel ourselves becoming too riled up. It is only when we're calmer that we can have a more rational, contained, and focused discussion. Think of this as a time-out—essentially, the same thing as the strategy recommended for young children who have lost control.

Because time-outs are temporary, they're not an ideal, long-term solution (though far preferable to continued loss of control and escalation). That's why I generally recommend them only at the beginning of therapy, before patients have learned more sophisticated problem-solving techniques. But for couples or individuals who are emotionally inflamed, simply deciding to go to a neutral corner represents an enormous personal struggle for self-control.

For instance, at one of our first sessions, Nella and Vic recounted a series of fights filled with mutual recriminations, hysteria, and ultimatums. Each fight would end with Nella in tears and Vic desperately afraid that she would leave him. I was concerned that their marriage would fall apart if these fights continued, so I suggested that the next time one of these fights flared, they should agree to take a one-hour break and go to separate rooms. I told them, "Don't blame each other for walking away from the fight. It's my decision. If you still feel worked up about this issue later on, rather than pick up the gauntlet again, just table the problem until our next therapy session. Whatever you do, don't perpetuate the fight."

Sure enough, at the following session, Nella and Vic described yet another emotional shoot-out. This time, though, they had followed my instructions and gone to separate rooms. Vic had found it to be a relief, whereas Nella said it had been a terrible struggle to restrain herself from going back in and letting Vic have it. They felt relieved knowing they had an appointed time to talk through the problem with an impartial mediator—especially Nella, who otherwise might not have been able to resist the temptation to continue the battle. And by the next morning, both of them had cooled off enough to reach a compromise.

The fight, it turned out, had been over whether Vic should accompany Nella the next weekend while she looked for a summer house or spend his time studying for an upcoming final exam. Taking time to cool off and "sleep on it" had allowed them to see that if they returned early on Sunday, Vic would have enough time to accompany her *and* study for his exam. It was an obvious solution, but neither had been able to reach it in the midst of a fight that centered not on a potential solution, but on Nella's feeling she was not being taken care of and on Vic's sense that he was being pushed around.

Fights escalate because of the need to win. But, as I tell my patients, fights should not be about winning and losing. They should be about solving problems and resolving disagreements. Time-outs work because they allow both partners to let go of an issue without there being a winner and a loser.

Modulating Our Feelings

The second part of my approach to dealing with anger involves being able to discuss why we're angry, but without venting—in other words, modulating our feelings.

Venting is counterproductive in all the ways I discussed earlier. Instead of venting, we need to think first, consider what we want to say, tone it down, focus our thoughts, and speak with a clear purpose in mind. If we feel we're on the verge of venting or lashing out, then we should button our lips, count to ten, do whatever it takes to regain control. At first it may feel mechanical or unnatural to resist the urge to lash out. But doing so presents us with the opportunity to reconsider what we're feeling—and to anticipate the consequences of what we'll be glad later we *didn't* say. The more practiced we become at controlling our emotions this way, the more internalized and therefore more natural the ability to control ourselves becomes.

In our first few sessions, Nella learned quickly how to contain her fights with Vic. She recognized the value of self- restraint, but it still took all her effort to stop herself from yelling. However much her outward behavior had changed, she confided, inside she felt as raw as ever.

Yet over the next few months, subtly, and without her even being aware of it, Nella began to internalize her emotional self-control. Situations that would have provoked her in the past no longer fazed her. She achieved what she termed a "deep calm" and felt good about being so much more in control of her own emotional state. This was brought home to her when one day she proudly announced that she had finally gotten a payoff for all the months of working to control her temper.

The Friday night before, she and Vic had begun to disagree about what to do over the weekend. Vic was nervous about an upcoming test; Nella wanted to go dancing to relax after a tough work week. Instead of criticizing Vic for not having studied earlier in the week (as she acknowledged she would have done before therapy had begun), Nella took a sympathetic tone, saying, "I don't know how that professor expects you to get all this reading done. He just keeps piling it on." Vic, pleasantly surprised by this response (instead of the criticism he had expected), went over and gave her a romantic kiss. In this way, Nella managed to defuse a potentially tense argument. Not only did she avoid a fight, she got what she most wanted—Vic's affection. Moreover, later on that night, Vic decided he had studied enough, and they went out dancing.

When patients talk with me about their fights, they feel that it is next to impossible to resist picking up the gauntlet when they are provoked. The answer, I suggest, lies in their own inner sense of safety. If we feel safe, we won't be prone to launch into anger. But what is it that helps us to feel safe in relationships? How do we learn to turn the other cheek?

There's something about anger that automatically makes us afraid. When somebody yells at us, we feel intimidated, whether or not we lash back. And when we feel threatened, we're most likely to react defensively.

To help patients gain a better perspective on their partners' anger and resist reacting defensively, I often ask them, "How would you deal with a temperamental child in a similar situation? What if your child started throwing a temper tantrum because you wouldn't let him have sweets before dinner? Would you retaliate?" Of course not. We're not threatened by the child's anger, however difficult or demanding it may be to manage the situation. We know that the child's mood will change, usually in a matter of minutes.

When I play out this hypothetical situation with my patients, they invariably say that their partner is not a child, meaning that they have different expectations of an adult than of a child. To which I respond, "The psychological issues driving your partner's anger are the same ones that cause your child's anger. He or she is frustrated, or is feeling hurt or disrespected. We're all children at heart. It's just that adults hide it a little bit better. What gives you perspective with your child is the fact that you're not threatened. Why be threatened by an adult? If we can achieve the same perspective when in the midst of an emotional argument with our partners that we have with our kids, we're ahead of the game."

Problem Solving

Disagreements are problems to be solved, not battles to be won or lost. We can only resolve our problems if we listen to our partners, give credit to the other's point of view, and ground our love in mutual respect.

Mutual respect is based on the recognition that both of us are entitled to our feelings or position on an issue. It means understanding that there will be times when we have at least different ways of seeing things, perhaps slight differences, perhaps even major gaps. When we can no longer agree to disagree—or can't tolerate any degree of disagreement at all—that respect breaks down. When we feel that our partner is just dead wrong, we invalidate and delegitimate his or her position. Similarly, when we feel our partner is being gratuitously contentious, we often react in kind.

One of the most difficult ideas for embattled couples to accept is that they need not think alike on every issue. The ostensible conflict may arise over issues such as: Should we spend money on your fur coat, or my car repair? If I take a golf vacation, will you get lonely without me? If I work late at the office, then you're left to do all the babysitting. Beyond that, though, couples often argue out of a sense that their partner is not entitled to think or want something different from them. We may be threatened by the fact that our beloved has such different priorities. When that happens, the relationship has no room for a live-and-let-live philosophy.

It's crucial for a relationship to allow both partners to be comfortable. Even though we're partners in a marriage, we also remain individuals. As such, we don't always have to think alike. In fact, because our interests and reactions diverge, we should actually expect disagreement. The inability to accept differences is what makes so many of us feel invalidated in our relationships.

But once we accept that our partner is entitled to see things differently and to disagree, we can begin to find common ground. For example, at one session, Vic and Nella told me about their frequent conflicts about driving: how fast is too fast and how slow is too slow. Nella complained that her husband was a lunatic who drove seventy miles per hour, while Vic countered that his wife was a nervous Nelly who wouldn't go over forty. Naturally, they wanted me to decide who was right and who was wrong.

"There is no right answer," I told them. "You have to reach a joint decision that will satisfy you both. If this becomes an issue of who's going to give in, then there's no room for compromise." It seemed obvious to me that a middle ground of fifty-five miles per hour was possible; the question was, could they themselves reach that conclusion? Indeed, at first each refused to concede a single mile per hour to the other. For Vic, every mile under seventy was an insult to his sense of masculinity, while Nella perceived every mile over forty as causing her far too much anxiety. I tried to show them that Nella was not insulting him, nor was Vic torturing her. But it was no go.

Finally I asked Vic, "What's wrong with her being anxious?" He seemed taken aback; the thought hadn't occurred to him. He had simply assumed that Nella's anxiety (a quality he did not respect) was neurotic and illegitimate. Nella appeared similarly caught off guard when I reminded her that she had often said that when the weather was bad, the only person she would trust behind the wheel was Vic because he was such an experienced driver. Why hadn't her trust in Vic's driving ability lessened her anxiety?

So caught up were Vic and Nella in their sniping that they could not see beyond their own arguments. Once they were able to step back and shift perspectives, they could acknowledge that this was not an either/or choice between his seventy and her forty. Once they understood—and respected—each other's feelings, they realized there actually was room to negotiate. But the only way two people can arrive at compromise is if each feels the other is *entitled* to his or her position and emotions: in this case, Nella to her anxiety, and Vic to his impatience.

You may ask why I go into such detail about an issue that seems so minor. Trivial arguments over issues like driving speed may seem insignificant, but they're the fodder of everyday life in relationships. More important, they generally reflect deeper emotional issues. such as "You don't care enough about me." Vic and Nella each read into the other's "speed limit" a malevolent motive that just wasn't there: Nella's suspicion that Vic enjoyed making her anxious, and Vic's suspicion that Nella tried to control him just to show him who was boss.

In eventually reaching their compromise of fifty-five, Vic and Nella established a sense of mutuality and partnership. They were able to learn from this small achievement that reaching a compromise is usually not a matter of giving in or giving up. More often than not, most successful negotiations, personally and professionally, involve relatively minor, incremental changes, not a radical abandonment of our position. But such minor changes can make a huge difference.

I often compare personal change to adjusting the focus on a TV set. Turning the dial only a slight amount can make a blurry picture suddenly take on great clarity. Similarly, slight changes of attitude—of mind-set—can make big differences in how we feel. Nella learned to be comfortable when Vic drove at fifty-five, whereas she could never have learned to tolerate his driving at seventy.

As a final note on the importance of mutual respect, it's useful to look at individual therapy for a perspective on couples therapy. One of the ways that individual therapy works is that people don't feel judged; they feel accepted by the therapist for who they are and what they are. In couples therapy, I try to communicate the same kind of acceptance and get my patients to do the same with each other. I take as a starting point that each side is reasonable. There are no rights and wrongs. All I try to achieve is for people to listen to each other. They don't have to concede at all, but they do have to listen. In fact, this capacity to accept differences, respectfully, is an important indicator of the strength of a relationship.

The Rules for a Fair Fight

When I work with couples, I lay out early on in the therapy a set of rules for fighting fairly. I know the therapy has truly taken hold when couples begin to self-correct without my having to say anything to help keep them on track.

Here are ten rules to help you fight fairly, constructively, and with respect:

1. Preserve a sense of safety in the relationship at all times. Security breeds trust. We need to know that a single

argument will not break the relationship; a disagreement will not cause your partner to run away. Contain the fight. Don't let it escalate. Protecting the relationship shows how much we value it.

2. View the fight or disagreement as a problem to be solved, not a battle to be won. When we're on the same team, there are no winners or losers, no points to score. If one of us loses, we both lose, so don't try to prove your partner wrong. Be constructive, not destructive.

3. Show respect by listening. Help your partner to feel heard. Accept differences. Even agreeing to disagree is a sign of mutual respect. ("I get what you're saying, but I don't know what to do about it.") Have a clear sense of boundaries; that is, don't impose your own views and attitudes on the other. Own up to what's going on internally, and look inward for solutions. (If we're looking for improved self-esteem or lessened anxiety, we can't expect our partner to achieve this for us.)

4. Blame less and make fewer accusations. Make "I" statements, rather than "you" statements. If we complain rather than criticize, our partner will feel less threatened and defensive. As we talk more about ourselves, we attack our partner that much less. ("I felt hurt when you cut me off in our dinner party conversation last night" rather than "You're so selfish, you never listen to me.")

5. Stay focused on the issue at hand. Rather than making global statements, make concrete points. Avoid reference to past misdeeds. Set achievable goals. The more concrete we are, the more likely we are to reach a consensus or compromise.

6. Avoid "therapizing" each other. Not only is this kind of psychological analysis usually wrong, it's done as a means of one-upmanship, and with such an unsympathetic tone

that it only intensifies the conflicts. (I tell my patients to leave the psychological comments to me.)

7. Don't issue ultimatums. Threats usually make people more entrenched and defensive. Even if the point made is fair, expressing it in an all-or-nothing way squeezes our partner, making him or her feel ambushed or cornered. Give your partner room to compromise. Remember that we all need to save face.

8. Don't demand a confession or force an apology. We may get it, but it will probably be hollow. If we're measuring results, it's better to look at our partner's behavior more than his or her words. Our partners may give us what we want even though they can't acknowledge that they're doing so.

9. Remember that venting anger—at others, or at the world in general—may give us momentary satisfaction, but it's usually counterproductive. Mastering our emotions represents a much better solution. Just because a spouse knows which buttons to push doesn't mean we are compelled to react to the button, for example, by launching into a harangue. Our tempers are under *our* control, and if they are out of control, it's our problem. To blast our spouse is to overreact—especially since, however loud and long we rant, the same old enemy is still right inside us.

10. Rather than making a preemptive strike to avoid what we assume will be mistreatment or rejection, sift through the preconceptions that led to that assumption. Try to clear the air by approaching each other with a more open view. Before lashing outward, look inward.

Finally, we need to pick and choose our conflicts. It doesn't hurt to let some problems just go by.

Don't Get Discouraged

As couples like Vic and Nella begin to understand how they turn their anger inside out, how to contain their fighting, and how to forge a sense of mutual respect, they make significant strides. But progress is not linear. For every step forward there is also some backward movement. Change and personal growth are incremental and hard-won. That's why I always advise my patients to expect discouragement and disappointment.

It takes time to grow comfortable with a new way of facing our emotions, ourselves, and our partners. Blaming and acting out serve to help us avoid feelings of depression, anxiety, and doubt; consequently, when we stop acting in this way we are forced to face rather uncomfortable, complicated, and ambivalent feelings that exist within us. As we confront them, we may not like everything we discover, and we may choose (at least temporarily) to return to our old ways of blame, anger, and mistrust.

This is what happened with Vic and Nella. Through the work of therapy, they had learned to treat each other with more respect and politeness, and when disagreements arose, there was a willingness to compromise. Yet it seemed to me that they were treating each other too cautiously—better, certainly, than when they staged their knock-down-drag-out fights, but still not optimal. To my mind their caution reflected their continued doubts about each other's fragility.

Then, after five months of good progress, a major battle destroyed much of the hard-earned trust they had built. Nella lashed into Vic with a barrage of perceived faults that burst like a pent-up dam. Criticisms that had been saved up over many months suddenly spewed out. Vic, too, regressed, storming out of the house in stony, withdrawn silence. This fight caused such a breach that when Vic did not return home that night, Nella worried that he had left her for good, was having an affair, and wanted a separation.

None of this proved to be true. Vic showed up the next morning in my waiting room, where he met Nella in time for our regular therapy session. But it was hardly a calm reunion. In fact, they yelled at each other so loudly I heard every word clearly right through the waiting-room door and had to interrupt a session with another patient to ask them to quiet down.

A few minutes later, at our appointed session, they told me what had happened: In line with their old pattern, Nella had felt ignored, while Vic had been intimidated by her threats. I said, "I'm less concerned that you had another fight than I am with how quickly you seemed to give up all your progress." I continued, "Personal growth is like climbing a slippery mountain. Each step is difficult, and backsliding is inevitable. The problem here isn't that you fell back a few steps. It's that you then let yourselves go into a free fall. If you had contained the fight and found your footing on that mountain, you would have stopped the backsliding. It would have required extra effort to retrace your steps, but the climb back up would have been less difficult than falling back to where you started."

Fortunately, after continued therapy, Vic and Nella were able to regain their footing and grew comfortable enough with their anger to contain future fights. As I said at the outset, we all get angry, raise our voices, and throw up our hands in despair. The strongest relationships are those that can tolerate anger and disagreement. We must protect our relationships from our anger, and protect others from it as well. In so doing, we protect ourselves.

Eventually, Nella and Vic were able to develop that level of comfort and trust as they demonstrated better mastery over their emotions, and so can you. Only then, I believe, is it possible to let go of anger and move forward.

4

When Happily Ever After Isn't

Blaming Each Other for Our Own Disappointments

In the previous chapters I focused on how we turn our anxiety, insecurity, and anger inside out. Here I'll describe how we turn our disappointment and sadness inside out and blame our partner for our feelings of depression, disillusionment, and frustration.

"He wasn't who I thought he was," we say, or "He let me down" or "He's stopping me from doing what I want." We may blame our partners for our discontent, or accuse our spouses of being the obstacles to our happiness, but who really is at fault?

When we become frustrated and angry with our partners for not fulfilling our often unspoken hopes and dreams, we're turning our disappointment inside out. Unable to tolerate frustration and unwilling to face our own limitations, we externalize our disappointment, blaming our partners for our feelings. If we examine our preconceptions about what we want from our partners, however, we generally discover that our sense of disappointment has less to do with our lovers and how they treat us than with our own elevated assumptions about the relationship and our negative feelings about ourselves. It's our difficulty in accepting people's limitations, not the limitations themselves, that are the problem.

To begin to take responsibility for our feelings of disappointment and frustration, we must look within. We must sift through our ideas about relationships, separating reasonable from unreasonable expectations, realistic hopes from unrealistic ones. We need to ask ourselves: Are we setting our hopes so high that they can never be met? Are we not getting our hopes up at all for fear that they will be dashed, a stance that also leads to frustration and hopelessness. How do we face our own limitations (and our subsequent sense of frustration and disappointment), and how do we respond to our partner's? Finally, when our lovers do not meet our needs, does that mean they have let us down irrevocably?

Confronting the answers to these questions will help us understand the source of our unhappiness. The more we are able to own up to our feelings, however uncomfortable they may be, the better prepared we will be to align our expectations with reality and stop blaming others for our own limitations. Once we learn to better tolerate life's inevitable frustrations and disappointments, including the ups and downs of romance, we'll discover that our partner is not the obstacle to our happiness. Only we are.

Disappointment Is Inevitable

One reason disappointment is so difficult to confront is that it represents a loss—the loss of a dream, hope, or ideal. And any kind of loss, large or small, is painful.

Yet loss and disappointment are inevitably woven throughout our lives. In terms of our romantic relationships, no one person can be everything to us all of the time. People will invariably let us down. They won't be available when we need them, or their interests will take precedence over ours, or they won't be able to give us all we want because of their own limitations. Sadly, even when we promise to love each other forever, there are no guarantees of permanence; we need only look to the divorce rate for confirmation.

And so when patients tell me they believe relationships can't or won't work out, they aren't wrong. You're right, I reply, relationships inevitably do lead to disappointments, sometimes quite painful ones. Yet it is as impossible as it is unwise to shield ourselves from disappointment entirely. The world is full of difficulties, quagmires, and assorted interpersonal conflicts large and small that can be difficult to solve. We may have financial problems, feel frustrated in our jobs, need to confront a medical illness, or be unable to get our romantic partners to care for us in the way we want. The challenge lies in how we confront these disappointments, frustrations, and limitations, and how we then align our expectations and actions with reality.

The mistake many of us make is to "act out" our feelings of disappointment. We blame others for our disappointment, rage at them, run away from the problem, or withdraw into a shell. When we think we can escape the obstacles to our happiness by taking these emotional shortcuts—whether it's by quitting a bad job, walking out of a relationship, or copping out of all relationships—we are generally fooling ourselves. It may be enticing to declare the grass is greener somewhere else and leave our partner behind, but often we end up repeating the same pattern in a new relationship.

Coming to terms with disappointment as a fact of life is important because a certain level of disappointment is a by-product of the very ideal of romance itself. When we love, we idealize our beloved. We imagine that this idealized lover will gratify all our possible desires, never abandon us, repair our defects, heal our emotional wounds, and assuage our humiliations. We endow him or her with an omnipotent capacity to correct and repair all that is wrong in our lives, as in a fairy tale.

But fairy tales are not reality. No one is perfect, and we will _____ably become disillusioned when we discover that fact. _____ to the way we may idealize a doctor whom we believe _____ ulously cure us. Eventually, we end up railing against the doctor when we discover that he cannot cure us after all. Doctors are not gods any more than our lovers are Apollo or Aphrodite.

We've all experienced this cycle of romantic idealization and disappointment in some form. No one can live up to all our fantasies. Even the best-matched partners will be crushed under the burden of such high hopes and elevated expectations. For no one, however beloved (or however loving), can sustain a sense of perfect, uninterrupted bliss forever.

In the first throes of love, we feel swept up, fascinated, enchanted. The sensation is that of an emotional high. If only we could live in paradise forever! But we can't. Unfortunately, our fantasies and preconceptions don't usually account for this fact—or take in the mundane reality of day-to-day life. If a relationship is to last, the initial stage of highly idealized romantic hopes and yearnings must give way to the more "normal" rhythms of work-a-day life, along with the limitations of work, family obligations, child-care responsibilities, and outside factors ranging from illness to job layoffs to something as mundane as a traffic jam. When we're unable to accommodate this ebb and flow, the every-day disappointments of boredom and monotony can loom large as problems.

Does the fact that this kind of letdown must follow the initial ecstasy of romance mean we should try to avoid idealizing our partner? Not at all. It's a testament to love's power that we're able to see Prince Charming in a balding man, or a beautiful woman in the ordinary person the rest of the world perceives. Moreover, in some respects, we need to view our loved one as a prince or princess and treat them accordingly; this is the way in which love can and does repair us, and helps buoy us through all kinds of hardships.

At the same time, we must acknowledge that no one can live up to such high hopes and elevated expectations all of the time.

Even Superman needs to be Clark Kent some of the time. When we are disappointed or frustrated, instead of blaming our partners, we need to look within, identify, and confront the interior emotions our disillusionment reflects. We may have a need to idealize our lovers, but their falling short of that idealization is not their fault. Our disappointment says more about our romantic wishes than about our partner's limitations.

When we do look within, we discover a deeper source of our disappointment, hidden in the emotional baggage we bring from childhood to our adult relationships. Our childhood experiences create a template for understanding our romantic lives, so much so that in many ways our relationships can be seen as a recapitulation of our earliest experiences.

Childhood endows us with a full history of experiences that teach us what to expect in loving, as well as what others should expect of us. We each bring to adulthood our personal legacy of developmental wounds, frustrations, and other attitudes about love and loving. Experiences need not be traumatic or abusive to leave their mark; wounds can also be caused by a parent who worked more than we would have liked, or the arrival of a younger sibling who competed with us for parental attention. The key to our satisfaction as adults is not allowing these earlier disappointments to undermine or dominate us.

In fact, how we deal in adulthood with this re-evoked disappointment from our early lives will determine the trajectory of our romantic relationships. If we rail against our lovers for their imperfections—for not giving us everything we want (just as our mother frustrated us), and for falling short of our expectations (just as our father had feet of clay)—we will be mired in anger and frustration. No one, no matter how loving and beloved, can wholly compensate for our childhood losses and disappointments. At the same time, the fact that a person had an unhappy childhood does not mean that he or she is fated to lead an unhappy life. We don't have to continue to be defined by our childhood experiences if we choose not to.

It is true that we are all predisposed to repeat the past, whether in our choice of romantic partner or in the patterns that we establish in our relationships. But through insight, mastery, and tolerance, we can overcome our pasts. If we are disappointed, it has more to do with what we are seeking than with what we have found. The more realistic we are in owning up to the flaws and imperfections that life has dealt us and that have shaped us, the better able we'll be to tolerate love's disappointments, and the more open we'll be to enjoying its gifts.

Aligning Expectations with Reality: Arlene

I've long held the view that the cycle of idealization and disappointment can be a healthy growth process. As our expectations evolve, they will inevitably be tested by reality, and in that way eventually come into closer alignment with it. When our expectations don't mesh with reality, disappointment will inevitably result. But we can learn from those experiences: first, how to confront and manage disappointment itself; second, how to shape our expectations in such a way that they can be more realistically met.

These are the lessons that Arlene learned through therapy.

All through her twenties and into her thirties, Arlene, who was thirty-two when she started therapy with me, had one intense love affair after another. None lasted more than a year, and all were strikingly similar in that they more or less followed the same pattern of idealization and disappointment. There would be a whirlwind romance, when she was head over heels in love, and then a sobering-up period, when she saw her lover's limitations. Rick was too committed to his work to dote on her as she wanted. Hank didn't earn enough money for Arlene's expensive tastes, and Len proved to be sexually unfaithful. In each case, Arlene felt "crushed" (as she told me) by her discovery of her lover's "true" character.

Arlene described each of these affairs as if the men had misled her and were therefore to blame for her disappointment. Yet the more she described the course of each affair, the more I wondered whether she had ignored or misread certain clues in a way that had led to, or contributed to, her feelings of disappointment. Who or what was to blame for Arlene's disappointment? Was it each man's shortcomings, or was it Arlene's own elevated expectations and preconceptions?

To help sort through the "responsibility" for her disappointment, I asked Arlene to review each boyfriend in a more objective way. For instance, Rick, a doctor-in-training, certainly was overwhelmed by his work schedule, and he certainly did not have much time to spend outside the hospital. But in the larger scheme, Arlene did not take into account other facts: that Rick spent every free afternoon or evening with her, rather than studying or visiting his family, who lived nearby. Hank was a struggling musician who needed to count every penny. But he adored her, and in order to go halfway toward meeting her need for security, he had sought and been offered a university teaching position that would have provided stability and more. As for Len, from their first date, he talked about his former fiancée in a way that made it obvious that he remained emotionally attached to her; when he went back to his "ex," the only one who was surprised was Arlene.

Perhaps none of these men would have been right for Arlene. But repetitive patterns are generally a clue that our own emotional baggage is influencing our choices. Arlene's pattern was to blame her boyfriend for the relationship's failure and her own disappointment. This suggested that she was playing out a psychological pattern that came from inside her, rather than merely responding to external happenstance (as she claimed). In my view, what led Arlene to be disappointed again and again was the way she framed her expectations and then projected her preconceived notions about romance onto each man.

Indeed, as we delved deeper, Arlene revealed a childhood history that began to shed light on her love affairs. Arlene's initial idealization of each boyfriend was, in my view, an attempt to compensate for a childhood in which her divorced father rarely visited or paid her much attention. Rather than face the disappointing reality of her traveling-salesman father's absence and disinterest, Arlene created a romantic image of a globe-trotting, James Bond–type father who would eventually swoop into town to rescue her from the workaday sameness of her suburban life with her mother. But this was just a fantasy. Instead of showing up to "rescue" her, Arlene's father made and broke repeated promises to visit her or take her with him on vacation. The excitement was all in the expectation of something that never came to pass.

Similarly, as an adult Arlene imagined that a man would inject excitement, romance, and an enormous sense of possibility into her otherwise stable, steady life as a high school teacher. Her romances always began with the same heady fantasy she had attached to her father's wished-for appearance. Soon enough, though, reality would set in. Just as her father never kept his promises, her boyfriends didn't live up to the exciting billing she had created for them.

To Arlene's credit, she had some awareness of how she would at first inflate her lovers, only to deflate them later. On some level she knew that as soon as the relationship progressed to the point where the inevitable disappointments of daily life would creep in, the "romance" (or her idealized conception of what a romance should be) was over. Yet time and again, she would become angry at the boyfriend in question for "leading her on." But who was leading whom, and where?

After listening to Arlene tell her story, I encouraged her to step back from her romantic history and ask herself who was responsible for her disappointment. Was it her boyfriends for not living up to her expectations? Or should she take at least partial responsibility for what happened? I suggested that a closer examination would reveal that Arlene had led herself on, acting out a cycle of idealized hope followed by disappointment, ignoring her more realistic perceptions and better judgment. Having projected her own fears and fantasies (which derived from her childhood) onto the relationships, Arlene felt justified in blaming her boyfriends for her sense of disappointment.

"So it's not me, it's my father who's to blame for my feeling so disappointed?" Arlene asked.

"Not exactly," I said. I pointed out that it was true that her father had, during the formative years of her childhood, initiated a long-term pattern that led to her creating inflated expectations of men. But she could not blame him for the ways in which she herself continued and perpetuated the pattern well into adulthood.

As her therapy progressed, I was able to help Arlene see that in blaming her boyfriends, she had turned inside out the disappointment and anger originally directed at her father. The disappointments of her early life had long predated these boyfriends, but her inflated expectations set in motion a continued pattern of unrealistic hope followed by needless disappointment. Could she break free? Her insight into the contributions of the past was a good first step.

Is the Glass Half Empty?

As we worked together in therapy, Arlene increasingly came to realize that only by facing up to disappointment are we able to move forward from the disappointments and developmental wounds of childhood. She also gradually learned that gauging expectations realistically did not mean focusing primarily on the missing elements that will disappoint us. We must also acknowledge and give equal weight to those aspects of a person that will please us.

In this, too, Arlene needed practice. Instead of feeling "crushed" and disillusioned by a boyfriend's imperfection, she needed to balance that flaw within the larger picture of what the relationship offered. For instance, Arlene told me how she had felt betrayed when Rick (the doctor-in-training) had not been sufficiently supportive during a time of great work stress for her. The year before, because of school budget cuts, Arlene had been forced to take on an increased teaching load as colleagues were laid off, and for a time there was a possibility that her position would be eliminated altogether. It was true that Rick did not do as much for her as Arlene would have liked, and after his own pressure-filled day, he often felt too emotionally drained and just plain physically tired to stay awake listening to her worries. Arlene was particularly miffed one night when Rick said he thought she wanted to be alone to think about her worries, and that's why he went to sleep without discussing what she had gone through at work that day.

I acknowledged that Rick was wrong to leave her alone when she was so upset, but whereas to me Rick seemed flustered by Arlene's emotionality, Arlene saw him as emotionally depriving. His behavior struck me as inept, not malevolent. Obviously, Rick had limitations: His work was so demanding that he had extremely little free time, and even when he was with Arlene, he was not always emotionally available. "But what about the things he does do to try to comfort you?" I asked. In dwelling on the ways in which she felt deprived, Arlene had glossed over the fact that several times when she was feeling particularly blue, Rick had surprised her by leaving the hospital early and cooking a special dinner for her. And when he was admittedly too bushed to keep his eyes open he would snuggle up to her and say, "Cuddle close, I'm here for you."

"Because you were so preoccupied with what Rick could not give you, you weren't able to clearly see or appreciate what he could give you," I told Arlene. Sadly, she had rejected what Rick had to offer because it was less than the fairy tale she wished for. Rick, like her father, wasn't the protective figure she had hoped he would be. He didn't protect her from disappointment any more than her father had. But rather than own up to this unrealistic expectation, Arlene blamed him. Indeed, Arlene said that Rick's failure to soothe her during this period was what led her to "see his true, narcissistic character."

After this incident, Arlene had harped on Rick's imperfections, initially hoping he would change, and later pointing to his flawed character as the source of her disappointment with the relationship. But people don't change easily, and almost never under pressure from others. To paraphrase that esteemed philosopher Popeye: We are what we are. Even therapy doesn't change us so much as help us to make the most out of who we are. To stay with Rick, Arlene would have had to learn to accept his limitations without getting angry about them. Unfortunately, at the time Arlene wasn't aware of her pattern of idealization and disappointment.

Sure, there was an element of truth to Arlene's perceptions of Rick. But like Arlene, many of us tend to focus on what we're missing (or what our partner lacks), rather than on what we have and what our partner has to offer. It's just as much of a mistake to minimize what we are fortunate enough to receive as it is to exaggerate what we have.

Arlene displayed another tendency that showed her expectations were out of kilter with reality—her penchant for being repeatedly "crushed," shocked by relatively small disappointments in life. When the landlord failed to send someone immediately to perform a repair in her apartment, Arlene felt "duped," she told me—as if landlords were known for being the most dependable people in the world. Another time, when a case of the flu kept her from taking a weekend trip to visit an old friend, she railed against her bad luck. "Why does everything have to happen to me?" She seemed to lose sight of the fact that she had already been able to reschedule the trip. Even in these little incidents, Arlene was not able to accept the fact that life is not always fair. The same unwillingness to accommodate to life's unfairness was characteristic of her larger disappointments with men. Arlene repeatedly failed to come to grips with this fact, like a child who hasn't yet learned to cope with frustration.

Like all of us, Arlene would have to learn to live with the chilly winds of reality, and with the disappointments and imperfections every potential mate has. We need to face our own problems, stop trying helplessly to seek protection from "bad" things by means of a fantasy version of a parent.

We must recognize that we have the strength to tolerate the pain of disappointment. I'm reminded of one patient whose treatment began shortly after she had attempted suicide in the wake of her boyfriend's leaving her. When I first saw her, she told me, "No one is worth dying for." I replied, "You misunderstand what it means to die for something. People are worth dying for. But in trying to kill yourself, you were not dying for him. You were terribly disappointed, and found the pain intolerable." I helped this patient see that she could draw on reservoirs of strength she did not realize she had, and that no despair was too great to bear.

Disappointment is definitely painful. There's no hiding from it or cushioning the blow. If we're especially fragile, disappointment can be devastating. But strong feelings do abate, even if we don't believe they will at the time. In the interim, we need to understand our susceptibility and live through the disappointment.

Denying Disappointment

As I got to know Arlene, I would marvel at her capacity for unrealistic hope. With every new relationship, she would just reinflate her balloon and set herself up for more disappointment. I witnessed this firsthand with her next boyfriend, Gary. As she described him to me, it struck me that Arlene was ignoring significant clues about his personality. But whenever I began to point these out, Arlene would use what I call the "ostrich" technique: bury her head in the sand. Apparently, after so many failed relationships, it was just too painful for Arlene to face up to the potential problems at the very start of a relationship; her attitude seemed to be: Get involved now, deal with the difficulties later. In fact, the more elusive a man was, the more attractive he appeared to Arlene.

Gary, a good-looking architect and designer, wined and dined her royally. If she mentioned the fact that a music group she enjoyed was playing in town, he would run out and buy the best seats available. At restaurants, he always seemed to know the maitre d', and he regaled her with the latest gossip about his well-to-do clientele. She loved his attentiveness and extravagance. But Gary also had a slippery quality, becoming elusive whenever physical intimacy was in the air. After an evening out, he would kiss her quickly on the lips and disappear, even when she invited him in for a nightcap. Similarly, when she planned a quiet, romantic evening at her apartment, he called at the last minute to cancel.

Although it was obvious that something was amiss, Arlene refused to acknowledge disappointment and instead denied that anything was wrong. She saw Gary as she wished him to be—a dashing figure, like the father she had dreamed of—not as he was. Instead of facing up to the fact that Gary seemed afraid of touching her beyond a brush on the lips, she would lose herself in fantasy, imagining that if only Gary were less stressed by work, he would be more physically open with her. Rather than acknowledge the disappointment in her current situation, which would mean doing something about it (such as confronting Gary), she remained in her fantasy world. Possibly Arlene was protecting Gary from her disappointment, believing he would be hurt if she brought up her sexual dissatisfaction; but I believe that her motivation was the need to protect herself. She feared that the disappointment reality might bring would hurt *her* too much, and she did not have the strength to acknowledge it.

Many of us are buoyed by fantasy and prefer not to deal with the frustrations of reality. I'm reminded of the patient who played computer games all day rather than face the challenging tasks of meeting his life goals—finding a job, meeting a romantic partner, buying a home. He preferred being "on top of the world" in his fantasy games to dealing with the inevitable frustrations of trying to achieve—and perhaps falling short of—his aspirations. But my position is that even the smallest reality-based gratification sustains us more than imaginary gratifications. We need to confront our frustration head-on to improve our lot in life. Perpetuating a fantasy won't get us anywhere.

That's why the "ostrich" technique is so dangerous. It leads us to ignore our observations, insights, and good judgment about what's going on, in favor of a fantasy world in which disappointment and frustration can be denied. This is what's at work when we make excuses and remain with an inappropriate partner long after a "reality test" would have told us to leave. Many patients have confided that they could tell early on that their lover or spouse was not trustworthy, or was leading them into financial difficulty, or was not going to marry them. Rather than believe what they saw, they chose instead to believe in their idealized fantasy. If they had confronted the truth, they would have had to take the painful step of walking away from a bad relationship.

This is what Arlene did by ignoring Gary's skittishness when it came to physical intimacy. I knew, however, the therapy was beginning to take hold when Arlene came in one day and started talking openly about her dissatisfaction with Gary with no mention of being "crushed" and angry. She had finally pressed him on his reluctance to become physically intimate. In response, Gary revealed to her that for many years he had been uncertain about his sexuality.

"Of course, I'm disappointed," Arlene began. "But I'm not going to say I'm shocked, because as soon as we started talking, I realized that on some level I had known this about him all along. I was the one who didn't want to face up to it. I guess I needed him to be a fantasy date, and he gave me some wonderful evenings I could never have afforded on my own." Arlene exhibited much more equanimity in this instance than she had about any of her previous romantic disappointments. What seemed to concern her the most was that she had lost faith in her ability to size people up. "If I made such a big error in judgment this time, how will I know what to think the next time I meet somebody?"

At about this time, Arlene had a dream that captured her confusion about what to believe about the men in her life, along with the childhood origins of her predicament. The dream took place in the days before her parents' divorce. In the dream, Arlene, her mother, and her father were eating dinner in a brightly lit dining room; it was a scene that any outsider looking in would declare a typical happy family. Abruptly the dream cuts to a completely different scene: a dark view from beneath the bottom of the house. Now it can be seen that termites have eaten away at the house foundation; the floor beneath the dining room where this "happy family" sits is on the verge of caving in, putting everyone in jeopardy.

For Arlene, the dream conjured a familiar sense of dread that her world was about to fall apart. I further interpreted it as a study in contrasts, appearance versus reality: the contrasting outsider's view of a happy scene (appearance) versus the more accurate perception that the inside was on the verge of collapse (reality). This resembled the contrasting perceptions Arlene had of her childhood, when appearances had often been confused with reality. Her family was perceived in the community to be stable, but Arlene knew firsthand that her parents' marriage was an unhappy one.

This early-childhood disconnect had left Arlene unprepared in adulthood to trust her perceptions of people and relationships. On a superficial level, Gary looked like an appropriate boyfriend who planned exciting and extravagant evenings. But this appearance held up only if she ignored the reality she felt from inside— that he had no sexual interest in her.

Although Arlene wanted to maintain the fantasy that Gary was "Mr. Right," by this point she had gained enough insight to stop playing the "ostrich" game. When Gary suggested that they continue their chaste dates, Arlene was tempted to agree to this, but she also realized that he was not what she wanted. Without rancor or bitterness, Arlene was able to walk away from the relationship with Gary, happy that she had found out about his sexual ambivalence sooner rather than later. Arlene came to understand that she needed to take her own observations and inner feelings seriously, regardless of appearances. Neither she nor I was surprised when Arlene learned that Gary's next relationship was with a man.

Like Arlene, in facing our life problems, we need to use our judgment, perceptions, and emotional reactions. What else do we have? This means understanding the connection between how we feel and the people and events provoking our reactions. We need to look at things objectively as well as subjectively, taking in the whole picture. Denial is not the answer. To ignore our emotional responses is to throw away useful information and repudiate a part of ourselves. It only sets us up for continued disappointment.

Disappointment and Yearning: Coming to Terms with Ambivalence

A common mistake many of us make is to become disappointed and get angry with our partners because they aren't everything we want. No matter how much they have given us, we may continue to yearn, especially if we have significant developmental wounds.

I'm often questioned about this by patients who continue to engage in sexual fantasies even after they have fallen in love, become engaged, or married and who think they must not love their partner if a sense of longing remains. My answer is that it's like winning the lottery: Those who win didn't stop having dreams, sometimes even of winning again. Even when we achieve our dream, our yearning does not disappear. Desire and longing are part of human nature, and to some degree can never be completely satiated. The mistake we make is to believe that because we still yearn, there must be something wrong with what we have.

Some of us may feel that we should never be bored nor feel frustrated and abandoned when we're in a relationship. Well, we *all* feel bored at times, or frustrated, or abandoned and not taken care of. Those of us who have suffered more childhood disappointments may feel this all the more intensely. Our boredom may come from an inner sense of emptiness, not from deficiencies in the relationship itself. We can't expect others to entertain us all the time; we need to do that for ourselves. Similarly, if we're frustrated, our lovers can't make obstacles in our life magically disappear. And there's no way our partners can take care of us all the time, just the way we want. The problem is not that we have these feelings of boredom or frustration or abandonment. The problem is our expectation that we shouldn't have such feelings and, further, how we actually deal with them.

One thing is certain about love: Our feelings will get hurt at one time or another. It is unrealistic to expect otherwise. How we deal with our disappointment or continued yearning makes all the difference in the world. Getting angry with our partners for not fulfilling all our wishes serves no purpose except to perpetuate our disappointment. Blaming others is a crucial psychological mistake. We need to acknowledge our own limitations and developmental wounds, accurately assess what others have to offer (and how their traits mesh with ours), and learn to accept others' limitations, just as we must accept our own.

The term psychologists use for what I'm talking about here is *ambivalence:* our disappointments, frustrations, and continued yearnings that may exist alongside our satisfactions and tender feelings. No relationship is perfect and conflict-free. No one is wholly unambivalent. There are always facets of the relationship, along with personality features of our partners, that will grate on us, and there will be problems and differences to sort out and work through. Does the fact that we're ambivalent mean we shouldn't get involved, or deepen the involvement? By no means. What causes problems is acting out our ambivalence and blaming others for it. We need to find constructive ways of coming to terms with these difficult feelings.

I'm reminded of the couple I treated who broke up and got back together every other week, vacillating between "We're through" and "I can't live without you." If we act out our ambivalence, we never come to terms with it; we're either in paradise or in hell, unable to comfortably reside with the full mixture of good, bad, and everything in between that makes up objective reality. Too many of us are disappointed by one particular aspect of a relationship, and then that single disappointment comes to color or be emblematic of the whole relationship. We need to see our disappointments in the context of the whole.

Coming to terms with our ambivalence means allowing ourselves the full range of our reactions and feelings. We should not
see one side without also looking at the other. This open-minded-
ness can be quite confusing. But if, instead of acting out, we learn
to sit with our confusion and mixed feelings, a clearer and fuller
picture will emerge, and we will be able to bring these two (or
more) sides of ourselves together.

Arlene was absorbing these lessons about ambivalence, too.
Her dilemma over whether or not to become involved with Gary
had been difficult. Should she stay in a flawed relationship that
didn't offer sexual gratification but that gratified her in many
other ways? She was well aware of how many relationships she
had run from in the past, so she distrusted her inclination to
break off with Gary. But she also knew that something serious
was amiss.

Out of Arlene's ambivalence and confusion came her realization that she should reject Gary's halfhearted offer to continue seeing her. Not only was it the right decision in terms of
her happiness. It also put her in the position to meet a new
man, someone with whom she could break the mold of the
past.

Enter Kyle, a steady, goodhearted man who owned his own
sporting-goods store. Although Arlene complained that he wasn't
as spontaneous as she would have liked, she had begun to appreciate the fact that, unlike her father, he *was* there for her. And he
was capable of being flexible, within limits. Although they had
their ups and downs, Arlene was able to place her qualms about
Kyle in a more realistic perspective. Yes, he worked long hours at
his business, but that did not mean he wasn't attentive to her; he
always managed to call during the day and spent almost every
evening with her. His job was not glamorous and he would never
make millions, but he made a good living. He loved being associated with sports, and on occasion he got to meet—and introduce

her to—sports superstars. In his own way, Kyle had a James Bond–like quality, but one that was realistic and sustainable. He was truly devoted to Arlene, who gradually was able to accept and become comfortable with the fact that Kyle was not about to run off and disappoint her.

By the time Arlene completed therapy, she and Kyle were engaged. She had broken free of the old pattern by which she had courted disappointment. Arlene had learned to align her expectations with what Kyle had to offer, and was able to take pleasure in that. For her, the glass was more than half full. Not a small accomplishment.

Learning to Tolerate Disappointment

You can learn to work through your disappointment as Arlene did. With insight, she broke free of her old pattern of idealization and disappointment. She learned to base her new relationship on more realistic expectations. Instead of first ignoring, then being "crushed" by Kyle's imperfections, she was able to listen to (rather than ignore) her initial perceptions, and not be fooled by unrealistic appearances. She then could view minor disappointments and drawbacks within the larger context of all the positive attributes Kyle had to offer. In this way she came to terms with her ambivalence. She didn't hold Kyle responsible for the monotony and boredom of her job, and she came to appreciate the excitement he did offer.

When problems arose, instead of looking for shortcuts—acting out, getting angry, blaming, or denying by means of the "ostrich" technique—Arlene confronted them and worked to resolve them. She recognized that difficulties do not go away of their own accord, but only through chipping away at them, day in and day out; eventually, through consistent effort, she and Kyle together were able to achieve their goal.

Personal growth is not a magical process, and neither is therapy. Growth comes from trying and failing, and after learning from our mistakes, trying once again. If we let our disappointments stop us cold, if we blame others, we get nowhere. Instead, we can, like Arlene, learn to tolerate disappointment, accept people on their own terms, and accept ourselves with all our emotional baggage and sensitivities. If we do, romantic relationships will have the power to heal, helping us to overcome our developmental wounds.

In a way, dealing with disappointment is like mourning lost dreams: If we become angry about and fixated on what does *not* exist, we will be unable to derive gratification from the connections that *do* exist. Finding this balance is not easy, and facing up to disappointment can be scary indeed. So scary that rather than acknowledge disappointment—and act on our insight—we may try to hold on to an idealized hope that clearly will never come close to reality. By facing up to our disappointments we can learn not only what we can expect of others but also how to align those expectations with what others have to offer.

These, then, are the points we must remember in learning to tolerate disappointment:

1. Only by seeing people for what they truly are—not what we wish them to be—will we make sensible decisions about relationships.
2. Unrealistic ideas about others usually reflect bad feelings about ourselves. If we let our projections and preconceptions distort our perception of others, we'll run into serious problems when they don't turn out to be what we expected.
3. Even when we've suffered deep developmental wounds (such as a narcissistic mother who was unable to care for

us or an alcoholic father who flew into scary rages), the notion that we didn't have a good enough parent doesn't mean we can't have a good enough life. Some part of us will always feel we haven't been well enough taken care of, or that at some level we've been abandoned. None of us had perfect parenting. All of us chase after lost dreams and seek to compensate for early frustrations. But we don't have to remain stuck in our patterns of disappointment; we need to come to terms with them. I tell my patients, remember that love does have the power to transform and heal. We need to give love that chance.

4. Dealing with disappointment means accepting our past, our sensitivities, and our sense of early loss, without projecting those templates onto people in our present life. We need to understand the expectations we bring to relationships and how they emerge out of our emotional baggage.

5. When something bad happens, we need to remind ourselves that all is not lost. People are multifaceted; we should not mistake one negative part for the whole picture. It is natural to have mixed feelings about people, and this ambivalence is not in itself an obstacle to romance. We must learn to accept from others what they have to offer, even if it's not everything we want.

6. Finally, tolerating disappointment means not acting out or blaming others. When we learn to sit with this uncomfortable feeling of disappointment, we feel stronger inside and much more in command of our own destinies.

Is our disappointment our partner's fault—or ours? In this chapter, I have tried to help you answer that question by examining the complicated ways in which our expectations are tied to our own emotional baggage, our attitudes and feelings about ourselves. Only after we have looked within can we begin to sort through, work through, and master the disappointments. They are only partially due to our partner's personality and behavior.

5
The Dance of Mutual Dependency
Why We Fight It, and Why We Shouldn't

Today's books on love tend to focus on our capacity to care for others. But to me, this is just one side of the dependency equation. Of greater concern are *the problems we face when we don't allow ourselves to be cared for.* Just as we blame our partners for our own disappointments, we blame them for not taking care of us as well as we would like them to. But is it that our partners are poor caretakers, or is it our own discomfort with dependency that prevents us from receiving what we want?

Many of my patients act out their discomfort with dependency. They're ashamed of their dependency wishes, and as a result don't put themselves in a position to be well taken care of. They refuse to make their wishes known, and then complain that they don't get what they want. Or they set up obstacles to intimacy, what I call "escape hatches," to depressurize the scary intensity of budding romantic relationships. Other patients repeatedly become involved in dead-end relationships with inappropriate mates; these debacles then serve to justify their skeptical attitudes. Instead of fighting our dependency needs, we must learn to become comfortable with them. For dependency is not only healthy, it's a necessity.

Dependency Is Not a Dirty Word

American culture dictates that we should avoid dependency—which it is assumed will become the dreaded codependency—and be as self-sufficient as possible. Given society's generally negative message about dependency, perhaps it's not surprising that so many of my patients see dependency as a psychological failing.

In truth we should embrace dependency, revel in it, learn to be comfortable with it. What undermines romantic relationships is not dependency but our resistance to the dependent pull of love and romance.

Dependency is a part of human nature—from infancy, when our parents cater to our every need, to adulthood, when we rely on others for human contact, to old age and infirmity, when we once more need help to survive. It is unnatural and ultimately futile to deny, suppress, or reject dependent urges. Instead, we need to find ways to become comfortable with the intense feelings and neediness that develop in all romantic relationships. We fare best if we can learn to help others to help us.

Being fearful and even shameful about our feelings of dependency, we struggle against them. We may choose to fight the powerful emotional current that propels us into relationships. Or we may equate feelings of dependency with being at the mercy of others and become afraid that they will exploit or take advantage of our vulnerability. It's no wonder that our relationships pay the price of these struggles.

Many people have come to believe that others can't or won't give them what they want. This belief becomes a self-fulfilling prophecy, as we reject that which is offered. For instance, one patient was so disoriented and confused by a new boyfriend's genuine show of affection that she decided not to go out with him anymore: "I just don't understand guys like him. What does he want from me? He didn't even pressure me to go to bed with him."

Underlying the belief that we won't be taken care of is the notion that we are not entitled to being taken care of, that we are not worthy of being gratified. We may say that our partners are negligent, withholding, or, even worse, so malevolent that they enjoy depriving us. But what we're really saying is that *we* aren't lovable, that our wishes aren't acceptable, and that we have something to be ashamed of. Until we change these internal beliefs, we won't be comfortable in a dependent position where we are able to receive love. This is another example of the fact that our expectations of others are completely interwoven with our ideas about ourselves.

My patients' feelings about dependency are reflected in statements they make such as the following: "I've screwed up so much, who would want to get involved with me, anyway?" "People only care about themselves." "If she really knew me, she'd run as fast as she could." These are all examples of inside-out thinking. If we believe we deserve to be gratified, we'll expect others to gratify us; if we feel undeserving, we'll expect to be deprived.

No matter what my patients say about the others in their lives, the major stumbling block to satisfying relationships, time and again, is their own self-image—their core beliefs about themselves. As intimacy deepens, they even try to keep certain key facets of themselves hidden—even though they are convinced that sooner or later, their "inner badness" will be revealed and their partners will be repulsed.

When I hear such deeply ingrained beliefs, I invariably look to the past, and often find that these patients' parents selfishly imposed their wishes and subtly discouraged their children from expressing their own. These children grow up ashamed of their needs. They not only deny or suppress their wish to be cared for, but they doubt that others could truly enjoy caring for them. If you feel at your core that you are not lovable, it is impossible to believe that another will love you.

Let's look at the model for dependency, the parent-infant bond, where we first develop core ideas about ourselves and our expectations of others.

When babies are unhappy, they make their discomfort known through a cry or a grunt or a gurgle. Sensing and responding to that discomfort, the mother shifts the baby's position, hugs her, smiles at her, feeds her. The baby who lets herself be taken care of eventually settles down.

When this feedback loop works, it is automatic, intuitive, and almost magical. The need is communicated, duly noted, and then gratified. And then, and this is important, a sense of appreciation is expressed, which closes the feedback loop.

In this model, one person, the mother or father, is the giver, and the other person, the baby, is the taker. Both giver and taker are fulfilled. The parent wants someone who is receptive to his or her gifts just as much as the baby wants to be gratified.

This is the prototype of healthy dependency in adulthood as well. The difference in adulthood is that it's mutual, not one-sided; both parties move flexibly between the dual, interchangeable roles of giving and getting.

I'm not referring to some kind of quid pro quo: If you give to me, then I'll return the favor. Although this rationale is certainly true, the psychological basis of giving and getting runs deeper than that. Because we identify with our beloved so strongly, in a way it does not matter whether we are giving or receiving; in giving to a loved one we are in effect giving something to ourselves. This is why when people are in love, they selflessly sacrifice for their beloved.

We may contrast this model of healthy dependency with a model of unsuccessful dependency. Imagine the child who is always uncomfortable in our arms, squirming around, and rebuking us with tears and screams for not being able to console her. Babies like this do not know how to or cannot let themselves be taken care of. They fight our efforts to care for them. Not only do they fail to make their wishes known, but even when love is offered, they angrily reject and resist comfort. I call these infants "unhuggable." Unlike the huggable child, they do not respond to nurturing efforts and refuse to show appreciation. It is a remarkably frustrating experience for the parent who can do nothing to improve the situation, and may ultimately withdraw or give up trying to care for the child.

As adults, these unhuggables seem to embrace their dissatisfaction. Many years later, they still do not make their wishes known, and they still reject and resist others' attempts at giving. On the rare occasions when they do let others do for them, they can't show appreciation because that would mean owning up to the fact that they did need something. Thus, they live in tragic self-imposed isolation, even though they may be surrounded by loving people. Blaming their partners for frustrating them, they don't recognize that it is their own discomfort, shame, and hopelessness about their dependent longings that are at the source of their unhappiness.

The healthy dependency of adulthood is not the passive, helpless experience of an infant. As adults, we are self-sufficient, and if we allow ourselves to be dependent on another, it's not because we have no other choice. It's because we freely accord to another the privilege of caring for us.

There is nothing wrong in developing the capacity to care for yourself, but this should not be at the expense of depriving yourself of the pleasure of allowing someone else to take care of you. In learning how to let ourselves be cared for properly, we are indirectly caring for ourselves. Letting ourselves be cared for is an important psychological talent and one that resides within. This is the mirror we need to hold up before we blame our partner for being uncaring.

Fighting Against the Current of Dependency:
Phil and Rachel

What makes dependency feel so dangerous? Why do we jump to blame others when we feel bruised and vulnerable? The answer is straightforward. Romantic relationships have a regressive pull that makes us feel childish, emotional, and dependent. And when we feel this vulnerable, we are likely to become defensive.

Love is an extraordinarily compelling emotion, but even as we feel the exhilaration of being "swept away," we may fear losing ourselves in powerful emotional forces that feel out of our control. In this regard, love resembles the hypnotic lure of the ocean surf: We can be so fearful of getting caught in its currents and swept up and out to sea that even as we take our first step in the water, we fight against the tide.

Sometimes the surf really is too heavy to approach, and there are romantic relationships that can prove too chaotic or destructive. What concerns me most, however, are the inner fears and inhibitions that can make us shudder at the calmest current. If we let the fear of being swept away prevent us from going in the water at all, or if we draw back even as we begin to get our toes wet, we will never allow ourselves to fall in love.

These are the issues Phil struggled with. He fought against the current of his dependency, and nearly let his inner fears derail his relationship with his girlfriend, Rachel. But through therapy he came to an understanding of how he had turned his discomfort with dependency inside out, and eventually he gave Rachel a chance to care for him.

The minute Rachel, whom he had been seeing for close to a year, went on a solo monthlong vacation, ostensibly "to tour the Far East while I still have the time," Phil began fighting with everybody—his coworkers, his friends, members of his extended family. Initially Phil did not make the connection between his irritability and Rachel's absence, but when he told me that he was sneaking cigarettes for the first time in many years, I asked what he was worried about.

Phil denied that he was worried, but then he let drop the fact that Rachel had mentioned on the eve of her departure that she needed time to "think about our relationship." Although anyone would be anxious and perplexed by such a bombshell, Phil found it nearly impossible to admit out loud how much he missed Rachel and how worried he was that she would break up with him.

Phil then told me he was so ashamed of his longing for her that he felt he had to hide it:"I have to be strong while she's away. I don't want her to know what an emotional basket case I am. And when she returns, I don't want her to stay with me just because she feels sorry for me."

Phil saw himself as a pathetic figure, evoking pity rather than respect and reciprocity. He felt embarrassed by his love and his longing and hadn't told her that he wanted to accompany her on the trip. Phil could not accept the fact that missing a beloved partner and being concerned that a significant relationship might be on the rocks was absolutely normal.

Here was the inside-out dynamic at work: Phil was attributing to Rachel thoughts and feelings he was having about himself. As a result, he was confused about who was disgusted by his neediness—was it Rachel, as he imagined, or was it Phil? By turning his feelings inside out, Phil had convinced himself that Rachel would look down on his longing for her. Even though there might have been a grain of truth to that, it was mostly his projection.

At the core of Phil's fears was a feeling many of us harbor that it is not okay to love wholly and with abandon. We may be ashamed of ourselves in our core being, believing that the love we offer has no value in the world and that we are undeserving of reciprocity. The fact that we love at all is experienced as a humiliation to be ridiculed rather than something to be glorified and cherished.

On the basis of his inside-out logic, Phil believed that if he hid his love he would appear stronger, and so he fought his feelings for Rachel. But this strategy was a mistaken one. It is not conceal-ing our love that makes us strong, I told Phil, but proclaiming it despite our lover's doubts and uncertainty. When we feel entitled to our love, we project strength; it takes guts and courage to put yourself on the line. Expressions of love by no means guarantee reciprocity, but the only people they turn off are those who have their own neurotic problems with loving.

Although Phil was uncomfortable with his feelings of yearning and longing for Rachel, he needed to learn that lovers, unless they are sadistic, usually are complimented by (rather than contemptu-ous of) the unqualified, uninhibited expression of someone's love. In loving Rachel, Phil was bestowing on her the greatest gift he had to offer. Whether or not it was reciprocated, he needed to believe that he was entitled to his love, and that it was worth something.

To better understand Phil's fear of dependency, it is important to understand that he was a recovering alcoholic who, like many people with addictive tendencies, was well aware of how out of control he could become and how much damage he could cause when he wanted, or needed, something too much.

Alcoholics and drug addicts are driven by the conviction that ingesting a substance will make them feel better. Like any inside-out way of thinking, this line of thought tempts us to believe that something outside ourselves will assuage our inner pain. This belief is by no means held only by addicts. The "cure" for much dissatisfaction can be seen in the hope that a new piece of cloth-ing, fancy car, different girlfriend, or change of city will promise relief. Since the source of our dissatisfaction resides within us, these external changes will not make us feel better inside, whether or not we continue to chase after them.

As it happened, Phil and Rachel had first gotten to know each other at an Alcoholics Anonymous meeting in their church basement, and they hit it off right away. Interestingly, Rachel as much as Phil was petrified of ever again letting anything dominate her life the way drinking had. Thus, they each feared becoming too intensely swept up in their growing relationship, which they worried would become a "dependency," as alcohol had been. They engaged in an odd back-and-forth, with each one trying to do for the other while simultaneously refusing to accept the same kind of care in return:"Let me buy you a cup of coffee.""No, it's my turn to take you to dinner." Their courtship had the pace of an elaborate Japanese ceremony in which Person A offers a gift, but Person B refuses, insisting that Person A must accept his gift first, and on and on in an endless round of polite offerings and firm refusals.

Their quandary was to find a way to get comfortable taking from each other without reverting to their prior addictive behaviors. This is where they were when Rachel took her solo vacation.

It seemed to me that they were both struggling with their growing mutual dependency as if it were an addictive tendency. Phil was uncomfortable with his intense hunger for love. He felt small, empty, and passive. Just as he had believed in his drinking days that alcohol could make his inner pain go away, he felt that Rachel's presence promised relief for him. Having experienced the destruction inherent in an addiction for alcohol, Phil was reluctant to let his desire for Rachel (which he compared to an addiction) get so out of control. He was further afraid to become "hooked" on her because of his fears that she would be revolted by him, exploit him, and ultimately abandon him. When she went on her solo vacation, he was certain this was just what she was doing. He felt that his "addiction" to Rachel would lead to ruin as surely as alcohol had.

In its own way, Phil's reasoning had a certain logic. As people satisfy our needs, they create a taste for more. But emotional dependency is better compared to our need for air; it can sustain us *without* being destructive, spiraling out of control, causing us to lose our ability to regulate our needs. The problem for Phil was not that his emotional dependency was actually dangerous, but that he wasn't comfortable with the experience of being dependent.

I knew Phil was beginning to approach a new level of insight when he told me the following dream. Coming across two subway tokens thrown down in the snow, he feels conflicted about whether or not to pick them up. On the one hand, he needs the money to visit his parents; on the other, he thinks that his parents deliberately threw the money in the snow in order to demean him. He finds it humiliating to pick up the tokens, much less use them; it makes him feel as if he were a homeless person begging for change.

To me, this dream dramatized Phil's ambivalence about dependency. He wanted to visit his parents, but he was ashamed of his neediness. The dream further reflected his perception that his parents were not receptive to his visit; they were insulting him rather than generously giving him the money he needed. He connected this insight to his present dilemma: He missed Rachel and longed to join her on her trip, but he didn't have the funds to go and had been too ashamed to ask her to lend (or give) him the money to accompany her. He thought she would not be forthcoming. As with his parents, he assumed she would not want him to come.

Phil thus began to acknowledge his complex feelings and ideas about dependency: how his shame over dependency was interwoven with his expectations of others, including Rachel and his parents. With this insight in mind, Phil decided to call Rachel and let her know how much he missed her—something he had refrained from doing until then. When he did, he was surprised to discover that she missed him, too. Without his even having to ask, she suggested that she pay for his airplane ticket so he could join her for the remaining two weeks of her vacation. Perhaps predictably, Phil's first reaction was to be ashamed of his financial plight and say "I'll have to think about it." But with my encouragement, he called Rachel back and accepted her generous offer. For one of the first times in their relationship, Phil let Rachel take care of him without fighting it.

Six months after their return from this vacation, Phil and Rachel became engaged and were married in the church where they had first met. They had become increasingly active in their church, doing community work and helping the poor, activities that they were able to share and both enjoy. The way I see it, Phil and Rachel were able to work through their fears of dependency by jointly caring for others. Only as they got comfortable with their ability to care for others did they eventually began to allow themselves to be cared for by each other.

Love's Roller-Coaster Ride: Connie

Love's powerful emotions can make us feel as if we're on a roller coaster filled with euphoric ups and also frightening dips. Rather than get caught up in the excitement and the immediacy of the experience, we may feel uncomfortable with the all-consuming feelings and sense of urgency that inevitably accompany the initial stages of love. The wide range of intense emotions that love summons may catch us off guard: the sense of elation each time our partner says "I love you"; anxieties about our partner's falling out of love with us; despondency when our beloved is absent or grows distant.

Falling in love evokes such extraordinary emotions that it is difficult, if not impossible, to remain on an even keel. It can feel like a threatening ride, undermining our usual equanimity and sense of who we are. We lose ourselves in our beloved, and however enriching that may be, it can also be remarkably scary. Getting swept up in a passionate romance is, by definition, disruptive of normal life, and the more passionate and intense the experience, the more destabilized we may feel.

Indeed, as someone once observed, falling in love is in some ways like being in free fall. What better image to characterize how out of control we feel when we are in the throes of a power-ful relationship? Equally evocatively, we commonly say that love enthralls us as if we were a slave; love strikes like a lightning bolt out of the blue; being in love is like being on fire, and so on.

Roller coaster, free fall, slave. Whatever turn of phrase we use, this loss of control can be frightening. If we become too anxious, we may well decide to skip the ride entirely. If we do get on the roller coaster, we'll be constantly on guard, reaching for the brakes, unable to let ourselves go, wondering all the time what danger lurks just around the bend.

It is this feared loss of control that causes us to try to put the brakes on a relationship at the very moment when things heat up. Yet the perception of danger, the fear that we'll be hurt, is a projection of our own vulnerability. Similarly, attempting to slow down the relationship is our way of acting out our inner fears on the canvas of the relationship. Our romantic partner isn't causing our fear; the fear comes from what is stirred up within us as we make ourselves vulnerable.

This was the case with Connie, a social worker in her twenties. Her fear of losing control kept her from getting beyond what I call the "half in, half out" point in a relationship, and caused her to repeat dead-end patterns that only confirmed her internal fears and projections.

Connie had a good time with Paul, her recent boyfriend, but she was petrified of becoming too involved. She was relieved early on when he agreed to her suggestion that, because they both had long work schedules, they should limit seeing each other to weekends only. What she didn't tell him was that she felt safer knowing that the workweek was entirely her own. "And who knows, maybe I'll meet someone else?" she told me with a smile.

All seemed to go well on this even, if lukewarm, keel, until Paul told Connie that his company was sending him to Paris for a two-week business trip. Why didn't she come with him, all expenses paid, and they could take a romantic vacation together? At first she hesitated; two weeks together nonstop seemed too intense for her. She didn't know if she could handle it. "What will we do all day together? It'll be too much. I've been on this roller coaster before. I get too attached, and then what happens when we get back? Are we supposed to revert to our once-a-week schedule?"

Connie was scared by Paul's invitation. He was asking her to release the brakes she had placed on their relationship and see where it could go. This was unfamiliar territory, and she was hesitant. When Paul persisted, Connie offered a compromise—she would go, but only on the condition they each take separate hotel rooms. Her thinking was that if she needed her own space and time away from Paul "to do my own thing," it would be there.

I think of ploys like separate hotel rooms as escape hatches that allow us to control and regulate the intensity of our feelings in the relationship. Like Connie, many of us can only tolerate the intimacy of a romantic relationship for so long. Knowing there is an escape hatch helps us to contain our fears, and therefore lets us stay in the relationship. *We can only be in a relationship as long as we know there is a way out.* With no way out, Connie never would have been in the relationship at all.

This is what I mean by half in, half out relationships. Interestingly, in the same way that Connie refused to be pinned down in a relationship, she also was half in, half out of therapy. She had a diffuse, quicksilver quality, never focusing on topics for too long, in a catch-me-if-you-can style that precluded me from probing as deeply as I would have liked. I'm sure Paul would have said the same thing about her.

Connie acted on her fear of being hurt by holding back and reserving a separate hotel room. She imagined that by manipulating the external conditions of her relationship with Paul, her fears would lessen. And they did. As it turned out, Connie never used her separate hotel room. She slept with Paul every night. Knowing that she had her own room allowed her to feel comfortable enough to remain with Paul—in the hotel room, in a foreign land, and in the relationship itself.

But the escape-hatch strategy had its cost. First, her need for an escape hatch corroded the intimacy she and Paul could have shared. Further, her belief that she required such an escape hatch served to confirm her underlying belief that she couldn't handle intense emotions and romantic connections. That's why, ideally, the best solution to dealing with the fear evoked by falling in love is to learn to tolerate and become comfortable with these intense emotions, without having to escape them. The keys to our emotional life reside within, not in changing external conditions.

This helps to explain why, when Connie returned home, she was essentially in the same place emotionally as before. Paul wanted to become more seriously involved. But Connie still could not tolerate ongoing, open-ended contact, and she began to feel trapped. Unfortunately, Connie did not recognize that these fears and feelings came from within, and she decided that the best way to regain her emotional equilibrium would be to cool her relationship with Paul. Although she did not officially break up with him, she put up significant roadblocks to deepening the relationship: she canceled dates, didn't return phone calls, and when they did spend time together she refused to go to bed with him. Paul was confused by Connie's behavior. He was in limbo, unsure if they were still going out together or had broken up and were now platonic friends.

Connie appeared to be in the relationship, but she wasn't actually—at least, not wholly. She was always putting on the brakes, looking for a way out, letting Paul know that she wasn't interested and had other priorities. But if we're always thinking about how to get out of a relationship, we're not focusing on how to stay in. In holding back, she was acting out her ambivalence about dependency.

This half in, half out quality is a perfect dramatization of how we act out our inner ambivalence—the simultaneous desire to be in the relationship and anxious need to escape it. It's unclear what we fear more: being in, or getting out. One solution is to straddle the relationship, as Connie did. In doing so, Connie was like the party guest who rushes in, declares she can only stay for a minute—and then stands around for hours chatting, never taking off her coat and all the while looking at her watch. Clearly, the guest is not in that much of a rush, or she would have left sooner, or not stopped by at all. Just as clearly, she is reluctant to commit herself to staying and acknowledging what a good time she's having. The problem with this noncommittal approach is that she never lets herself get fully comfortable.

Similarly, many of us won't fully immerse ourselves in our relationships. We may appear to be involved, but we're actually quite ambivalent, calibrating our level of involvement to our partner's level of involvement: The more deeply Jack cares, the less Jill will; as soon as Jill shows serious interest, Jack gets cold feet and withdraws."

Our halfheartedness is quite apparent by the kinds of statements we make about our relationships: "I'm willing to go out with her for now, but she's not good enough to marry." "I can't get more involved because my work is too demanding; I just don't have the time." "Wouldn't you know it, the same week he gets a job offer across the country I realize I'm madly in love with him." I hear this kind of ambivalence in the person who keeps telling me he plans to get a divorce, but never follows through; he seems to enjoy talking about how bad his marriage is, but is unable to acknowledge how attached he obviously remains.

On the surface, these ambivalent people are the "undecideds" of romance. Yet their ambivalent behavior reflects the ways they act out conflicts around dependency, rather than any problem with decision making. They resist the magnetic pull of the relationship. Afraid of what the relationship sparks in them, they look for a way out. They act out in their relationships the fears they feel within.

When I see patients doing this, I ask them: Why not take your coat off and stay awhile? Yes, you're uncomfortable right now, but why not find ways to get comfortable in this relationship? It's insulting to your partner to constantly let him or her know how lukewarm you are, and it ultimately causes the partner to be distant with you. The fact that you do feel something does not trap you; you'll always have a chance to decide, as time goes on, whether or not to commit. Get on the ride and see where it takes you.

After Connie put the brakes on her relationship with Paul, she became involved with a series of dead-end relationships with other men. She described these men as "losers" who she knew from the start she could never get "seriously serious" with because their backgrounds and aspirations differed too much from hers. One man was too old for her to have a family with, another was married, and a third was a ne'er-do-well. But, she told me, they were "fun, low-maintenance" relationships that she never had to worry about precisely because "I knew they were never going anywhere."

Paradoxically, Connie enjoyed and felt much more comfortable in these meaningless flings than she did in the more serious relationship with Paul, which made her feel tense and edgy. Connie could be as slippery and carefree as she wanted with her flings. But with Paul, whom she considered "marriage material," there was much more pressure, many more doubts, and lots of questions to be answered. When she went out with Paul, she worried too much; when she went out with the other men, she didn't worry at all.

Why did Connie seem to prefer the dead-end relationships to the one with Paul? Because with Paul, the emotional stakes were enormous. Our tendency to suspect others, doubt them, and test their sincerity is in direct proportion to how much love we feel: the more risk of getting hurt, the more guarded and protected we become. But if we're indifferent, we feel well protected and may be more willing to take a chance. There's nothing at stake—no humiliation, no expectations—so we are not vulnerable. This explains why we may subconsciously choose partners who can't or won't give us what we want: We won't ever have to make the decision to become more intimate. The minute we meet a potential partner who is more intimate and giving, we put on the brakes.

Unfortunately, Connie seemed determined not to confront this paradox in her relationships and showed no awareness of the vastly different attitudes she herself brought to them and projected onto the men. For instance, when I asked her why she did not pursue what seemed the more appropriate relationship with Paul, Connie listed his many faults. She complained that he wasn't smart enough, well-read enough, perceptive enough, dependable enough—statements that contradicted all the previous information she had given me about him. "I just can't count on him in a crunch," she concluded. In response, I suggested that her criticisms exaggerated the problem and did not give him the credit that was due him. Further, I asked her to consider the possibility that her doubts might reflect her own conflicts about dependency more than anything about Paul. The reasons she gave to justify her reluctance to become more involved with Paul seemed to apply not just to him, but to any partner who might be an appropriate match for her. In my view, Connie's uncertainty as to whether or not she could count on Paul "in a crunch" was her way of saying she felt that becoming more deeply committed to this (or any) relationship put her survival at stake. Certainly, I said to her, when our survival is at stake, we become irritable and critical and overreact. But I questioned Connie's fundamental assumption: How was her survival at stake? I used the image of a "rubber band." With her "fun, low-maintenance" boyfriends, she could be loose and flexible and have a good time. But with "marriage material" she became taut and prone to snap, reject, or insult in an instant, at the slightest disagreement.

One of the most common ways of acting out dependency conflicts is to get involved with "losers" and then persist in the relationships even though they're not working. If we select obviously inappropriate partners, we have a clear explanation for why we're not getting what we want out of the relationship. This is what Connie did. She played out her inner discomfort with dependency by selecting men who would confirm her experience. These dead-end relationships said something fundamental about herself.

In fact, Connie told me she had a persistent feeling of being "out of place," as if she "didn't belong." She compared this to how she had felt growing up in a household dominated by a father who ignored her needs and wishes and who never went out of his way to make her feel as if she had a place in his household, much less his heart. After her parents divorced, Connie chose to live with this narcissistic father, hoping she could establish a more loving relationship with him. But his self-absorption was impossible to penetrate. Unable to let go of her failed attempt to connect with this elusive man, she unconsciously brought this pattern to her adult relationships. Even though her dead-end relationships were doomed to failure, she kept trying to make them work (because she was more emotionally involved than she could acknowledge), while she herself invented obstacles to derail the relationships that had real potential. In this way, Connie perpetuated her perception that men couldn't and wouldn't give her what she wanted. No wonder she felt out of place. Unfortunately, in recreating this pattern, Connie also perpetuated the idea that this was all she deserved.

Connie tried to pretend to herself, to the men in her life, and to me, that she didn't have any dependency needs, and that she didn't want anything from any man. But the fact that she bent over backward to prove that she did not need Paul or any other man in her life suggested not true autonomy, but what I call "pseudo-autonomy."

True autonomy reflects self-respect and pride, whereas pseudo-autonomy is a manifestation of shame and furtiveness about ourselves and our needs. Connie acted as if she had no needs, but on a deeper level she found it demeaning actually to ask for something. To her way of thinking, articulating a wish devalues that which is ultimately given because it makes the act of giving less voluntary. Connie thus put herself in a terrible bind: On the one hand, she was unable to admit to herself and others that she wanted things, and on the other, she felt much more needy and isolated than she thought she should be. In the end, she made her belief that men like Paul didn't genuinely care about her and her needs come true by not letting them know what it was she did want.

When Connie finally told me that she wasn't satisfied with her "loser" boyfriends, I wasn't surprised. I knew she wanted and needed more. She finally was able to see that she had been selecting "losers" over "marriage material" because she thought that was all she deserved.

Learning to Overcome Our Fear of Dependency

We can always find ample reasons not to depend on someone. No one is perfect and no one will care for us perfectly. The more pertinent question is: How can we learn to embrace a relationship that only partially meets our needs? How can we let ourselves go in a relationship that doesn't feel completely safe? How can we help others to make us feel safer? And how can we learn to tolerate the inevitable fears that emerge in any intense and dependent relationship?

It can be difficult and confusing to sort through the answers to these questions. Our feelings about dependency stem from childhood, and, as we know, love rekindles with renewed force not just the wonder but also the wounds of childhood. Too often, those reopened wounds from the past can make us raw, prickly, and oversensitive.

But love also affords us the hope, and the opportunity, of healing our childhood wounds. Indeed, love would not have its remarkable reparative powers if it did not evoke regressive feelings. It can truly be a "corrective emotional experience," helping us to move from mistrust and doubt to hope. But it can only do so if we become comfortable with the raw dependency that love evokes and with our hungry yearning for love. We must allow ourselves to be vulnerable, and we must learn to tolerate our sensitivity and bruised feelings.

Our struggles against dependency can be so great that I consider it a truly remarkable psychological achievement for two people to lay aside their fears and form a secure attachment. It is no mean feat. But our fears and our defensiveness are based on the fallacy that we must protect ourselves from potential hurts. As I've said throughout this book, just because we feel vulnerable does not mean that we must protect ourselves. Just because our feelings will get hurt is not a reason to avoid involvement. It's a waste of our time and energy to hide from imaginary dangers. We don't have to react defensively. Feeling vulnerable and dependent is more than just okay; it's a normal part of life.

Love is about accepting our dependency and passivity, feeling entitled to having our needs met, and allowing our partners to take care of us. Mutual dependency does not mean that we can't care for ourselves, only that we willingly and temporarily let someone else enjoy this privilege. The beauty of mutual dependency is that we can be dependent *without* relinquishing our autonomy. This is how it works its creative magic on our wounded psyches. But it can only do so if we let it.

I find it useful to compare romantic relationships to dancing. As two people come together on the dance floor to form a single entity, the members of a couple move fluidly back and forth between the dual roles of giving and getting. Like dancing, romantic relationships require that we find a shared rhythm. In order to get in sync with each other, we must give ourselves over to our partners. Like dancers, lovers in a couple are separate yet together, part of a team.

When we see a couple dancing together with seamless rhythm and grace, we cannot tell who is leading whom, only that they fit together. Similarly, when we fall in love, it's as if we meld, merge, commingle. Our boundaries begin to blur, and we become confused over where "I" ends and "you" begins. There's mutual enjoyment as we bask in the reflected glow of a shared spotlight.

But we may also be threatened by this fusion, and by the loss of control over a part of ourselves that is now roaming freely in the world in the guise of our lover. In the same way that stubborn or awkward dancers refuse to lead or be led, we may be uncomfortable with loving and being loved, with caring for others and being cared for by others. Like clumsy dancers, we'll step on each other's toes, and then blame our partner for the misstep. But

blame and pulling away is not the answer. We must let ourselves
be swept up in the rhythm of the dance.

The only way to become part of a seamless, graceful dance
couple is to stop holding on to our old, familiar, singular self. We
must begin to feel comfortable with the sense of fusion that love
brings. Most important, we need to recognize that as our boundaries become blurred with those of our beloved, we are not losing our selves. We are creating a new self that is part of a couple.
In this way, we transcend our self rather than give it up. To hold on
to our separateness is to deprive ourselves of this achievement in
partnering and connectedness.

Romantic relationships, like dancing, have an ineffable chemistry.
There are innumerable subtle, almost unnoticeable, communica-
tions back and forth between well-matched partners. With a slight
pressure of the hands, we signal the other to move in a certain direction. As the music changes, so does our rhythm. Similarly, as romantic
relationships change and evolve, we and our partner learn ever
more precisely what each of us does and does not want: to be held
this way, not that way; we like cotton shirts rather than polyester; we
prefer beach vacations to touring European museums, and so on.

This rhythm can't be manufactured. That's why relationship
books, such as this one, can't simply prescribe Step 1, Step 2, and
so on. Even so, there are certain general principles that apply,
which are listed below. The advice I give is intended to help you
understand the basic psychological mechanism of dependency
and the fears and feelings it evokes:

1. Our dependency does not pose problems for relationships;
   it's fighting against our dependency that undermines our
   romantic connections. If we can achieve this insight, we will
   realize that if our relationships aren't giving us what we
   want, it is probably because we do not put ourselves in a
   position to get what we want.

2. When we feel entitled to want what we want, we will find people who can do a good job of giving it to us. It's okay to yearn; it's okay to long for somebody; it's okay to fall in love, wholly and with abandon.
3. Instead of pulling and pushing at each other, we should give ourselves over to the rhythm of the dance. We should allow ourselves to be swept up by the powerful emotions love evokes, however intense, regressive, and irrational they may feel. Yes, there will be ups and downs, but we can learn to tolerate and be comfortable with these feelings.
4. We need to be comfortable enough with ourselves to give ourselves over to each other. Even as we continue to chart our own course, our boundaries will blur with those of our partners. We must realize that we are becoming part of a whole, even though we still remain separate individuals.

6
Confusing Love with Emasculation
The Fragile Male Ego

We all use the inside-out dynamic to blame others for our feelings and attitudes, some of us more than others. Although neither gender employs this psychological defense more than the other does, men and women differ in how they use it. Because of the impact these differences have on relationships, the next two chapters focus on the specific ways in which gender determines the ways in which we turn our emotions inside out. Let's begin with men.

As we saw in the previous chapter, feelings of loss of control and dependency are evoked naturally in romantic relationships. Because romantic relationships necessarily entail giving up power to another person, they can be deeply threatening, especially to men who feel inadequate. (In extreme cases, the need for control can further lead to sexual obsession or domestic violence.) It's not intimacy per se that's terrifying; it's the sense of powerlessness and submissiveness that goes with the territory.

Through the inside-out mechanism of projection, men frequently transform their anxiety about feeling powerless into anger. A man will convert an internal problem having to do with his fragile ego into an interpersonal conflict with an external adversary—the romantic partner. He'll become overly suspicious and prone to rage, trying to compensate for the fears and feelings that come from within.

Men, especially those with insecurities, tend to view love in terms of control and power. When that happens, instead of experiencing the relationship as a pleasurable giving over of oneself to a beloved partner, love is seen as a display of weakness. Instead of perceiving love as enriching, enlarging, or empowering, these men view love as synonymous with the loss of freedom and thus of self-respect.

It's a twisted, perverted logic that leads men to feel emasculated in relationships; instead of feeling at the height of their manhood in a relationship, they feel *less* masculine. Their anger and suspiciousness serve as a defense weapon against an enemy whom they fear will charm, disarm, and humiliate them. Frequently, they lash out preemptively to protect themselves from anticipated criticism, humiliation, or rejection.

But there's a major flaw to this reasoning: The enemy is an illusion. It's not the women in these men's lives who are out to get them; it's their own inability to deal with vulnerability.

Men whose relationship difficulties stem from this psychological defense usually exhibit the following reactions. They

- hear criticism where none is intended.

- feel burdened by women's expectations.

- feel emasculated when they should feel empowered.

- blame women for their own self-consciousness.

- strive for freedom against what they perceive to be the constraints of a committed relationship.

- use physical intimidation and violence to buttress their fragile egos and to exercise control.

When Men Don't Feel "Manly": Will

These turned out to be some of the issues that concerned Will, a tall, husky advertising executive in his thirties who came to me ostensibly about problems at work. He told me that his new boss, a woman, had criticized him at his annual review for the way he handled their clients. He was hard-working and had creative ideas, but she had received several complaints from dissatisfied clients.

"She wants me to suck up to them, to get their okay on every little detail, as if I were in kindergarten, needing permission every time I had to go pee," he said, clearly agitated by the image he himself had conjured up.

"For some reason that bothers you," I said.

In response, he stuck out his broad, square jaw as if he were squaring off in a football lineup. He crossed his arms, further reminding me of a defensive linebacker, and said, "What is it about women? I feel like they're on my case nonstop. At work, my boss says I'm too blunt. Then my girlfriend Jackie complains that I'm insensitive. But if I think a client's idea is no good, I tell it like it is. It's the same way when Jackie fishes for a compliment about a new dress. She's got to be prepared for honesty. I just tell the truth. But women want it sugarcoated. I say, if they can't hack it, it's their problem."

I told Will his monologue reminded me of Henry Higgins in *My Fair Lady*. Like him, Will wondered, "Why can't a woman be more like a man?"

Will laughed. "That guy had a point. I never had any trouble with my old boss, Gus. He knew how to take it on the chin."

I nodded, because Will reminded me of many men for whom a female boss represents a blow to their ego.

Will felt similarly threatened by his girlfriend, Jackie. I wondered why he was really here—to straighten out his work life or his love life? A pattern began to take shape, and despite his bravado, it seemed as if Will was ready to acknowledge his contribution to his problems.

"What's wrong with sugarcoating things once in a while?" I probed. "People have feelings and you need to take them into consideration."

Will shook his head. "If I soften up, I'll lose my edge. Besides, it makes me feel like a sissy," he told me. "I can't stand it when Jackie calls me Honey. As if she expects me to go all mushy."

"Why is that?" I asked.

"It gives her the upper hand. Like I'm being made a sap." It was the same at work. "When I do what my boss wants, I feel like her secretary, instead of my own man."

"Yet that didn't bother you when your old boss Gus gave you orders," I interjected.

In both spheres, in love and at work, Will's ego was on the line—frequently when the issue at hand had nothing to do with his ego. He kept imagining that people thought he didn't "measure up." And so he had to prove himself. He was ultracompetitive in all things: sports, work, even dating. For example, Jackie's mere mention of one of her old boyfriends got Will's dander up. Although she was clearly head over heels for Will and had no lingering interest in her former beau, Will's fragile ego still felt endangered by her past. However much she might reassure him, he could not let go of his anger. As Will thrust his fragile ego into his interactions with women, it kept getting in the way and tripping him up.

By working hard and pushing himself (and others), Will had gotten very far. But at this point, his hard-driving personality was becoming counterproductive. Although Will was afraid he would lose his edge, I told him that softening his edges could only help him. It wouldn't affect his work ethic or productivity. On the contrary, paying attention to people's feelings would make him that much more effective.

As therapy progressed, Will began exploring the emotional baggage that had led him to this uncomfortable impasse with two important women in his life, his boss and his girlfriend. He became aware of the link between his inner insecurities and his gruff, heavy-handed behavior. He gradually realized that not everything had to do with him, that women weren't trying to put him down. He gained some insight by examining his attitudes toward his parents' relationship.

Will had always seen his mother as a weak, fragile figure for whom he had little respect. In contrast, he had tremendous respect for his father, despite the fact that his dad had gone bankrupt due to serious financial misjudgment and had, in fact, led a dishonest double life. But by keeping up the appearance of strength even when his world was caving in, his father had managed to retain his son's respect. "He always acted like a man," Will said admiringly. (This was actually selective memory on Will's part, since his father had been afraid to own up to many failures, professional and personal.)

By contrast, Will's mother had acknowledged her problems and disappointments. Although she in fact tried to save the family by going to work and paying the bills, in Will's eyes she was a "crybaby complainer," who wanted to turn his father into "a wimp who should beg her forgiveness." Will had idealized his father's brittle veneer as adult and manly, while deriding his mother's complaints as feminine and weak.

I pointed out to Will that in adulthood, whenever he emulated his father by playing tough and ignoring his problems, he found himself in one sort of trouble or another. I reminded him how, for example, when he continued training for a marathon despite worsening pain and against the advice of his girlfriend at the time, who was a nurse, he had suffered permanent joint damage. Several previous relationships of his had foundered over the issue of his insensitivity. And now, his boss was giving him a warning that if he didn't become more tactful with his clients (and, presumably, toward her), his job was in jeopardy, no matter how creative an ad executive he was.

"You know, your father was just as vulnerable as anyone," I said. "It was denying his problems, and acting as if nothing was wrong, that got him into worse trouble and further in debt, and undermined his marriage. The same thing happens when you make yourself blind and deaf to what others say, and decide to tough things out. Is that being manly, or is it just running away from the problem?"

Gradually, as Will examined his preconceptions, he grew to learn that people do have vulnerabilities and emotional needs that must be taken into consideration. The more he came to accept this fact about himself, the more he was able to cater to similar needs in others. Thus, he learned it was okay to take care of himself—that he, too, needed a good night's sleep and healthy meals, that he could leave work before ten p.m. every night, and take a vacation without calling the office every thirty minutes.

He also found that he could tell Jackie how much he cared for her and not be ashamed to admit that he felt lucky to be involved with her. He then began to own up to the fact that he had a drinking problem—which further hindered his handling of stress. Acknowledging weakness, he came to understand, is part of being human—these were not "flaws," as he had always imagined. He could be strong, even if he did have needs and weak spots. And it didn't take anything away from that strength to be more sensitive toward his girlfriend, respecting her and other people's weak spots, too.

Will learned that he needed to deal with his problems from the inside and grapple with his own insecurities—about himself, his strength, his accomplishments, and about what it meant, and did not mean, to be a strong male. Eventually, he learned that relationships did not have to revolve around his ego needs. But it was a long, hard therapy, with as many steps backward as forward.

Like Will, many men see it as a sign of weakness to give in to even the most mundane requests: from giving a compliment that has been "fished for" to showing interest in a woman by asking her out for a date well in advance.

To turn these simple gestures inside out and convert them into power struggles is an indication of how low some men's self-esteem is. To do what someone else wants is not to be submissive or unmanly. Yet that is the template through which many men experience these interactions. The mere fact that a woman has any needs at all can be experienced as controlling.

One day, for instance, Will came in complaining about how demanding Jackie had become. "Her brother's getting married, and she expects me to go to every family event that weekend. I told her I would. But I hate feeling like some new puppy dog she's showing off to her relatives."

I pointed out to Will that anyone in that situation would feel on display, and in fact he would be on display. But what's wrong with that? It was a compliment to be included in all the festivities, but he was treating it as if he were being sentenced to twenty years of hard labor.

It was an indication of the progress Will had made that he overcame his instinctive initial reaction and agreed to go. When a patient resists following an ingrained pattern, such as Will's reaction to the wedding invitations, he puts himself in a position to exercise better judgment. Will proved that he was growing more generous toward Jackie, accepting her needs and seeing them as less of an imposition. His going did not mean he was powerless, or just doing "Jackie's bidding." Instead, it demonstrated how much he cared for her. She was proud of him, and that reflected well on him, not badly.

Even so, Will still felt uncomfortable about other aspects of what he perceived to be the balance of power in their relationship. At one point, Jackie's job as an accountant required her to work long hours during a particularly hectic tax season and she was not as available to him as usual. Will felt that Jackie was "calling the shots" and became quite upset with her. In an attempt to reduce his anger, I reframed the problem: "Don't you expect Jackie to understand when you have a big work deadline?" I asked, knowing that Will often had to work long hours himself. In any relationship, people have to accommodate their partner's outside commitments. Making things easier for her did not mean he was getting the short end of the stick. Once again, Will needed to reconsider his view of power and strength, and weigh the possibility that he was feeling humiliated when there was no reason to be.

One night Will went drinking with his buddies and got so drunk that he "blew off" his date with Jackie. She was left waiting in a restaurant for over an hour without getting so much as a phone call from Will, before she gave up on him and returned home. Late that night from the bar, he drunkenly called her to offer a rambling explanation. She told him to sober up and hung up the phone. As you might imagine, Jackie was furious, but the next day when Will called, he couldn't bring himself to apologize. Instead, he stubbornly tried to justify his behavior by asserting his "right" to see his friends. Jackie didn't question his freedom to see his friends; she was angry because he had stood her up. But for Will, an apology meant giving her the upper hand.

Will was gradually able to realign his perceptions of what it means to be involved in a caring relationship and to develop a more egalitarian notion of power. He came to realize that it takes more strength to share your life and yourself with someone than to remain guarded and withhold love. It takes more self-confidence to admit a vulnerable side than to hide and deny one's feelings behind a tough facade.

Similarly, Will gradually became more comfortable articulating his emotions and owning up to the fact that he had a tender side. Being "mushy" or apologizing when he was inconsiderate did not mean he was a "wimp," nor that Jackie would take advantage of him. Rather, it takes a different kind of strength to show vulnerability, admit need, and accept another's care.

Commitment as Emasculation

In turning his feelings inside out, Will had converted his relationship with Jackie into a power struggle. He read into her every action a desire to deprive him of his autonomy. Then, in order to assert his freedom, he had to pull away from and struggle against the bonds of their relationship. In subtle ways, Will perceived Jackie as an enemy—one who symbolized his loss of autonomy and signaled the end of his cherished bachelorhood. And so he fought her, along with the commitment, dependency, and powerlessness she represented. He was caught between his wish to be involved with her and his countervailing wish to move away from her. But to give in to the commitment would make him feel less like a man.

As a therapist, I'm often struck by people's use of language. Will spoke of being a "wimp," a "sissy," "getting the short end of the stick," "needing permission to go pee," "not measuring up." The connotations all have to do with emasculation. It is the sexual overtones of power and powerlessness that make love and intimacy such a troubling issue to so many men. They feel as if their sexual potency is on the line, even when the particular interaction has nothing to do with sex.

Let's take men's well-known fear of commitment. Many psychologists conceptualize this in terms of a madonna/whore complex—that a man treats a woman either as an object of awe, respect, and tenderness or as an object to be sexually dominated. This separation makes it difficult to integrate intimacy with sex, and thus men are unwilling or unable to make a wholehearted commitment to one woman. Although I do not wholly disagree with this psychological explanation, I'm much more concerned by the problems posed by men's image of women as powerful figures to be feared and hated. This fear of women's power is, in my opinion, what underlies "male fear of commitment."

Men are reluctant to commit to women because being in a romantic relationship seems emasculating. It's a convoluted logic: Rather than feeling they achieve sexual potency in a relationship, they believe they lose their potency. Even though men in relationships obviously have more sex than men who are not in relationships, they still feel as if they have been castrated. Why? They feel that once the woman has hooked her man, she will abuse the power she has over him. It may be an exaggerated fear, but it reflects their discomfort with giving up power and control.

The kinds of fantasies men have about how they will be "abused" are varied: The woman will tie them down; or spend their money; or, being fickle, will abruptly change her mind and dump him. Many men believe that women are too emotional, and therefore not to be relied on—an especially scary thought when we feel dependent. Regardless of the specific fear scenario, the men feel that the women are not on their side and are not to be trusted.

Many men fear a woman as soon as they perceive her to be strong and powerful. Men identify with the biblical character Samson and his downfall at the hands of Delilah. You'll recall that

Samson's strength resided in his uncut hair. When Delilah, working at the behest of Samson's enemies, took scissors to his long locks and cut them, he became a weakling, no longer able to perform his great feats of strength. Delilah seduced Samson and stole his potency. Although she spoke words of love, she was untrustworthy.

As a psychologist, I interpret Delilah's cutting of Samson's hair as a displacement of an underlying male fantasy of "vagina dentata"—the idea that the very act of sex with a woman will emasculate or castrate him. This perception of women as figures to fear and distrust reinforces men's sense of inadequacy and fuels their anger.

Like Samson, many a man fears that his very own temptress will work her charms in order to lull him into a sense of false comfort and security; once she has him in her grasp, she'll seize all his strength. To my mind, this is the underlying fear of men who describe their girlfriends or wives as fencing them in, acting like their jailer holding the keys, or, as Will imagined, keeping him on a leash, or treating him like "a puppy dog to show off." One patient was so uncomfortable letting a woman know of his interest in her that he told me that every time he called to ask for a date, he felt his ass was "flapping in the wind"—a most evocative image!

Like Will at the beginning of therapy, many men are reluctant to make a commitment to the women in their lives. They protect their freedom at all costs, seeing themselves as perennial bachelors—an image synonymous with eternal attractiveness and youth, freedom from responsibility, and possessing limitless choices. Even men who marry may fight against their feelings of attachment by retaining a fantasy of perpetual bachelorhood.

The idealization of bachelorhood is a way to deny the passage of time. Unfortunately, as soon as some of these men begin to feel secure and established at midlife, they realize that their choices are limited, that life is finite, and that they may not achieve many of the dreams of their youth.

These men, married or single, hold out (and hold back) on love, waiting for the exact right time and place and woman. For them, love is a scarce resource to be conserved and parceled out in infinitesimal portions. They fear that in loving, they will be drained of their power and potency. And so they wait, rejecting any number of possible partners because of some perceived flaw or another, ever fearful of losing control.

I try to help my male patients like Will change their view of love and begin to see it as an ever-replenishing commodity. The more love we expend, the more we have to give. By contrast, if we continually hoard, and never expend what we have to offer, we risk becoming a modern-day Scrooge, alone and unloved. My message is that by loving, we're gaining, not losing.

Image Isn't Everything

To understand why so many men struggle for freedom and feel so powerless in relationships, it's important to refer back to their feelings about themselves. Like many men, Will felt burdened by others' expectations of him. Will felt that both Jackie and his female boss put enormous pressure on him to live up to impossible standards. This stress contributed to his drinking, and made him tense and irritable much of the time.

To shore up their fragile egos, many men feel compelled to project an image of strength, even if it's not how they feel inside. This discrepancy between the "true self" and the "outside persona" can only be straddled at great emotional cost. The wider the discrepancy, the greater the cost. To some degree, our society reinforces this tendency with the public relations message used by André Agassi: "Image is everything." Although this ad contains a note of irony, many people do believe this. But the truth is that image is not everything, and people, especially men, cannot compensate for inner insecurities by projecting a false image, however impressive it may at first appear.

This is the underlying reason many men feel pressured to live up to other people's expectations and at the same time feel burdened by the image they have to project. Whether they focus on their physique or their clothing, their earning power and financial resources or other status symbols, they push themselves to measure up to certain standards. They think this pressure is coming from outside, but it's coming from within.

This dilemma is well illustrated by Will's problems with money. Following in his father's footsteps, Will lived a lifestyle that exceeded his means. In spite of having enormous student loans to pay off from college and business school, Will wanted to project an image of being well-to-do; to do otherwise, he felt, would detract from his manliness and make him less attractive to women. Despite his large debts, Will felt obliged to pick up the tab for each of his dates with Jackie. To make matters worse, he kept trying to impress her—despite the fact that she was obviously in love with him—by continually taking her to fancy restaurants or pricey plays and clubs. Will knew he couldn't afford this kind of extravagance even once, much less on a regular basis. Instead of dealing directly with the problem, though, Will would get angry at Jackie for putting pressure on him by expecting lavish evenings out.

Will sometimes canceled a date rather than scale down his image. Still, he refused to even consider my suggestion that he allow Jackie to pick up a check; as he put it, it was "the man's responsibility." And even though Jackie did not expect one expensive date after another—in fact, she called them "show-off dates"—Will still attributed this expectation to her. Nor did this belief soften even after they became more deeply involved. "She may say I don't have to spend so much on her, but if I stopped, she'd dump me as a cheap date."

Similarly, when Will and Jackie reached the year anniversary of their first date, Will felt obliged to buy her a costly piece of jewelry. He still hadn't told her about his financial situation ("It would make me look bad"), and he believed she expected extravagance. "I'm afraid to disappoint her. There are any number of guys who'd be happy to buy her a diamond bracelet. I can't afford it, but if I don't she's going to think I don't care. I don't know what to do."

But from what I knew about Jackie, Will greatly exaggerated her expectations. I don't know many women who wouldn't love a beautiful bracelet, but that does not mean they expect it or that they'll be disappointed with a more modest gift. In fact, Jackie was not especially materialistic, and had even told him she much preferred a simple celebration, such as a quiet, home-cooked meal enjoyed at home alone together. Will thought he was afraid of Jackie's anger, but her anger did not exist.

One of Will's dreams illustrates the psychological dilemma he had created for himself. In the dream, he was transformed into a statue. As I interpreted it, Will felt compelled to project to the world (including Jackie) a heroic image. Unfortunately, one can never live up to such an unrealistic standard; statues are static, dead, and lacking in human qualities. If you're a statue, you don't have natural human needs and vulnerabilities (except possibly the need for adulation), and you don't let yourself be cared for. In fact, Will did not let Jackie help him—with their dinner checks, or anything else. But the pressure was coming from within, and Will was mistaken in thinking it was coming from Jackie.

This dream was crucial in helping Will accept his own vulnerability. He recognized that he had not allowed himself to be more human and humane, that the excessive and unrealistic expectations were his own. By the end of therapy, Will was able to accept the chinks in his armor, and no longer believed that the women in his life would take advantage of them or him.

Male Performance Anxiety: George

The internal pressure to live up to an image is commonly known as performance anxiety. And who wouldn't feel pressured, anxious, and self-conscious, if he thought he was constantly onstage, surrounded by judges, in a continual performance that never allowed him to let down his guard? Like Will, the men in these next two cases both turned their anxiety inside out and transformed it into anger at the women in their lives. Although they are in quite different phases of their lives—George at twenty-two is unmarried and at the beginning of his career; Steven, forty-five, has been married for over twenty years, is the father of three children, and has already achieved significant stature in his profession—they represent two sides of the same coin.

George was a recent college graduate who felt hampered by his shy, bashful manner. He wanted to come across to women as someone cool and strong. Instead, he was so self-conscious that he froze and was perceived as being aloof and distant. As a result, when Jean, a colleague at his new job, began flirting with him, complimenting him on a new tie one day and asking him what kinds of movies he liked the next, he became so anxious and tongue-tied that he began avoiding her. One day, Jean sought him out in the coffee shop she knew he frequented and coyly asked why he didn't invite her to sit down with him. Feeling pressured to say something clever, and not wanting to appear too interested, George blurted out, "It doesn't matter to me if you sit down or not." Insulted, Jean turned on her heel and left.

George tried to justify his behavior by telling me that Jean was just teasing him and wasn't truly interested. But it certainly didn't look that way to me. When I asked if he was interested in her, George admitted that in fact he was attracted to her. Trying to link his inner emotional state with his behavior, I pointed out to George that the more attracted he was, the angrier he appeared.

By examining his interactions with Jean in microscopic detail, we were able to see the effects of his anxiety. George worried that he was "no good at banter" and feared that if he tried to be witty, his jokes would fall flat. So he clammed up and made Jean do all the work making conversation. By acting cold (rather than "cool"), he avoided putting himself on the line. It was a defensive strategy meant to protect him from rejection, but it only served to turn her off. Even when Jean continued to show clear interest, his anxiety caused him to actively insult her.

In this way, George transformed his internal anxiety over performing well (saying something clever) into fights with an external adversary, even though that seeming adversary was actually on his side. He had converted an internal enemy into an external one.

Something similar happened with another woman. One night at a bar, George met Felice, who, having just turned thirty, flirted with him, saying, "You're cute, even though you're probably too young for me." George was so insecure that he took her joke seriously, accepted it as a rejection, and left the bar. Even though Felice clearly had wanted to pursue their repartee, George managed to turn a possible romance into a self-inflicted failure. In his view, Felice was "just some old witch." Although I knew it was his insecurity talking, George did not.

As therapy progressed, however, I helped George see the pattern: He blamed women for his own insecurity. It was true, strictly speaking, that first Jean, and then Felice had made him anxious by flirting with him and arousing emotions both pleasurable (attraction) and uncomfortable (fear). But it was a mistake, I told him, to conclude that they were responsible for his anxiety and discomfort.

It turned out that George was an only child who attended an all-boys prep school and then an all-male college. He had carried over into adulthood an adolescent mentality that cast women as the medium through which men compete with their buddies, the kind of thinking that puts a notch on the belt for every "score." Given the pressure he felt, George had little interest in these women other than the ways in which they might bolster his ego and reputation. He saw every interaction with a woman as leading to some kind of competition, as though he were one prep school jock trying to outdo another.

For him, dating was all about performance—how clever his conversation was, whether he had a more attractive date than his friend, and how good a lover he would be (at the time of the therapy he remained a virgin). Under such pressure to perform, it's no wonder he froze up and lashed out on occasion.

I tried to help George get beyond the performance issue and see women as real people, not as commodities in some male competition, and not as judges out to evaluate his performance and humiliate him. The women George told me about had just been trying to get to know him, and I encouraged George to take the pressure off himself and reciprocate. George would have to open up and expose more of himself if he became more intimate, but that wasn't going to lead to humiliation. More often than not, the woman would reciprocate in kind. I wanted George to learn that women weren't so different from himself, not nearly as harsh as he imagined. Finally, he needed to realize that talking to a woman was not about competing with other men. Once he gained these insights, his performance anxiety would begin to abate.

George and I discussed ways for him to "practice" being with women in nonthreatening, low-pressure situations. One possibility was to talk to, and eventually socialize with, colleagues like Jean. Despite his trepidation, George was able to tolerate his anxiety enough to approach Jean with an apology for his rude behavior, and she accepted his offer to go out to lunch.

Step by step, George learned to master and tolerate the emotions and sensitivities that had derailed him in the past. The key for George was to resist the temptation to lash out at the moment when he was most anxious. If he could hold himself back, it would give him time to reconsider what he was feeling, why he was feeling that way, and what would be the best course of action. He began to ask himself whether the woman he was with was in fact going to be as critical as he anticipated. But what really took the pressure off was his realization that even if she was critical or rejecting, he would not be harmed by it.

Always in Control: Steven

George's tendency was to transform his performance anxiety and self-consciousness into anger by acting out and lashing out. Although Steven, a successful investment banker, would appear to be quite different from the younger George, he too felt self-conscious. The difference was that Steven dealt with it by always remaining in complete emotional control and never letting anyone see the slightest flaw or vulnerability.

Again and again men tell me they need to remain in "the driver's seat." They're afraid to let themselves go, to let their emotions fly. The underlying motivation is that if we can completely control our performance, making certain that people see only what we want them to see, then we'll feel more secure about their evaluation of us. But such control only comes at a great cost to us and our relationships, and in any case it's impossible to control everything.

Typical of this buttoned-up style, Steven was remarkably self-contained and reserved. He always presented himself impeccably, wearing suits on dress-down days at work, speaking in soft tones even when he got angry, and seldom showing more amusement than could be conveyed by a wry raising of the eyebrow. He himself never would have come into therapy to deal with his constricted emotional life; as he saw it, the problem was external. Steven became visibly uncomfortable, he told me, when his wife behaved in what he felt was a less than restrained manner. Through the years, he told me, he had come to hate the sound of her laughter, which he considered boisterous and uninhibited. Despite the fact that everyone else seemed to find her good humor infectious—and he himself had originally been attracted by her openness and warmth—whenever she laughed now, he felt ashamed of her. Steven would communicate his disapproval to his wife and subtly try to inhibit her.

I asked Steven, "What's wrong with your wife showing people how she feels? Even if you choose not to, why shouldn't she? It makes her happy, and everyone else around her seems to appreciate that quality."

"She's lacking in self-control," he replied. "She has no self-discipline." Further negatives in his wife's behavior were what he considered her excessive generosity in terms of buying extravagant presents for their children, and her contributing so much time and money to charitable organizations. Worst of all was her habit of trying to draw him out in conversation. "But when I'm not in the mood to talk, I like to keep to myself," he told me.

One day right after the winter holidays, Steven walked into my office looking especially distressed. "Merry Christmas, Happy New Year," I said, but Steven only frowned. The holidays had been trying, he told me in his typically understated way. His wife and daughters had decorated the tree with a beautiful display of antique ornaments that his wife had recently inherited but had kept hidden in order to surprise him. When it came time to open the presents, as a further surprise, his wife had made reservations for a romantic weekend, just the two of them, at a small New England inn they had visited on their honeymoon.

Steven was so taken aback by this cheerful scene and show of affection that he felt momentarily paralyzed. Like many men who need to keep a firm grip on the reins, Steven didn't like surprises. Secretly, part of him had adored watching his wife and daughters enjoy the exquisite decorations, and he himself admired the tasteful way in which they had adorned the tree. And despite his complaints about his wife's extravagance, he knew in his heart of hearts that this was a small price to pay for the holiday spirit she brought to the family.

Yet instead of exclaiming, "What a wonderful present!" he had held back, scolding, "You're going overboard here." His wife had been understandably hurt, and what should have been a joyful evening had ended in tears.

I asked, "Why do you resist your wife? What are you afraid of?"

Steven changed the subject slightly, complaining anew about how many bills of hers he had to pay; all she wanted to do was spend money.

I countered, "But this is not going to break the bank. You can afford it." Steven had a quick response: "But if I show her that it's okay to be extravagant at Christmas, she's going to think I've given her the green light to waste even more money. By showing my disapproval, I'm stopping her from doing something worse." His intricate logic, based on all sorts of preconceptions about his wife's behavior, was completely off base.

I challenged his view. "What do you mean? Your wife's never shown bad judgment. You're anticipating something that has never happened." He replied tersely, "There's always a first time," as if his wife was going to change after twenty years of marriage.

Steven was stingy, both financially and emotionally. He wouldn't let himself go with his wife because he was afraid of not being fully in control. In therapy, I tried to show him that it was okay to loosen up.

We began by examining the emotional baggage he brought to

his feelings about being in control. After his father's sudden death when Steven was in junior high school, he eventually became the primary provider for his family. He took pride in shouldering responsibility and, having started working diligently at a relatively young age, he became very successful. Yet despite the fact that he had been able to restore equanimity to his and his family's life after such an tumultuous childhood, Steven still did not believe that life was "in control."

Having missed out on a strong protective male role model during that critical period of his life, Steven felt there was no one who could establish order. Without a father figure to identify with, Steven always had a sense that things were falling apart. As a result, he felt he needed to have a tight grip on everything in his life—from his business dealings to the way his wife expressed her feelings. He was unable to let himself go emotionally, or even allow himself to be "drawn out" in conversation, much less agree to a surprise romantic trip. Steven further revealed that although he had been married for twenty years, he had so much difficulty expressing himself emotionally that he had never actually told his wife, directly, "I love you." Doing so would have meant opening himself up to unknown emotional territory where he no longer would feel completely in control.

Steven's therapy began to make progress as I reconceptualized the problem from being a conflict with his wife over behavior styles to its being another manifestation of his own fragile ego and self-consciousness. As Steven revealed what lay beneath his highly controlled exterior, I discovered that he constantly compared himself to others in all things major and minor, from physical appearance to the amount of money he was making to what type of car he drove to the cut of his clothing to the prestige of his country club to the status of his hairline. It's what we commonly think of as "male vanity," but its causes lie deeper than mere vanity.

For example, Steven had his suits tailored quite carefully in order to mask the fact that he was slightly bowlegged—a minor physical flaw that I would never have noticed if he hadn't mentioned it but that bothered him a great deal. In his imagination, he magnified this "flaw" a hundredfold. He felt that revealing a weakness (whether it was physical, like his bowleggedness, or educational, like his not having gone to college) would humiliate him. He was as anxious to avoid revealing any weakness to his wife of twenty years as to his business partner of over fifteen years.

Because he was so aware of what he viewed as his defects, Steven felt uneasy in another person's presence unless he knew of some comparable (or preferably, more troubling) flaw in that other person's life: anything from financial difficulties to a physical illness to a bad marriage to a family member who was an alcoholic. As soon as he discovered that comparable flaw, Steven immediately became much more comfortable.

In therapy, I helped Steven see that this perception was distorted. His fragile ego led him to exaggerate the kinds of flaws and imperfections from which we all suffer. More often than not, no one saw the hidden flaws he worried over. If and when they did, like any trusted companions, they accepted him, and certainly would not laugh at him.

Even though Steven was at a much different point in his life than the younger George, and even though Steven never lashed out in anger, their self-consciousness led them both to believe that they didn't "measure up." In therapy, they each needed to come to terms with their own failings, put their flaws and imperfections in perspective, and be willing to reveal them when appropriate.

Once we had identified Steven's extreme self-consciousness, we were in a better position to deal with his marital problems. Steven was uncomfortable revealing his own flaws, and he was equally uncomfortable when his wife revealed what he perceived to be her flaws—her effusiveness, her extravagance, her general uninhibitedness. As with many married couples, Steven was so closely identified with his wife that she had become part of his self-image. He could control his own behavior in an attempt to hide his perceived flaws, but he had little control over his wife's behavior, and she saw no need to conceal these personality traits. This is what led to his disapproval and discomfort around her, and to his efforts to constrain her.

Predictably, perhaps, as Steven came to terms with his own failings, he began to be more comfortable with other people's imperfections as well. Once he felt less of a need to control and perfect his own performance, he also felt less of a need to control others, especially his wife and children.

Thus, the perceived interpersonal problem that had brought Steven into therapy was ultimately understood to be an internal problem that was playing itself out in his marriage. Steven had begun therapy believing that because his wife made him feel self-conscious, he needed to get her to change those personality characteristics and behavior patterns of *hers* that made him uncomfortable. But changing others is not the solution to our problems. What Steven came to understand was that by getting more comfortable with himself, he became more comfortable with his wife.

Overcoming the Fragile Male Ego

Simply put, men need to change their ideas about love. They need to become comfortable with the submissive feelings and lack of control that inevitably accompany romantic relationships. Instead of viewing love as tying them down, humiliating them, or emasculating them, they must begin to see love as enriching and empowering.

Unfortunately, the men who most need to learn these lessons

are least likely to enter therapy. Because therapy itself recapitulates their feelings of powerlessness and humiliation, it is particularly difficult for them to swallow. Because men fear dependency and are reluctant to give up power, they experience the therapist-patient relationship within that template as well. In fact, my male patients all tell me at one point or another that they feel humiliated or embarrassed at being in therapy, and transform this discomfort into competition and antagonism toward me. In therapy, as in their romantic relationships, they try to establish who is in charge.

For example, when George, the insecure young man who felt humiliated by every flirtatious woman he met, was nearing the end of his therapy, he could not acknowledge his anxiety and sadness about stopping treatment and going off on his own. As often happens in therapy, he had developed a level of attachment to me. But instead of being able to voice his fears out loud, he reverted, turning his anxiety into angry denial. During the final month of treatment, he said, "Hey, I got along fine without you before, and I'll do fine again." It was the kind of bluster he had used when he first met Jean. It was now nearly a year later, and George and Jean had started dating, but he still stumbled over how to handle our leave-taking.

But the year's treatment had made a difference: This time George caught himself in midsentence and said, "You shouldn't take me seriously, you know? I'm scared about stopping treatment, and I'm truly grateful for all your help." George now knew enough about himself to recognize that he had turned his own feelings inside out. I felt proud that George had gained a good enough grasp of his fears to be able to own up to his feelings. His acknowledgment of his fears also provided me with the opportunity to reassure him that my door was always open and that he could contact me whenever he wanted. Although George struggled with me throughout the treatment and often felt humiliated by the things I said, he had let me help him. George had come a long way.

I tell my male patients that the greatest mistake they can make is to blame the women in their lives for their own inadequacies. I urge them to learn the following lessons:

1. Relationships are not fundamentally about power or control. Nor are most women out to castrate or entrap men. As men change their perceptions of women, they will find it easier to tolerate the submissiveness and dependency that develop with love and intimacy.
2. Love is not humiliation; it can build a man's ego rather than tear it down. Men need to find ways to feel better about themselves in relationships.
3. Showing love does not turn men into ninety-eight-pound weaklings. They should be less stingy with their emotions, for they have nothing to lose and everything to gain.
4. Men must change their ideas about what it means to be a man. People do have expectations of men. But the pressure many men feel comes from within, not without.
5. Men must protect their relationships from the destructive effects of their anger and aggression.
6. Finally, for the female readers of this book, I don't believe that they can change the men in their life; it's not their job to shore up a man's fragile ego. But understanding men's psychological dynamics will make it easier to apportion responsibility when it comes time to sort out the question: Is it you or is it me?

Now, let's turn to women's psychological dynamics.

7
Raw and Vulnerable
Women's Fear of Intimacy

As discussed in the previous chapter, men tend to view falling in love as a loss of power, and consequently transform their discomfort with dependency into anger and a need for control. Women, more comfortable acknowledging their vulnerability, tend to blame men for not treating them gently enough. In fact, their hurt feelings are coming from their own oversensitivity.

Many women have become sensitized to the ups and downs of the romantic roller coaster, and they are ready to feel bruised and hurt. Above all, they believe they must protect what they feel to be their raw inner selves. Fearful that even the gentlest brush with romance will cause them pain, they guardedly avoid, or defensively vent at, their partner or potential lover. Because they consider themselves to be unlovable, they assume that others will hurt them by rejection or by not loving them enough. They turn their vulnerability inside out and blame their lovers as the source of their pain. I suspect this is the case when I see the following patterns emerge in a female patient's relationships:

- The woman feels so defenseless that she clings to the shards of a relationship, seeking love or commitment that obviously are not forthcoming.

- She submerges herself and loses her individual identity in her partner.

- She believes she is damaged goods, the product of an inner "fatal flaw."

- She oversexualizes the relationship to distract the man from seeing who she really is.

- She finds herself unable to move past abusive relationships from the past, and revictimizes herself in new relationships.

In this chapter I tell the stories of three women who, each in her own way, tried to fend off their internal pain by blaming someone else for it. Belying their different circumstances and situations, they all acted out and externalized quite similar feelings of inner fragility and vulnerability.

China Doll: Suzanne

I begin with Suzanne, a woman whose perception of her own unlovability and lack of value in the world led her to cling needily to an unsatisfying and insulting relationship. Convinced that her current partner, who was quite ungiving, was as good as she would find, she held on to an empty shell of a relationship in a futile attempt to make it work.

As she walked through my office door, the first thing I noticed was that she carried herself with the grace of a dancer. Suzanne was tall and thin, with high cheekbones, an aquiline nose, and thick blond hair worn in an elegant bun that showed off her long neck. She had worked for several years as a model before turning to the business end of fashion and cosmetics. Now in her late thirties, she was a senior public relations executive at a well-known cosmetics firm.

On the outside everything in her life seemed to be in perfect order, just like her makeup. But inside, she told me, she felt as if she had just stepped in from a torrential storm that had left her face smudged and dirty.

I asked her what had happened to make her feel that way.

She said tersely, "John." Three months before, she had ended their three-year relationship, and she was despondent. She had really believed he was "Mr. Right" and couldn't get over her disappointment that he was not. He had not wanted to marry and have kids, as she did, but preferred to "stay in the dating mode." She laughed weakly. "I guess he was Mr. Wrong."

Still, she remained preoccupied with thoughts of him, clinging to memories of their time together as if they were precious possessions. She also spoke at length of a troubling incident that had taken place shortly before she left him. At a party one evening, they had run into one of Suzanne's old friends from her days as a model. John couldn't get over how beautiful the friend was, and compared the two in terms that derided Suzanne: "I can't believe you're both the same age. She looks at least ten years younger. She really knows how to keep fit." He had played into her worst fears about her lovability and made her feel like an old hag, Suzanne remarked.

This kind of incident had led Suzanne to decide to break off the relationship. All too often when they were together, Suzanne ended up feeling insulted. Even when John wasn't overtly hurtful, Suzanne felt she wasn't getting what she wanted from him or the relationship. For a long time, Suzanne had attributed her dissatisfaction to her own neediness. Believing she was too "hungry and needy for his love," Suzanne had at first tried to hide her need for John to be more committed and giving. She thought it was her problem, not his, and so she put up with the status quo and remained in the "dating mode" (afraid that if she gave him an ultimatum, she would lose him). Over time, she hoped, he'd come around and be the kind of lover she wanted him to be.

But as time went on, John did not come around. On the contrary, his thoughtless behavior suggested that he took her for granted. His subtle and not-so-subtle insults became more frequent, and he spent less and less time with her. Suzanne's decision to break off the relationship was a long time in coming.

Yet without his love, Suzanne told me at the start of therapy, she felt bereft, as if she would "wither away." Breaking up with John had "knocked the wind" out of her. Most striking of all was the image she used to describe herself: She compared herself to a fragile China doll that would break at the slightest touch. So brittle did she feel that she believed that the only reason John had stayed with her for as long as he did was because he thought she would fall apart if they broke up. In this and other ways, she attributed to John her own feelings of worthlessness. It was he who had made her feel unattractive, unlovable, and unmarriageable.

She said, "It's as if he robbed me of myself. I used to have such self-confidence, and he took it all away. One glimpse of him across the room, and I feel sick to my stomach."

I asked why had she allowed John to hold such power over her and her opinion of herself? Any objective observer would say that she was attractive, poised, intelligent, successful. At work she could certainly hold her own. Why did she feel so vulnerable and lacking in value in her personal life?

Now Suzanne's sadness took on an angry edge. She blamed John for her unhappiness, and said in disgust, "John should pay your bill," as if he were responsible for her emotional state. Interestingly, not only did she refuse to accept responsibility for the choices she had made throughout the relationship; she still refused to do so, despite her insistent clinging to the remnants of an affair that she herself admitted had been unfulfilling from the very start.

"I should tell him off once and for all," she continued. "That will get him out of my system."

I disagreed. In the wake of so many hurt feelings, Suzanne understandably thought that she would feel better if she could vent her anger. In fact, however, I told her that to do so would be a mistake that would only draw her more deeply into a dead-end and perpetuate her feeling of being unlovable.

Then I gently explained that she was erring the way many women do when they cling to a relationship that has ended, or when they remain in one they know should end. In clinging to John (even in clinging to the memory of her relationship with John), Suzanne was perpetuating a sense of herself as empty, bereft, robbed. In order to get over John, she needed to build herself up from within, not see her strength as contingent on how another treated her.

In fact, as our sessions continued, it became clear that the deeper source of Suzanne's depression was her low self-esteem, which had predated the breakup but was also exacerbated by it. By focusing her anger *outside*, on John, I noted, she would remain stuck where she was. If she were able to improve her self-esteem, she would be able to find a man who really would love her the way she deserved to be loved.

More than that, she had already shown more inner strength and resolve than she gave herself credit for: She had taken the step to end the relationship, because she knew that he wasn't treating her well. Contrary to what she had suggested at our first session, John hadn't stayed with her because he was concerned about her vulnerability; that had been a projection of her attitude about herself. Actually, he had stayed with her because he loved her in his own conflicted way. Several weeks into therapy, when Suzanne bumped into John at a party, she was able to stand up to him again. Taking advantage of their chance encounter, John had suggested they spend the weekend together, "for old times' sake." Tempted though she was to take him up on the invitation, Suzanne knew he had no intention of their getting back together, much less deepening their relationship, and she possessed the good sense to turn him down. Though Suzanne thought she lacked resilience, she had shown plenty already, if she could but see it.

As Suzanne told me more about her relationship with John and her previous affairs with other men, a pattern became clear. She had consistently selected men who did not treat her well; doing this had validated her masochistic sense that "I don't deserve better."

With John, for instance, she had always put herself in what she called the "sub" position, submerging her own preferences (concerning everything from where to go on vacation to when and how often to have sex) rather than risk threatening him. She compared herself to an "emotional sponge" who soaked up John's emotions and desires but was unable to express her own. Like an ever-changing chameleon who seems to obliterate its own character, she became so caught up in understanding and responding to John's needs that she relegated her own to insignificance.

When I asked her why she did this, she told me she had felt safer submerging herself beneath John's protective umbrella. She was ashamed of her own needs and believed that asserting them would be a turn-off to John. As a result, there was "no place" for what she herself wanted in this relationship.

For Suzanne, becoming involved in a relationship posed a fundamental boundary problem. It's not an uncommon one. Boundary blurring is especially difficult for those whose sense of self is as tenuous as Suzanne's. Like Suzanne, as they become involved, they fear they will (or they actually do) merge so completely with their partner that they become overly masochistic, submissive, or clingy. They feel as if they're being swallowed up by the relationship. In the absence of their lover or his acknowledgment, they almost feel as if they don't exist.

In this light, Suzanne was convinced that her hunger for love was so voracious and all-consuming that it would overwhelm

John. She compared herself to a drug addict, and was unable to envision the possibility of anything in between the extremes of intense neediness and "just saying no." She didn't believe that she deserved to be with someone who found her attractive, treated her well, would accept and meet her needs, and wanted to marry her.

I told Suzanne, "You don't have to become completely submerged, submissive, and dependent to be in a relationship. Just because John or any other man doesn't acknowledge you or reciprocate your feelings, that doesn't mean you don't exist."

This was a revelation to Suzanne. As thoughts of John gradually faded, and she began to date other men, she realized that clinginess was neither a solid foundation for a relationship nor healthy for one's self-esteem. "You know, I think men actually feel relieved when women say straight-out what they do and don't like. It takes the pressure off them."

More important, I reminded Suzanne, asserting herself took the pressure off *her*. She could be herself, not a "sub."

Even as she started going out again, though, Suzanne remained self-conscious, particularly about her appearance, and was considering a face-lift. Again she brought up the story of how John had compared her so unflatteringly to her model friend. She also told me how, when a previous relationship had ended (also with a man who, like John, was hypercritical of her appearance), she had gone on what she called "a makeup binge," obsessively trying to compensate for what she believed was an unattractive appearance.

When we explored this preoccupation, Suzanne revealed that her father had been extremely critical of her mother's appearance, and her mother had tried so many hairdos and worn so much makeup that there was a family joke that all by herself she was keeping their local beauty parlor in business. At this, I reminded Suzanne of how she had described herself at her very first session as feeling "smudged," like poorly applied makeup. Perhaps, I suggested, it was not an accident that she had gone into the cosmetics business, or that she responded to her various breakups the way she did. In her mind, not measuring up to a standard of beauty was equivalent to not being lovable.

Like many women, Suzanne felt like damaged goods. She projected this feeling of ugliness outward onto her physical appearance. Her discomfort with her body reflected her discomfort with herself. Her greatest fear was that men would view her as she perceived herself, as someone fatally flawed, lacking in positive qualities, and unworthy. She repeatedly chose men who perpetuated this negative self-image.

Suzanne had mistaken a single aspect of which she was ashamed (her appearance) for the very core of her being. Lacking perspective, unable to place the perceived flaw within a larger context, she had magnified its importance out of all proportion.

I said, "So what if you have a wrinkle. Don't we all have blemishes, defects, physical attributes we can only do so much about? Not everyone is Miss America, and Miss America herself can only maintain that level for one year." I pointed out to Suzanne that she, like her mother, mistook outer beauty for the more important qualities that reside within.

When Suzanne looked in the mirror, she distorted what she saw. Sure, we all get wrinkles and bulges as we grow older, but there is beauty and dignity to maturity, as well. To me, as to most outside observers, Suzanne's appearance was quite lovely. Indeed, wasn't that one reason she was so effective in her job in the cosmetics industry? When she listened to critics like John and her other ex-boyfriends, I told Suzanne, she was filtering out key information, ignoring all the men who paid a great deal of attention to her. Instead, she was hearing, in memory, the taunting voice of her father berating her mother. Her enemy was this inner voice that insisted she was not worthy of love, that she was unattractive and therefore too needy, too clingy, too angry, too hungry for love. As long as she allowed that enemy within to rule her relationships, she would continue to find herself in relationships that made her feel ugly and damaged.

I noted that as Suzanne started dating men again, one strategy she used to hide this "fatal flaw" and keep men from seeing her as she saw herself was to oversexualize her relationships. By going to bed with men early in the relationship, or by focusing predominantly on the sexual aspects of the relationship, Suzanne tried to deflect attention from what she felt to be her "fatally flawed" inner self. As she explained, "If we really spent time together, not in bed, he might see the real me."

Suzanne was so sure of rejection that she didn't know how to handle relationships when they were in limbo. So she would bring them to a premature resolution: go to bed or break up. But to confine a relationship to the sexual arena is to block off the possibility of a deeper, more fulfilling romance. Instead, Suzanne needed to learn how to sit on her hands and let the relationship play itself out, however much emotional uncertainty that left her in. The real issue was how to sit still and just "be" with someone, without going to bed. Without getting drunk. Without having to come up with a lot of nervous, distracting talk to deflect attention from the "real me." Moreover, in using her sexuality, Suzanne did not get her needs for love and intimacy met; her "hunger" remained.

But Suzanne felt so burned by her experience with John that she did not believe she could handle another serious relationship. If the same thing happened again, she said, "I'd be such a basket case, I'd have to rent your couch on a permanent basis." She was afraid to rekindle the hope and desire that develops in the course of budding intimacy.

I told Suzanne, "I know it sounds paradoxical, even frightening.

But because a loving experience gives you the strength to handle hurt, loss, and potential rejection, you actually *protect* yourself by loving—not by avoiding love. To remain afraid of love is to be constantly reminded of your fragility. The only way for a fragile person to believe that she's not going to break is to go through a painful experience and recognize that, however wrenching it is, she will survive."

I then pointed out that she had not fallen apart during the breakup with John. This not only proved her resilience; it also showed she wouldn't fall apart if she went through another breakup. Although I also reassured her that I'd be willing to see her again if such a crisis occurred in the future, I helped her realize she was not an "emotional basket case" requiring an IV line to therapy.

By this time, Suzanne had met Alan, a solid, dependable man who, to my mind, clearly adored her. But because Suzanne felt so vulnerable, she did not see how much he cared, and set up tests of love that he was sure to fail: "If you loved me, you'd think of these things without my having to tell you." Or, "The fact that you didn't call right on the dot is proof that you forgot."

Tests like these remind me of the kinds of impossible tasks that the Greek heroes of ancient myth were asked to perform to prove their devotion. Alas, even when the heroes succeeded, they were doomed to fail because their lovers would ask for yet more proofs. In truth, these tests are not given to elicit proof of a lover's interest, but are manifestations of fear and vulnerability of the person setting the "test." No amount of reassurance or protestations of love can make the doubting person who is convinced she is unlovable suddenly believe that someone really loves her.

Thus, when Suzanne wanted "proof" that Alan's commitment was as real as he proclaimed it to be, he responded by proposing to her. "But he only proposed because I cornered him," she told me. So she put off saying yes by asking for additional proof that he really loved her—and again rejected and dismissed the ample evidence of his continued devotion. For instance, she was unhappy in her job and asked him to promise to support her if she quit; he said fine. Would he show her his financial records to make sure he wasn't hiding any secret debts? He set up a meeting with his accountant, who vouched for his financial stability; in fact, his successful business dealings had made him quite wealthy. Finally, forced to admit that Alan had passed each of her tests with flying colors, Suzanne said yes and they celebrated their marriage at a reception worthy of Cinderella.

Interestingly, even after the wedding, Suzanne was still not completely certain of Alan's love. She had had the courage to take a chance with him, but she wouldn't let go of the reins on her emotions. She remained tense, mistrusting, doubtful—waiting for him to change his mind. She feared that their marriage would recapitulate her experience with John, and Alan would be transformed into a hypercritical man like so many other men in her past. All of Alan's reassurances could not compensate for the emotional scars of her upbringing. She complained increasingly about her husband's long work hours and the time he spent going over plans with her for the country house he was having built for them. "He wants me to give the house the kind of makeover he probably thinks I need," she said bitterly, as if looking for a reason to doubt him.

When Suzanne recounted these episodes, I helped her see that her attitudes reflected her feelings about herself. Alan thought of the new house as a gift to Suzanne, a place where she could relax and let her creative bent flow freely in decorating and gardening. John had mistreated her, but Alan certainly wasn't doing that; Suzanne needed to distinguish between the two. With hard work and in time, she did succeed in changing her preconceptions about love, and learned to let Alan love her.

The Career Excuse: Marguerite

Marguerite, a highly successful businesswoman in her late thirties, shared Suzanne's sense of raw vulnerability. Instead of clinging to another or submerging herself in him, however, Marguerite used a different strategy for self-protection. She built artificial boundaries that warned "Keep out," and whenever someone came too close, she was ready to lash out aggressively in self-defense. Like Suzanne, Marguerite turned her feelings inside out, and they both shared the fear that any man who came close enough to see their authentic selves would be repelled and ultimately rejecting. They differed only in style: Marguerite's anxiety had taken on a hard edge, and she blamed her partners for not being able to cope with her, or her business success.

Marguerite had a razor-sharp intelligence and had succeeded, she told me, by being "as tough as the guys." She was rightly proud of herself when she was promoted to a senior position in a Fortune 500 company but felt "lonely at the top." At the same time, she experienced relationships as an intrusion on her time and responsibilities at work. In fact, Marguerite had come to see me in the aftermath of the disintegration of her marriage. "My career comes first. If a man can't accommodate that or tolerate a powerful woman, forget it. My husband couldn't, and that's why our marriage didn't work." She also quoted him as saying he had left her because she had acted like "the C.E.O. of the relationship." Clearly, Marguerite's competitive spirit and uncompromising manner had served her well in business, but when it came to marriage and romance, this style proved less than ideal.

I found it interesting that Marguerite described marriage in much the same way as many men did—as forcing her to give up her freedom. The way she saw it, relationships required that she relinquish some of the control she so jealously guarded. Getting involved with a man was tantamount to setting out on the road to becoming "barefoot and pregnant, with no professional life whatsoever." Her career became a way to guard against becoming involved, and having to yield to another person's needs.

Where had Marguerite's rigid, either/or view of romance vs. work come from? Of course the conflict between work and private life, especially family life, is quite real. But in Marguerite's case, her devotion to work appeared to be a way of excusing herself from serious relationships. I suspected her negative image of romance had a deeper origin.

In therapy, Marguerite and I traced her attitude toward romance to the unbalanced union of her parents: an overpowering father and a helpless mother. Marguerite had grown up fearing that when she married she would become a victim, like her mother, and her husband a tyrant, like her father. Even though she despised her father, in her marriage she had found herself taking on his aspects of control and power. In the same way that she was unable to achieve a balance in her marriage, she could not find a workable compromise between these two major figures in her past. In fighting against becoming like her mother, she had become as overpowering as her father. However much she tried to escape these core beliefs, they were deeply internalized.

Marguerite's dilemma illustrates how influential our parents are in forming our basic ideas about relationships and about what it means to be feminine and masculine. Marguerite was struggling with how to be feminine without becoming as helpless as her mother—how to give up some control without feeling completely out of control. It was this middle course that she was unable to forge. Instead, she had overcompensated for her fears by attempting to keep as much control in her personal life as she did in her work life. Where Marguerite had miscalculated is that there is no way to be a C.E.O. in romance. Like many women who fear being overpowered by or manipulated by men, she had defended herself by refusing to submit to another's will. The catch was that, given her childhood images of male and female behavior, Marguerite viewed such a refusal as "unfeminine."

When I asked her why she did not feel more "feminine," she compared herself to a piece of broken glass. In her heart of hearts, she felt she was, like her mother, brittle and easily breakable. More than that, she viewed her jagged edges as dangerous to those who were "unlucky enough to get involved with me."

Marguerite was owning up to her discomfort at being unable to find a balance between being hard-edged and competitive at work but loving and feminine at home. Lacking a positive role model, she was at sea when it came to knowing how to assert herself in a romantic relationship without "being bitchy." In her experience, the only way to feel strong was to be angry. With the help of therapy, Marguerite began to make the distinction between assertiveness and aggression. She learned that by acting assertively, she could be effective without having to resort to hostility; that being feminine did not mean being passive or helpless; that it was indeed possible to be both feminine and assertive.

Marguerite had begun therapy unable to see that she was in any way using her career as an excuse to stay away from romantic involvement. Yet as therapy progressed, she disclosed two dreams that evoked important psychological aspects of how she had done just that.

In the first dream, Marguerite found herself riding on a subway car that had no strap to hold on to. As she wandered through the car, she felt unmoored and off balance. I interpreted her not having anything to hold on to as a reflection of the lack of emotional commitments in her personal life. "Even though you say you don't need or even want a man who won't fit himself to your schedule," I told her, "in the dream you seem to be searching for a relationship that you can hold on to." Although Marguerite had begun therapy with the deeply held assumption that life was better without the complications and intrusions of a romantic entanglement, this dream showed her beginning to question that belief;

she was starting to see that something was missing from her life, and that part of her did want a relationship.

Marguerite's second dream was even more thought-provoking: She dreamed that she was a cat being shot by a man with a rifle. I interpreted this to mean that although Marguerite spoke of herself as being tough and steely outside, internally she felt as vulnerable as the cat in her dream. Whether or not we want to interpret the rifle as an explicit phallic symbol (as I did), the dream still reflects her sense of vulnerability. The dream indicated that she was more afraid of the pain relationships can cause than she acknowledged.

The dream also spoke to Marguerite's "bitchiness." She identified not only with the vulnerable cat in the dream, but also with the man with the rifle. She was both victim and aggressor, identifying with her mother and her father. She was well aware that her competitive, angry, controlling manner had disrupted her marriage, and was now interfering with her dating. Although she claimed to want a man who "could take it," she was convinced that once men saw how angry she was, they would first be repelled by her "unfeminine" personality, then they would retaliate in kind. This dream, I suggested, showed Marguerite's anger being turned back against her. It reflected her belief that her anger made her unlovable, and it demonstrated how her brittle sense of self made her view relationships as dangerous. In all these ways, this second dream showed that Marguerite's avoidance of attachment was not simply a conflict between work and love.

Together, these dreams illustrated Marguerite's growing realization that relationships can thrive only when the split-off parts of the self (in her case, her fear of being hurt) are integrated with the whole. She saw relationships as dangerous because of her own aggression and vulnerability; but this was the inside-out dynamic at work. Thus, Marguerite's "career excuse" actually was less about work than about her fraught sense of lovability. As therapy continued, I helped her feel safer in relationships, so she did not have to be so vigilant, controlling, and hostile. As she began to feel less brittle, her jagged edges softened. The less angry she felt in herself, the less danger she felt in regard to men. And the more progress she made in confronting her fears, the less she had to rely on turning them inside out.

Destabilizing the Relationship: Gillian

Gillian, an attractive woman in her early thirties, exemplifies a third tactic many vulnerable women use in dealing with love's riotous feelings. They attribute their chaotic inner experience to a chaotic relationship they themselves have destabilized.

Even at our first session, Gillian struck me as an impulsive, flamboyant woman who experienced herself through others. If she didn't get a reaction, or didn't elicit the reaction she wanted, she felt that she did not exist. To me, this was a warning that inside she felt very much at sea.

She began by telling me about her love life, which was, by her own definition, "all confused and topsy-turvy."

"How so?" I asked.

"Well, I've had my ups and downs with a lot of men. And I mean ups and downs. There's always a rush and then something screws up. Take my boyfriend, Sy, for example. He says he's going to leave his wife, but he never does," Gillian told me. "He wants to wait until after his oldest daughter's wedding, but that is five months off, when she finishes medical school. I can't get over the fact that he expects our engagement to be as long as his daughter's. And then, who knows what will happen? He has two younger daughters. He'll probably expect me to wait until they're married, too."

Gillian went on to tell me that her relationship with Sy, a fellow partner in a large law firm, was as intense an experience as anything she had ever gone through. From the moment they met there was electricity in the air. She hadn't cared that he was married with children; she hadn't even thought about it. They couldn't keep their hands off each other. They saw each other whenever they had a moment to spare, and they would talk and talk and talk, about anything and everything. In fact, Gillian bared her soul to Sy, telling him about her struggle with bulimia, her chaotic childhood, and her mother's four marriages; she even confided in Sy that as a preteen she had been sexually fondled by one of her stepfathers. Sy had responded to her traumatic history with great sympathy. In this, and in all ways, it seemed to her, they connected at a gut level so profound that it excluded everyone else in the world, including his wife and kids.

Like Gillian, Sy had also let himself go emotionally and wanted to marry Gillian. But unlike her, Sy would occasionally "sober up" enough to recognize that there would be consequences to their passion. His delay in leaving his marriage put Gillian in what she felt was an untenable position. She felt betrayed and taken advantage of. As she saw it, there were only two positions he could take: Either their love could conquer all obstacles, or he didn't truly love her. She told me, "When we're together, I know he loves me, but when we're apart, it's as if he doesn't know I exist. I need to get his attention." So Gillian took action. Unfortunately, her solution was to go to bed with Bill, one of Sy's associates.

Sure enough, Gillian got Sy's attention. When he heard about it (from Bill himself, who hadn't known of Sy and Gillian's affair), Sy stormed into Gillian's office. "Sy got so red in the face," Gillian told me, "I was afraid he would have a heart attack right then and there. I could tell he really loved me, and I had been a fool to doubt him. But the damage was done. Sy said he could never look at me the same way again. I tried to tell him I was sorry, but he didn't care." She paused and threw her arms in the air dramatically, as if to absolve herself of all responsibility. "Sometimes I just get impulsive and then regret it later on."

But to me the deeper issues were, why had Gillian gotten so angry at Sy? Why hadn't she had the patience to wait out the five-month delay? Why had she behaved in a way that was sure to destabilize the relationship? Were her "chaotic, topsy-turvy" feelings a result of the relationship? Or were those feelings already present inside her, and then acted out in the relationship?

As I learned more about Gillian's background, I came to see that Gillian did feel terribly chaotic inside. With each of her mother's marriages, Gillian had moved to a new city, a new home, and a new school. She tried to make the best of it, but her life lacked stability. Adding to that, her father had faded from the picture early on, only showing up for "state occasions," as she put it, such as a birthday party or high school graduation, and even then he couldn't be counted on.

Given her history, it was little wonder that Gillian had serious misgivings about whether passion and intimacy could be sustained. It even seemed that she preferred an unstable environment precisely because it reflected the precariousness she had always known.

I suggested to Gillian that her unconscious intention had been to destabilize the relationship with Sy. By acting impulsively, she had irrevocably damaged and derailed it. Afraid that she would be consumed by their passion, and convinced that it was impossible to sustain such intimacy, she chose to get out of the relationship, while claiming that Sy was responsible for the problems. But despite her contention that it was Sy's delay in getting a divorce that made her feel so riotous inside, she had brought to the relationship the chaos that ended it.

Gillian attributed her inner reality to external circumstances—specifically, to her romantic relationship. When she went to bed with Sy's colleague, for instance, she said it was because she had felt so anxious she couldn't stand waiting around anymore. But how had she arrived in a position where she felt such anxiety?

She had done so herself by choosing to participate in a dangerous relationship with a married man, and then having an affair
with the same man's associate. It should have been no surprise
when everything collapsed around her. She may have felt that
events were happening to her, but she was at the whirlwind's vor-
tex.

This pattern was dramatized in a dream she had: She was walking on top of the railing on the George Washington Bridge. "I
knew it was dangerous, but I kept on going," she told me.

I asked, "Why are you intentionally putting yourself in so much
danger? Not only in the dream, but in your relationships? The
danger is not coming from the bridge; it's coming from your
choosing to walk along the railing. The same goes for your relationships. You create danger and provocation, and then, when
things fall apart, you have further evidence of how dangerous
your life is. But you're the one who makes it so precarious."

As her therapy deepened, I tied together her struggle with
bulimia with the conflicts in her romantic relationships. Like
many women with bulimia, Gillian felt ugly and empty inside,
but, unable to voice these emotional concerns out loud, she
instead acted them out through the binging and purging of
bulimia. The bulimia represented a ritualistic enactment of her
inner chaos and turbulence. Rather than giving vent to and purging her emotions, as she hoped, the bulimia just made her feel
that much more ashamed.

Although Gillian had outgrown the symptoms of bulimia by
the time she entered therapy, they could be seen to symbolize
her problems with intimacy. As she had with Sy, Gillian would
take in relationships with men "whole hog." She became completely consumed by the man, and consumed him in turn. Gillian
didn't "metabolize" or "digest" these relationships; she would
expel them as completely as she had taken them in. She did not
know how to take from the relationship the aspects she liked and

ignore or set aside the aspects she did not like. As soon as some aspect of the relationship turned sour, she had to "vomit" it out, as she had done with Sy.

In therapy, I tried to teach Gillian patience: how to sit with her feelings rather than purge them. Had she possessed this emotional mastery before, she might have been able to wait out Sy's delay and believe in his love for her. Gillian also needed to establish a more stable foundation for a relationship from the beginning: For instance, choosing a "dangerous" married man was not a good start. If she had chosen a more stable man, she would be much more likely to maintain a more stable sense of herself.

But the therapy wasn't going to make any real headway until we addressed her history of being sexually abused. Like many women, Gillian pointed to her experience of abuse to explain why she was so anxious and skittish. But to my mind, harping on the past is often an excuse for not allowing oneself to sustain a relationship in the present in which one is vulnerable.

As a psychologist who only treats adults and older adolescents, I occasionally see patients who are survivors of such abuse, but none of my patients have been actively being abused when I saw them. In therapy I focus on the fact that they are no longer helpless, even if they once were. And that's why, when Gillian kept repeating that Sy was going to take advantage of her just as her stepfather had, I challenged her. Yes, her stepfather had molested her when she was nine, but how did that relate to Sy? She had tested his loyalty by sleeping with his associate, virtually kicking Sy out of her life. Her history with abusive men was in the past; why was she constantly putting herself in a position to be taken advantage of in the present? Whose fault is it if you put yourself in danger's path? When she was a child, she was helpless and without recourse, but now she was an adult and had many resources. To recapitulate the emotions that were evoked by her abuse was to revictimize herself.

I helped Gillian see that although she was initially in a position of weakness with her stepfather, she no longer needed to yield power to him. The power, the strength, the inner resources to deal with the past were all within her as an adult. Thus, when Gillian told me she planned to see her now elderly stepfather and get him to admit what he had done to her years before, I asked her why she needed confirmation of something she knew had happened. Whether or not he confessed (and no doubt he would deny his actions), confronting him this way would only revive in her the same feelings of vulnerability and weakness she had had as a child. Eventually, I helped her see that just as she did not need to confront her stepfather, in future relationships she would not need to put her lovers through constant tests of love and loyalty.

Therapy with Gillian progressed slowly, but gradually she achieved some insight. Although the relationship with Sy was never resurrected, she did eventually conduct a more stable relationship with a more appropriate partner. As I told her at the time, we can only overcome our wounds from our past if we don't perpetuate them in our present relationships.

Opening Ourselves, Healing Our Wounds

The mistake so many women make is to guard themselves from further hurt by tightly bandaging their wounds or isolating themselves in virtual quarantine, fearful of the slightest touch. But wounds cannot heal this way. When bandaged, our wounds remain raw and vulnerable. It is only by exposing our scars to nature's healing powers—to love—that we become less sensitive and allow ourselves to become truly whole. Not by hiding our inner core, but by revealing it (under the right circumstances) can we mend. Only by feeling loved will we begin to believe that we actually are lovable. By bringing to the surface the inner self of which we're most ashamed, we can achieve a sense of dignity. That is why I encourage you to do the following:

1. Tolerate the intensity and the rawness that come with opening up. You're more resilient than you think.
2. Resist the impulse to act out, even when you grow uncomfortable or anxious. My motto is "Sit on your feelings for a while, and see where things go." When patients say "Is he trustworthy?" I tell them, "His behavior will show you in the long run; don't jump to conclusions."
3. At the same time, don't disregard signals. Take your partner's behavior seriously. If your partner acts in a callous or uncaring way, it is a clear sign that he's not right for you. Don't submerge yourself or "walk on eggshells" in order to preserve a bad relationship. You deserve better.
4. Don't cling to a bad relationship because you think that's all you're entitled to.
5. We all need an internal rudder, and however involved we get, we must continue to trust our own instincts. It would be a great mistake to give over control of the ship to someone going in the wrong direction, or board one vastly different from the kind of ship we want. As long as you and your partner are in sync, it does not matter who is steering the ship; but when your interests diverge, you need to assert yourself.
6. Don't let your fears of being swallowed up or submerged by a relationship prevent you from being loved by an appropriate partner.
7. Let go of the past traumas you may have experienced and allow yourself to experience relationships in new ways. That was then, and this is now.
8. Explore and test your inner resources. Be courageous about opening yourself up to another. Use the wisdom you have

gained. With time and patience, even the most painful wounds can begin to heal.

9. Remember that the only way to heal the inner wound is to allow others to see the real you. The only way we can believe we are lovable is to let somebody love us. This means owning up to our feelings and finding a way to confront, integrate, and balance our many different sides.

8
Exposing Ourselves
Splitting Off Sex from Emotion

Sex is an experience of particular vulnerability. As our physical boundaries merge, our psychological boundaries can also become confused. We feel exposed, literally (i.e., physically) and emotionally, and we may try to defend ourselves by turning our emotions inside out. This is what's happening when the following things happen:

- We feel we don't exist unless we engender desire in others. As a result, we become confused over whether we are responding to another's expectation, or to our own desire. Our inner vulnerability becomes split off from our outward sexual behavior and bravado.

- We split off our sex lives from our emotional lives, telling ourselves that sex doesn't matter. But sex does matter, which is why we may be confused about when to go to bed with someone, may have regrets about doing so, or may want to change our minds once sex has been initiated.

- We act out our fear of intimacy through adultery. Having sex with someone else distances us from our mate and diffuses intimacy.

Sex Matters

My patients often ask me, "How important is sex and sexual compatibility to relationships?" My answer: "When sex is good, it's not nearly as important as respect, trust, love, generosity, appreciation, and other kinds of compatibility. But when sex is not good, its importance cannot be overestimated."

Sexual love is so intense an experience that it can't help but heighten our every sensation and emotion. Like an exquisite thrill ride, its potent mix of physical and emotional passion can feel simultaneously exhilarating and engulfing, liberating and risky, ecstatic and terrifying. We become a jangle of raw nerves, responsive to our lover's every touch. The fusion between ourselves and our lover, the blurring of both physical and psychological boundaries, gives us the sense of joint ownership of our bodies even as we take pleasure in each other.

It's no wonder that our sexual lives represent a microcosm of our romantic relationships. In sex, we enact the patterns of intimacy that have developed in the relationship—as well as the problems. If we feel distant, angry, anxious, or mistrustful, these emotions will also be manifested in the sexual realm. Sexual pleasure can also be a powerful tonic, healing breaches and salving the wounds caused by anger; or, if we've felt distant or out of touch with our lover, sex can help us to reestablish a sense of intimacy. But if sex isn't working, there's no way to ignore the problem, however much we try.

Another reason sex can be so confusing is that it stirs up all our feelings about how we deal with trust and vulnerability. When we make love we entrust ourselves and our bodies to another. We need to have confidence in ourselves and in our partner that despite the sensation of being close to the edge, on the verge of losing control, that the experience of joining intimately not only will leave us whole, but will also enrich and gratify us.

When trust is lacking, however, we feel unbearably vulnerable, literally naked in our defenselessness. That's when we may turn our emotions inside out and use anger as a protective mechanism—either lashing out or holding back in order to guard against our unease and discomfort.

Sex can also cause us to be confused about intimacy—about how to maintain boundaries and, more important, how to let them down. This is another way of saying that when we're physically intimate with someone, it is difficult to decide how emotionally intimate to be. Being sexually involved with someone doesn't mean we should necessarily lay down our guard completely, especially if trust and love are absent. Moreover, if we're enjoying ourselves sexually, how do we know what the relationship will be like in other respects? Sex can compensate for certain problems in relationships, but it's not a panacea.

There are no hard and fast rules about sexual intimacy. Without a solid foundation of trust, sexual involvement may be premature, but sexual intimacy can also be a forerunner to emotional intimacy. In the latter relationships, sex becomes the vehicle whereby two people begin to take down their guard. The vulnerability shared during sex can lead to a kind of trust that never would have been achieved without sex as the catalyst.

Because our sexual identity represents such a core component of our self-image, some of us use sex to compensate for bad feelings we have about ourselves. I see this in men who need one conquest after another in order to feel manly; their voracious appetite has little to do with sexual desire and everything to do with ego. I also see it in women who like to observe the effect they have on men. If a man is attracted to them, they feel attractive; they look for the reflection of their own value in the mirror of their partner's sexual response.

These needs can lead us to jump into bed with someone much too soon, and often when it doesn't suit our emotional needs. We become sexually intimate prematurely, before we're ready to be emotionally intimate. Or we get caught up in a pattern in which we continue to look for the wrong thing in having sex, such as gratifying our egos or bucking up a poor self-image. When these things happen, a split develops between how we feel inside (our vulnerability, rawness, doubts, fears) and how we behave (our sexual bravado). As the split grows, the relationship evolves on two separate tracks, the internal, emotional one where we feel vulnerable, and the external, image-based one where we act with bravado. This leads to tremendous confusion about intimacy, as well as terrible misunderstandings and disappointment. We end up feeling devalued emotionally.

Sexual intimacy *is* confusing. Putting up and letting down boundaries is at best a complicated psychological process. In deciding whom to trust, how to trust, and when to be wary, we must rely on our intuition, emotional reactions, judgment, and experience. The process of developing intimacy is never static or final, but always is ongoing and back-and-forth. At one moment we may feel inclined to open up, and at the next feel uncomfortable and pull back. We must respect these reactions, but we also need to understand them in the context of our emotional susceptibility and personal history. The biggest mistake we make is when we feel we no longer have the freedom to make our own decisions. Because sex tends to accelerate the relationship process, we need to feel that we can change our minds. Just because we're sexually attracted to someone and have already given them the green light doesn't mean we can't give them a red light. We're not on automatic pilot, but must maintain control over our own destiny. In this, sexual intimacy is not much different from other forms of intimacy.

Putting On the Brakes: Anna

As a psychologist, I often see people whose difficulties with trust are expressed in the sexual arena: People who are promiscuous and who denigrate the value of sexual intimacy. People who have extramarital affairs to diffuse the intensity of their marriages. People who have sexual dysfunctions. These dysfunctions—in women, a lack of sexual desire or other sexual inhibition, and in men, premature ejaculation or impotence—are often manifestations of the inside-out dynamic.

Such was the case with Anna. The more intimate she became with her boyfriend, the more sexually inhibited she became. Her own feelings of fragility made her perceive her boyfriend as dangerous, and sex as perilous.

Anna first came to see me when she was in her late twenties and had been involved with her boyfriend, Joe, for two years. She was troubled because her enjoyment of sex, specifically her ability to achieve orgasm, was erratic. Although sex had been very satisfying early in the relationship, by this point, Anna told me, she hadn't had an orgasm in over a year. She wasn't sure if it was something that Joe was doing; she only knew that the more she focused on the issue, the more self-conscious she became around him. As a result, she had started to avoid going to bed with him, as if the problem would miraculously go away. But it hadn't; things were just getting worse.

When Anna told me about her dating history, I immediately noted that her difficulty with orgasm predated her relationship with Joe. She had had two previous steady boyfriends, and in each instance she had eventually developed a similar self-consciousness and sexual inhibition. With these boyfriends, too, Anna had attributed her sexual unresponsiveness to problems in the relationship. The first man had been her supervisor at work, was fifteen years her senior, and had a long history of prior lovers; all this had led her to believe she was not special to him. Nor did she ever feel entirely comfortable with her other boyfriend, who was her father's best friend's son.

I observed a pattern in Anna's sexual responsiveness. Early in relationships, she had no difficulty with orgasm. She also had a number of pleasurable sexual experiences with men with whom an ongoing relationship never developed. It seemed to me that Anna was unable to achieve orgasm with a man once she loved him, or, as she put it, "when I had gotten in too deep."

I asked Anna to describe what she called her "visceral" feeling of self-consciousness. "I become too nervous to relax," she told me. "I enjoy it at first when Joe is touching me. Then I get anxious. I feel like I've floated to the ceiling and I'm looking down from above at this couple making love. It doesn't feel like it's me down there, and Joe looks like a complete stranger to me."

I followed up with another question: "What would happen if you stayed focused on the sensual stimulation, and tried to stop yourself from getting detached?"

Anna said, "I feel the orgasm building inside me, and it feels like I'm going to lose control. I don't want Joe to see me that way. That's when I start to float away. Can't I have a more controlled orgasm? A smaller orgasm?"

As I understood the problem, Anna felt that in having an orgasm, she would reveal too much of herself. By holding back and remaining in control, she was guarding herself. Orgasm is often experienced as an abandonment of self, which although pleasurable, can be quite anxiety-provoking.

In working with Anna in therapy over the next few months, I discovered that her reaction was in part related to an interesting and not uncommon experience from her early adolescence. She and her father had always had a warm and physically affectionate relationship during her childhood. As Anna remembered it, her father would hug her every day when he returned from work, and give her a kiss every night before she went to sleep. She loved to sit on his lap and have him read her stories, and he appeared to enjoy their relationship as much as she.

Then, when she was thirteen, her parents' marriage suddenly

started to unravel, and her father had an affair with another woman whom he ultimately married. From about that time, the quality of Anna's relationship with her father changed markedly. He no longer expressed his warmth and affection. The hugs, kisses, and father-daughter closeness ceased, just at the crisis time of the divorce when Anna needed his affection most.

The divorce represented more than just the breakup of the family, and more than a betrayal of her mother. To Anna it constituted a personal rejection; she had lost her father to another woman. Anna maintained a relationship with her father, and they visited often, but they never recaptured their prior closeness. When she would go over to give him a kiss, she felt her father bristle, as if he didn't want that kind of intimacy. Anna was convinced that he no longer loved her or wanted to see her.

I suggested that Anna might have misinterpreted her father's feelings. Like many fathers of adolescent girls, Anna's father may have been uncomfortable with her burgeoning sexuality. He may have been self-conscious about showering physical affection on someone who was now a young woman. He may even have been embarrassed about seeing his daughter in those terms. What many fathers do in that situation is distance themselves, not out of rejection or a lack of love, but because of their own discomfort. Unfortunately, the early adolescent doesn't understand this, and learns to be ashamed of her sexuality.

Anna benefited from this round of therapy. She learned to let go enough with Joe so that more often than not she did have an orgasm. Both she and Joe became much more relaxed about the issue, and within another year they married. All appeared to be going well with Anna, until she called me about a decade into the marriage to discuss, as she put it, "something troubling on my mind."

Anna entered looking very much the same as when I'd last seen her, except perhaps for a few gray hairs in the dark curly hair that flowed down her back. (I guess I had a few grays as well.) Dressed casually in tailored jeans with a turtleneck and blazer, she began by putting on a cheerful face, taking out her wallet to show me candid snapshots of her kids at the beach. But the moment she snapped shut her wallet, her tone became subdued, almost mournful.

She and Joe were having trouble in bed again, she told me. "Sex with him isn't interesting anymore. We've been together too long, it's too predictable. I suppose it's natural for couples to lose that extra edge. Now I've met someone who's clearly interested in me, and I'm tempted."

When I probed further, Anna recounted that about three years ago, soon after the birth of their second child, Joe had had an affair that caused them both a great deal of anguish. Although she and Joe had reconciled and their life had returned to normal on the surface, she remained hurt by his betrayal.

Now Joe was more attentive than ever. Rather than golfing on weekends, he spent much more time at home, taking the family on country outings, and planning romantic evenings alone with Anna. I don't know what woke Joe up: He may have known of Anna's flirtation, and sensed her withdrawal. For whatever reason, he was clearly trying to salvage their marriage. Yet the more interest Joe showed in Anna, the more flirtatious she became with the other man.

After hearing this story in more detail, I began by asking, "Why do you really want to have this affair? It's not because Joe isn't paying attention to you; he is." I then challenged Anna's contention that her lessening interest in sex with her husband was merely a by-product of their longevity as a couple. To me, it seemed a reprise of the sexual problem she had experienced prior to her marriage.

I said, "You may think that having an affair will solve your sexual problems. But doesn't that remind you of the 'old Anna'? The

Anna who distances herself from a high-stakes relationship by withdrawing sexually? The same woman who feels perfectly comfortable throwing herself into a relationship that does not matter?"

I went on: "Clearly, the sexual realm creates a tremendous sense of vulnerability for you, as it does for everyone. This has been heightened by Joe's affair. It's understandable for you to have mixed feelings. You were hurt by what he did, and his actions fed into your longstanding ambivalence about intimacy, and into your residual feelings about your father's betrayal of your mother and yourself. But let's talk about the here and now. If you really do want to work things through with Joe, you cannot continue using his affair as a justification for your having an affair. You're the one setting up obstacles now. I urge you to look deeper, to your own fear of vulnerability which has been evoked once again by Joe's affair."

In essence, my message to Anna was one we all need to learn: We must tolerate our feelings of vulnerability—whether in the emotional arena or in sexual intimacy.

Anna's case is an example of another interesting phenomenon: Sometimes our attempts to accommodate a problem by minimizing it (as she tried to minimize the scars left by Joe's infidelity) or rationalizing it ("It's natural for long-term couples to lose interest in sex") can themselves cause new problems. Surely it seems easier to avoid confronting problems by sidestepping them in this way. But emotions find a way to reveal themselves, whether we fully admit to them or not. In the end, Anna wound up in my office again—fortunately, in time to work through her troubled state of mind and, with this new knowledge, to renew her marriage.

The key was getting Anna to focus her attention on what was going on inside her, as opposed to looking for a solution to her marital problems outside, in an affair. Anna had initially felt the problem was her husband (his betrayal); but she needed to acknowledge her own contributions to a discomfort that long predated her husband's betrayal. When she did, she and Joe were able to work things through.

Sexual Dysfunction: Submissiveness and Sex

The more secure our sexual identity, the more comfortable we are accepting the submissive aspect of sex. Many of us fear that to be submissive is to be humiliated and weak, yet sexual fulfillment is only possible when we are comfortable with our passivity, and willing to succumb to another person's desires. We can do that only when we feel comfortable about ourselves.

This is as true for men as for women. Impotence and premature ejaculation can usually be traced to a perception of women as dangerous authority figures. This is the unconscious male fantasy of "vagina dentata" (discussed in Chapter 6), the fear that women will castrate them during sex. Nonmedical impotence (i.e., with no known physical cause) generally reflects profound performance anxiety as well as fear of women as authority figures. Premature ejaculation is a compromise solution for these fearful men, reflecting a willingness to engage in intercourse, albeit only briefly.

Other men prefer masturbation to intercourse, or are unable to ejaculate during intercourse, or have delayed ejaculation. For these men, the only way for them to feel potent is to maintain their erection. Such a man is suspicious of his partner's motivation in enticing him into sex, perceiving her seductiveness as a kind of duplicity meant to weaken him. Only when a man views his partner as a peer, rather than someone to be afraid of or to submit to, can he begin to become more comfortable, less anxious, less angry, and more able to fulfill his own sexual pleasure, as well as his partner's.

Our sexual dysfunctions represent our attempts to play out our inner feelings, in the act of sex. Anna showed how anxiety about intimacy can manifest itself as sexual inhibition. In my next example, we'll see how anger gets expressed in bed.

Anger and Sex: Paul

Anger and sex can be a combustible mixture. For some, anger may fuel sexual desire and for others lessen it. Sometimes the angry envy of rivalry can spur us to increased sexual passion. And in ambivalent relationships, the anger itself may carry a certain erotic quality. To some degree, this explains the dynamic underlying many sadomasochistic practices and fantasies. Even at a low level, we may become very passionate after we've had an argument; anger is the spark that brings us together again.

But some men worry that their anger can grow so potent that it will actually endanger their partners. They avoid sex in order to protect their partners from themselves. This was the case with Paul, who was so uncomfortable with his hair-trigger temper that he avoided sex with his wife. He was afraid that in an emotionally charged sexual situation, he might be prone to rage at her. Was this his problem or hers? On the surface, he thought it was hers (she wasn't attentive enough to him). But underneath he recognized that he made excessive sexual demands, and that his fragile ego needed constant bolstering to avoid an angry eruption.

An actor in his early thirties who was always stylishly dressed and coifed, Paul carried himself with a commercial-perfect veneer: he always appeared very much in control, soft-spoken, rational, affable, smiling even when the inner clouds of his emotions engulfed him. But his actor's facade concealed a tremendous rage: a sense that he wasn't getting his proper due as a highly talented professional actor whose knockout good looks could (and did) turn heads wherever he went.

To my mind, he was a classic narcissist whose ego needed to be constantly fed, in his case by frequent reassurance about his handsome appearance and professional potential. Although some narcissists may become sulky and depressed when their egos are not bolstered, Paul typified a more common behavior for this personality type: he got angry at those who didn't provide him with the flattery he required.

It was interesting that Paul the actor initially came to see me about a performance issue—not onstage but in bed with his wife. He suffered from delayed ejaculation, something that embarrassed him to such a degree that he had come to prefer masturbation and extramarital affairs to sexual intercourse with his attractive wife. He told me he felt so on edge that he would easily fly into a temper if, in the course of making love, his wife did not do exactly what he wanted.

Paul stated his problem as being his seething anger, which scared both him and his wife, but I understood his underlying problem as having to do with his ego. Paul had chosen his wife in part because of her extraordinary beauty; as a couple, they were as picture-perfect as any two handsome people could be, and she had become an extension of his own narcissistic ego. As such, he would get angry at her whenever he felt bad about *him-self*, especially after a professional rebuff at an audition. He resented the fact that with her job as a television producer, she was the main breadwinner in the family. Having come from a traditional working-class family, where men labored hard and women stayed home, he felt impotent in more ways than he could say.

In therapy, we got beyond Paul's anger and began to explore his hunger for adulation. The only way he could feel good about himself was when he was convinced that a woman was sexually interested in him—not just one woman, but every attractive woman with whom he came into contact. The affairs and one-night stands served to bolster his brittle ego, and evened out what he perceived was the imbalance of power in his marriage. These secret affairs gave him power over his professionally more successful spouse.

Going further, I interpreted his preference for masturbation as choosing the pleasures of fantasy over the intrusive reality of his wife and her sexual needs. In the fantasy, his sexual partners did everything he wanted exactly as he wanted, and had no needs of their own. His one-night stands were the same kind of scenario. By contrast, if his wife didn't follow his direction exactly, he would become irritable, short-tempered, and fearful that, as he put it, "I'll really lose it." Thus, the masturbatory fantasy protected him and his wife from his rage, which had too often been elicited during sex with her.

Paul's insecurity had little to do with objective factors. No matter how many women he slept with, it did not change his need for further conquests. And when he eventually did achieve some success in his career—earning a rave review in a Broadway show that led to new theatrical opportunities—his narcissistic ego remained unsated. "Even when you do succeed in the world, it doesn't actually make you feel that much better about yourself," I pointed out. "You need to have your ego fed to be reassured. It's not your wife that's making you angry, or your professional status, or your friends' attempts to undermine you. Those feelings are coming from within yourself."

One of Paul's dreams illustrates the complex interconnection between his fragile ego, his anger, and sex. In the dream, Paul and a friend are sitting around drinking wine, when the friend suggests that they go out and "get laid tonight." Then the friend accidentally spills some wine on Paul's shirt, and Paul flies into a tantrum, shouting "Now, you've ruined it. I can't go out looking like this." And he proceeds to pummel his friend.

As I interpreted the dream, the stain represents his anxiety about his appearance, which then is transformed into rage at his friend. Feeling competitive with his friend, Paul views the friend's "accident" as an intentional attempt to trip him up, which explains why he felt his violent response was justified. Indeed, without its underlying context of sex and sexual performance, I suspect Paul would never have been as angry as he was in the dream.

Gradually, over time, Paul did start feeling better about himself, and not just in terms of his growing professional and career achievements, which were objective facts. He felt he was a better *person*, he told me, because he was able to treat his wife better; and the more gentle and accepting he was with her, the less he felt "like an S.O.B." (This was the first time he had made any reference to feeling guilty for his behavior toward her. A sign of progress.)

The more Paul was able to tolerate his ambivalence about his wife—without having affairs or venting his anger by lashing out—the more things improved in his sexual performance. His problem with delayed ejaculation disappeared, and he grew less interested in masturbation. Paul told me that in the past, the only time that his wife had really fueled his sexual passion was when other men were interested in her. That sense of rivalry was still a turn-on for him, he admitted. But as he became more interested in her as a person and her sexual needs, he was able to overcome his narrow narcissistic view of marriage. He began to develop a broader appreciation of the mutual gratification they could provide each other. Paul was proud of his newfound emotional maturity, and so was I.

The Dynamics of Adultery

Ultimately, both Anna and Paul were able to work through their difficulties, but as we saw, along the way Anna contemplated an extramarital affair, and Paul actually engaged in many. Although their particular motivations differed, there are underlying similarities to these and, I believe, all sexual infidelities.

The most important fact to remember about sexual infidelity is that it has little to do with sex. It has everything to do with egos, anger, triangles, and ambivalence about intimacy.

There are several corollaries to this basic fact. First, affairs are a means of restoring a balance of power in the relationship. If our egos have been battered, we might be tempted to believe that we will feel better about ourselves in the arms of someone else. We punish our spouse for his or her "mistreatment" of us. Unfortunately, this attempt to even things out is based on the misperception that an imbalance of power exists to begin with. Moreover, the affair doesn't assuage our ego; all it does is make us feel guilty and worse about ourselves. As we try to keep the affair secret, our spouse becomes the authority figure who will punish us if and when he or she discovers our transgression. Thus, an intimate relationship is transformed into a power struggle replete with secret betrayal and guilty fear.

Second, affairs are all about reenacting the Oedipal triangle, which binds a child and his or her two parents. Affairs play out in adulthood the rivalry and competition of childhood. In some triangles, a man will find a woman more attractive by virtue of her attachment to another man. Or, as in Paul's case, a sense of rivalry—seeing another man flirt with his wife—will spark sexual excitement.

On a deeper level, this sort of triangulation is a way of defusing the intensity of the dyadic (involving two individuals) relationship between the original partners. If we're unable to tolerate these feelings as the relationship becomes more intense, we may have an affair to diffuse the intimacy. Such affairs can lower the emotional stakes—but in doing so they can also destroy a relationship.

This is another way of saying that affairs reflect the inability to sustain ambivalence within the context of a loving relationship. As we know, ambivalence (simultaneously having negative feelings—such as anger, disappointment, and frustration—and positive feelings—such as affection and desire) characterizes all relationships. By having an affair we merely act out the ambivalence; the affair doesn't help us work through our ambivalence; in fact, it prevents this. If we're unhappy with certain aspects of our relationship, we may believe that the only happiness we will find is in an affair. We think that our spouse can't understand us, appreciate us, satisfy us—but that someone else can. Our ambivalence gets split into two separate relationships. We may even believe that these relationships are separate and can be kept separate, psychologically speaking.

But in acting on our ambivalence rather than owning up to it, we never do integrate the disparate feelings we have. We may think that the appeal the two lovers hold for us is mutually exclusive, but that is not possible, in psychological terms. Relationships are outward manifestations of what's going on inside, and inside we may try to split off two different sides of ourselves but psycho logically they remained linked. That's why affairs cannot be considered separate from the marital relationship. They are con ducted completely in the context of dissatisfaction about the marriage. That's also what makes it a triangle: The betrayed spouse is, psychologically speaking, in bed with the lovers.

This same dynamic applies to feelings of guilt for having an affair. It's quite common, of course, for an affair to evoke anger from the betrayed spouse. Instead of the unfaithful partner voicing remorse, however, I've often seen it happen that the partner will perpetuate the cycle of one-upmanship by erupting in anger in return, declaring, "He's so spiteful, no wonder I need to have an affair." This is merely another defense mechanism for overcoming guilt over the affair. Just as ambivalent feelings were intolerable before the affair, so the sensation of guilt and shame in its aftermath is intolerable and is pushed away.

And so the key remains this: Instead of turning our emotions inside out, we must learn to accept, tolerate, and integrate our ambivalence. We need to bring our feelings about sex and sexual intimacy together. And instead of splitting off parts of ourselves in sex or in an affair, we need to integrate what's happening in our relationship with how we feel inside. When we accomplish that, we're well on the way to a fulfilling relationship, both sexually and emotionally.

9
Whose Side Are You On?
When We Compete Instead of Partner

One of the most striking characteristics of the couples who come to me for therapy is that instead of being partners, they've become rivals. Instead of being able to negotiate and compromise, they wage never-ending contests with each other. Their relationships have deteriorated into competitions.

In my view, this competition is another manifestation of the inside-out dynamic. If we're uncomfortable with the feelings of merging inherent in relationships, we may choose to fight them. In so doing, we define ourselves in opposition to, rather than in partnership with, our mate. Instead of working together, we pull away from each other. In battling against each other, we fight the connection of the relationship.

Why is there so much envy and competition between partners in a couple who also feel so bonded to one another? Competitions over who's getting and who's giving. Over who's winning and who's losing. Over whose needs are being met and whose are not. It's as if we can only feel better about ourselves by comparing ourselves with those closest to us—but this competition frays the fabric of our attachment. Instead of finding compromises that will allow both of us to succeed, we try to get a leg up on our partner, or put him or her down. Like adversaries, we squabble, jockey for position, play on each other's weak spots, use "emotional blackmail," selfishly take advantage of each other, and spitefully use whatever leverage we have to get our way.

This kind of "winning" is a Pyrrhic victory at best. Since we are so closely identified with each other, every time we win we also lose. Because our relationships reflect who we are, when we fight our partner as though he or she were an external adversary, we are also fighting ourselves. Psychologically speaking, we do battle with and reject in our partners that which we don't like in ourselves. Therefore, the solution (and the challenge) is to reintegrate these split-off parts of ourselves. When we reach this peace within ourselves, we also renew our sense of mutuality with our partner.

Sibling Rivalry

When I see competitive couples I can't help but compare their relationship to that of children in the same family who act out sibling rivalry; they are like little kids squabbling over whose turn it is, who hit whom first, who got the larger portion of pie. When envy takes over, we feel we're not getting our due, and we angrily pounce on those who appear to be getting more. Alas, feuding siblings can and do spend a lifetime measuring themselves against the yardstick of their brothers and sisters. Unfortunately, embattled couples can waste years in similar struggles.

It's hard to think of any other emotion as nonconducive to romance as envy. (However destructive jealousy may be, at least it has the power to fuel romantic interest.) Envy undermines the very sense of teamwork and mutuality required to build a life together. How can we identify with someone we perceive to be an adversary? How can an individual sacrifice his own personal needs to the good of the team, if he feels that he won't succeed when the team succeeds? On a psychological level, how can we derive vicarious pleasure from someone else's gratification, if we feel that the other person's gratification deprives us? On a practical level, how can we reach workable compromises, both major and minor, in everyday life?

Rivalrous relationships operate according to a giant scoreboard, with each player watching carefully to see who's ahead and who's behind. It's a far cry from healthy mutual dependency, where one person basks in the reflected glow of the other's achievements, each enhancing the other. Instead of feeling bolstered by our partner's success, we may be threatened by it—like the wife who told her husband on the day he received a major promotion, "I hope you're not so important that you can't do the dishes tonight."

When we feel we're not getting what we want, and at the same time see that others *are* getting what they want, we can become consumed by indignation, envy, and anger. Feeling deprived, we may believe that even though we may do for others, others won't do for us. We feel easily taken advantage of and operate under the false assumption that if their needs are being met, then ours must not be. This is the sort of faulty reasoning that leads us to deprive our partners of the caretaking, ego boosting, and idealization that are necessary to sustain the relationship. Our conversations take on overtones of anger, whining, and entitlement. We may greedily conclude that the only way we can feel good about ourselves is to hog the spotlight and take more than our fair share. In this way, a dynamic of competing, rather than mutual dependency, develops.

But relationships are not competitions over scarce resources. On the contrary, in taking care of others, we are, psychologically speaking, taking care of ourselves. Generosity of spirit (the opposite of competitive rivalry) attests to our capacity to give. Indeed, only when we feel we have a rich inner life do we believe we have what it takes to give to others. When we feel connected to another, and have an expansive identification of self with other, giving yields benefits to us as well as to the recipient.

By contrast, when we feel empty, envious, and angry, we are unable and unwilling to give others what they want. These negative internal feelings reflect significant doubts about our capacity to gratify others. We may think we are (and in fact may be) too selfish and needy ourselves to care for others. When we are ashamed of our own needs and wishes, we become critical and contemptuous of our lover's needs, experiencing them as an overwhelming imposition or manipulation. As a result, when our lover speaks up and demands her piece of the pie, we may feel threatened, used, and convinced that we won't get our fair share. As we perceive (often accurately) others pursuing their own agendas, taking care of their own needs or asking us to take care of them, we might think that our own wishes will be given short shrift.

When in my practice I see couples competing with each other, following a pattern of sibling rivalry, I ask them, "What's wrong with being 'used' occasionally? If you have the resources to give, then give. Aren't you enriched by doing for your spouse, partner, boyfriend, or girlfriend?"

For relationships to work, we need to get back in touch with a sense of mutuality and of being on the same team. Rather than "Every man for himself," our motto should be "One for all and all for one." Unfortunately, the prototype of sibling rivalry sets us against each other and undermines our willingness to nourish our partners. Instead of competing against each other, couples need to forge a different model for the relationship. They need to give giving a chance.

When We Become Entangled and Enmeshed

As intimacy develops, we get to know each other well—perhaps too well. We learn how to push our partner's buttons and exploit our partner's weak spots. We can become experts on how to take our partner on a "guilt trip," playing on feelings and using emotional blackmail to get what we want. This dynamic is often at play in competitive couples.

But it is crucial that we not take advantage of our intimate knowledge of our partner's weak spots. We must refrain from abusing the privilege that intimacy offers. The complex ways in which couples emotionally blackmail each other or sadistically play on each other's weak spots reflects their degree of *enmeshment*, a term psychologists define as the mutual entanglement, or boundary blurring, of two people within a relationship.

In its healthy aspect, this kind of blurring of boundaries yields a positive mutual identification: When I give something to you, I feel as if I am also receiving. But in its more pathological aspect, enmeshment sets the scene for us to project onto someone else parts of ourselves that we have disowned—which we then proceed to reject in them. When we do this, criticizing someone else for something we cannot accept in ourselves, we may feel as if we are escaping it, as in a game of hot potato. But this reflects a struggle with our own ambivalence; we're merely splitting off unwanted parts of ourselves and reassigning them to our partner.

Embittered and embattled, the enmeshed, competitive couple often lives out the philosophy that misery loves company: "After all, if I can't win, I don't want you to win, either." Thus they drift to their lowest common denominator. Chained together by their shared low self-esteem, they identify with each other's failures, not their successes.

A seesaw develops: As one partner begins to achieve some personal growth, the other tries to pull him back down again. Similarly, when one partner begins to outgrow envy or greed, the other partner may try to rekindle it as best he or she can. The reason is that the competition and envy that may have drawn them together, however unhappily, will now be lost. This is why fundamental change in one partner can be so threatening and destabilizing to a relationship.

Needing our partners to have their weak spots so that we can play on them is another manifestation of the inside-out dynamic. We try to hold the other person back because we are afraid to move forward with them. We need them to be the way they are because they embody the neurotic aspects of ourselves that we have projected onto them. This is why when a marriage or a relationship leaves us no room to grow, we have to "outgrow the marriage" in order to successfully meet our personal psychological challenges.

Keeping Score and Triangulation:
Bob and Glynis (and Philip)

Glynis and Bob engaged in a covert competition in which each one secretly kept score on the other. To win a point, they would use inappropriate leverage—for example, guilt-tripping each other for their own selfish needs—and they undermined the marriage's foundation of trust in the process. Everything became a possible arena of competition, including their child. Unable to accept the fact that we don't always get everything we want, their logic sank to the level of squabbling siblings: "If I don't get exactly what I want when I want it, you're not on my side. You're depriving me."

I was first contacted by Glynis, who told me she had a problem with her husband, Bob. At her initial consultation, she told me she didn't know if she was crazy or if she was imagining it, but in a very subtle way, she always felt manipulated and controlled by her husband. It was a classic "Is it me or is it him" inquiry.

As Glynis elaborated, she said that she loved Bob very much, and she couldn't really pinpoint her complaint. She referred to a vague sense that their marriage revolved completely around him and what he wanted, never what she wanted. Her friends told her she was crazy to complain, that Bob was the most generous, entertaining, talented man they knew. Maybe they were right, she said.

When I asked Glynis to offer an example, she talked about Bob's gastronomical talent. He loved to organize elaborate dinner parties at least once a week, and invited a slew of friends to partake in his exotic creations. All the friends were enormously impressed, and invariably had a great time. Wearing his dapper chef's hat, Bob would be the center of attention and dominate the conversation. Whenever talk did turn to Glynis, he would contrive to return the conversation to food or another of his interests.

Glynis never liked these dinner parties. First, she had spartan tastes, and didn't really like the heavy French sauces and eight-course dinners that Bob prepared. Second, she could not get a word in edgewise. Third, she was responsible for cleaning up the enormous mess left in the aftermath of these mammoth meals. To make matters still worse, the meals took so long to prepare that they never had time to engage in the activities she enjoyed, such as having a picnic or going on a long bike ride with their seven-year-old son, Philip.

Whenever Glynis tried to address the problem, Bob successfully deflected the conversation by telling her she was lucky to have such a good cook for a husband. He also alluded to the benefit these dinner parties provided their son, who was allowed to sit at the table and converse with the adults. Bob acted as if he were the most generous, self-sacrificing man in America, and all of their friends agreed. But Glynis knew better. Whatever Bob might say, an adult dinner party held no appeal for Philip, who, as you might expect of a seven-year-old, thought the food was "weird" and felt by turns bored, ignored, or patronized by the adults. "Why can't my friends order pizza and have our own party?" he asked, but his feelings made no impact on Bob. No wonder Glynis saw Bob as solely focused on his own needs; he made certain that he got what he wanted at all costs and remained unconcerned about whether others got what they wanted.

It was a difficult position for Glynis to be in: She was fighting a battle over whose needs would be met, but it was a subtle, covert battle and her competitor was her husband, who swore he was taking care of her and their son the best he knew how.

Glynis went on to tell me that Bob had a reputation as a master negotiator at his real estate firm, gaining every edge he could in the deals he handled. He was equally vigilant in protecting his personal finances: Not only did he carefully monitor their investments but he also micro-managed the household bills to make certain that none of the local tradesmen ripped him off. At work and at home, he lived his life according to a perpetual calculation of getting the most he could in return for what he gave.

Although this approach worked well in business, it caused trouble at home. Glynis told me their conversations more closely resembled his business negotiations than they did a loving interaction between husband and wife. For example, Glynis told me that one night recently she was getting ready to leave for a rare evening out with an old college roommate who was visiting from out of town, when Bob started complaining about having to stay home to watch their son. "I've had a tough week at work," Bob grumbled. "I need a break, too." He would not drop the subject.

It was a textbook case of competing dependency. Instead of graciously saying, "You sure deserve it after all the time you put in at work and with Philip," Bob felt excluded and taken advantage of. Although Bob well knew that Glynis wasn't going to change her plans at the last minute, she sensed that he was intentionally grabbing the opportunity of trying to make her feel guilty, so she wouldn't complain about his upcoming golf game the following Saturday when he would be away all day long. Just as he would at work, he was setting her up for the next negotiation, extracting the highest price he could.

Bob's "negotiations" did not stop here. Through triangulation, Bob found a way to drag their son into the dynamic as well. *Triangulation* means creating a triangular dynamic by bringing a third person into a situation that actually concerns just two. As you would expect, triangulation makes the enmeshed dynamics of families that much more complicated. Through triangulation, couples not only project onto each other aspects of themselves; they play out these dynamics through the intermediary of a third person, usually their child.

Glynis told me that by harping on her night out, Bob had succeeded in making their son so concerned that Philip started asking her a long string of questions: "When will you be leaving? Where are you going? Who with? When will you return?" Sure enough, Glynis ended up feeling guilty about her rare night out, and Bob had made it seem as if the concern came from their son, not from him. Bob, the master manipulator, had induced Philip to play out and articulate his father's concerns, thereby allowing Bob to disown responsibility for them. It was a beautiful inside-out dynamic foisted on a third party and directed at a perceived adversary.

It was bad enough that Bob manipulated her, Glynis said. But she was especially concerned about the effect of his behavior on Philip. Philip was becoming just like his father: When he wanted something, he would play one parent off against the other. In fact, since Bob never wanted to be the "bad guy," whenever Philip asked him for permission to do something Bob didn't think he should do, Bob would defer the decision, telling Philip to ask his mother what she thought. In this way Bob forced Glynis to be the "bad guy" so that Bob didn't have to take responsibility for saying no.

At school, Glynis went on, Philip tried to manipulate his classmates as he had witnessed his father do with his mother so many times, expecting them no doubt to give in as his mother usually did. But his friends didn't accept being manipulated without complaint; they were blunt and confrontational. As a consequence, Philip was having difficulty making friends among his classmates.

This turn of events especially concerned me because at seven years old, Philip didn't have the emotional resources to deal with the family situation that Glynis had. I suspected that Philip was "identifying with the aggressor," a dynamic in which someone identifies with a more powerful adversary and models his behavior on that person. Having been a pawn in his father's game, Philip was now trying to use other kids as pawns of his own.

Without having met Bob, I was nevertheless reminded of Shakespeare's Iago, who appeared to be Othello's ally, while behind the scenes he manipulated him and controlled the action of all the other characters. Similarly, Glynis told me, she felt like a puppet on a string wrapped around Bob's finger. Not only did Bob get her and Philip to do what he wanted; she was uncomfortable with the roles he foisted on her. For example, Glynis didn't mind at all that Bob was going to play golf all day on Saturday, but Bob had framed the negotiation as if he had to extract this concession from her unwillingly. To Glynis, his desire to play golf wasn't a negotiation or quid pro quo; she was happy to let him do whatever he wanted. What she didn't like was being characterized as stingy and withholding. This was clearly a projection of Bob's own personality as someone who would never be so forthcoming without expecting something in return. Glynis felt that Bob had trapped her in a role she did not want to play, and that in some fundamental way her husband of twelve years didn't truly know her.

At the conclusion of this first session, Glynis asked again the question she had posed at the start: Was she crazy, and if not, what could she do about it? Glynis was not crazy, I assured her. She needed to trust her own perception of her marriage, whether or not Bob confirmed her reading of their family interactions. The issue, as I saw it, was how to stand up for what she wanted and make certain that she wasn't being manipulated. She had to be herself, regardless of the roles Bob tried to foist on her. I recommended they come see me together.

When I met Bob, he immediately told me his philosophy: "You have to fight for and pay for everything you get in life." In his view, nothing comes for free or is voluntarily given. By way of background, Bob told me he was the second of three brothers. Although I don't like to make too much out of birth order, middle children often feel that they have not received the attention, nurturing, and support that their siblings did—a phenomenon accentuated in same-sex siblings. This experience of deprivation may help the middle child become more autonomous, assertive, and self-sufficient at an earlier age, as it apparently had for Bob. But it can also leave him feeling that unless he fights for what he deserves, he will be left out.

When I asked Bob about Glynis's night out, it was just as Glynis had described it. He took no pleasure in Glynis's plans to have an enjoyable evening with her friend, and he made sure that she paid for it. Then, when Saturday came, he felt no appreciation for her letting him play golf all day. As he saw it, she owed it to him.

When Glynis got what she wanted, he felt deprived, and when he got what he wanted, he felt it was his due. Everything was toted up on the giant scoreboard he kept in his head. Among other unfortunate results of his way of thinking was his failure to realize his own potential gain from the situation: what fun it could be to have a special night alone with his son—a "boys' night" together. They could have ordered in pizza and watching basketball on TV. It would have done wonders toward fulfilling Philip's need to have his father all to himself.

After several weeks in couples therapy, an issue arose that struck me as emblematic of their problems. Prior to meeting Bob, Glynis had been actively involved in her local church in New

England. But after their move to the New York area, and in consideration of Bob's lack of interest in religion, she had not sought out a new congregation. Now that their son was old enough, Glynis wanted to enroll him in Sunday School.

Although Bob did not voice his objections directly, he managed to put the kibosh on Glynis's plan in numerous subtle ways. At first he expressed reservations about the minister at their local church. At another church, he criticized the way the service was performed. At yet a third church, Bob noted that the twenty-minute drive each way would be an obstacle. As I saw this story evolve week after week, it was clear to me that these were merely excuses. Bob definitely acted in bad faith toward Glynis, though he stopped short of actually lying to her. Wanting to get the truth on the table, I asked him directly, "What have you got against joining a church?" Glynis nodded her head as if to second my question, relieved that somebody was willing to confront her husband.

After a moment's thought, Bob acknowledged that he was concerned that the more time Glynis spent in church, the less time she would have for him. He anticipated that as she became involved in various charitable activities sponsored by the church, he would have that many more child-care responsibilities. The reason he had discouraged her interest in church activities was that he wanted her to focus solely on him and his needs. Bob mistakenly believed that he would be better off if she had no outside involvements.

I suggested that if Bob felt left out, there were better solutions than derailing Glynis's wishes. All that did was make Glynis feel stifled and not listened to. Further, he wasn't acting in Philip's best interest, either. Fortunately, Bob wasn't so selfish that he couldn't appreciate this.

"What if you got involved with the church and the community activities along with Glynis and your son?" I proposed. "That way, you won't feel excluded." Glynis wasn't choosing the church over him, I continued. She was looking for something to complement their family life. On a deeper level, I was saying: In order to get what he wanted, Bob didn't have to deprive Glynis of what she wanted. That which made her feel good and which was best for their son benefited him as well.

As time went on, I was happy to see Bob begin to participate in many church functions—not merely their son's Sunday School, but also family worship services and a variety of charitable activities. The three went together on clothing drives to pick up secondhand clothes and furniture for the church thrift shop, and Bob was proud of the fact that they raised more money than any of the other families. He came to realize that the church added to his and his family's life a new dimension that he had never before appreciated.

But it wasn't enough for me to be able to confront Bob; Glynis needed to be able to do so as well. She accurately perceived that Bob didn't know her, and that his primary concern was looking out for himself. But she didn't seem to be able to fight for what she wanted or thought was best for her family. To do so would threaten Bob, and the last thing she wanted to do was start a battle of wills, especially with such a masterful negotiator.

Glynis was in a bind, but she also had contributed to the problem. However much she might want to shy away from competition, I explained to her, she needed to assert herself more forcefully with Bob, both for her own sake and for that of her son. It was true that Bob became competitive about everything and anything, and he did so in very skillful and effective ways. He took competition to such an extreme that even the two people he loved the most in the world—his wife and son—were merely pawns in his game, to be used and sacrificed as he needed.

Glynis thought that it was better for Philip if she remained laid-back and avoided confrontation with Bob. But she was wrong.

She needed to stand up for herself and set an example for Philip
that people should not let others manipulate them. When disagreements arose between husband and wife, Glynis needed to
address her concerns with Bob directly, and do her best to keep
Philip out of the middle of their marital conflicts.

Eventually, I helped them see that life is less competitive than
Bob thought, but more competitive than Glynis wanted to recognize. There was nothing wrong with the fact that Bob pursued his
interests with unrestrained vigor. Couples don't have to want the
same thing or think the same way. However, I felt that there was
something wrong with the way Bob went after what he wanted—
indirectly, covertly, and using inappropriate leverage. Bob's vision
was too narrow; he failed to see that there are many areas of
mutual benefit, if only he were to define his identity more expan-
sively.

In the course of their yearlong therapy, Bob never once gave
ground without a fight. But as Glynis persevered, she achieved
what she wanted—and, interestingly, by showing she could and
would stand up for herself, she earned Bob's respect. Gradually,
without realizing it, Bob had begun to take Glynis's wishes into
account when he made his calculations. He still made elaborate
French dinners every once in a while, but they were much less
frequent. By dint of Glynis's repeated efforts, he had gotten the
message. Ultimately, Glynis forced Bob to see things from her side
as well. By going beyond his narrow interests, he finally got to
know and develop a new measure of closeness with his wife and
son. It was (and I'm sure continues to be) a hard-won success,
but certainly worth it.

Arguing with Ourselves: Jerry and Jane

Highly enmeshed couples often unwittingly push each other
to dig in their heels and take positions far more extreme than

they would if they weren't being pushed; unable to compromise, to give in and find a middle ground, they end up forcing each other (and themselves) to polar-opposite views, or what psychologists call *polarization*. Through projection, the enmeshed couple attributes to the other ideas or feelings that they don't want to acknowledge, because to do so would be to admit their own ambivalence. Jerry and Jane's story shows how, in struggling with our ambivalence, we split off unwanted feelings and project them onto our partner.

Jerry was an ambitious workaholic who claimed that his perfectionist wife was pressuring him to "go for the gold" and strive for a prestigious partnership at his law firm. He insisted that it was her desires, along with his wish to please her, that drove him to succeed and work such long hours. "If it weren't for her," he told me, "I'd have left the city ages ago. If I had my druthers, I'd move to the country and run a mom-and-pop law firm from our basement."

Jerry's wife, Jane, who as an in-house counsel for a Fortune 500 company was equally driven, saw things differently. She had grown up in a small country town and knew how limited it could be for someone who had wider aspirations. As a result, she didn't take Jerry's idealized view of country life seriously, and accused him of being too much of a city mouse to ever make it as a country mouse. Jerry sensed Jane's resistance, and blamed her for keeping him from what he thought of as his true happiness.

This couple had a finely tuned equilibrium: As long as they remained in their respective corners they achieved a wonderful balance. It was a classic case of polarization: On the one hand, the knowledge that Jane would resist moving freed Jerry to express his unquestioned desire to move. On the other, if Jane had been the one who wanted to move to the country, I suspect Jerry would have voiced many more misgivings about such a change. Similarly, Jane could express great certainty that a move to the country would be wrong for them because she knew that Jerry could be depended on to articulate the other side. She didn't have to consider her own doubts about city life.

This is how polarized couples work: Each partner expects the other to take the opposite position, and thus both can take their stances to greater extremes than they might otherwise have done. Jerry needed Jane to be resistant or else he would have to confront his concerns about the move. As long as Jane articulated misgivings that Jerry actually shared, he could deny having those feelings and blame her for being an ambitious "slave to work" without facing this quality in himself. As happened with Jerry and Jane's positions, over time these polarized positions become hardened, unchanging, and automatic.

The way they told it, Jerry and Jane were opposites. Yet the more I listened, the clearer it became that they were actually two peas in a pod, that Jerry was just as ambitious and competitive as Jane. He was blaming her for the inner pressures to achieve that he felt. Jane was no evil sorcerer forcing him to stay in the competitive rat race of New York City. In fact, if Jerry had wanted to, Jane would have been more than willing to discuss the realistic pluses and minuses of moving to the country. But with all the blaming and posturing, they never had this conversation.

Theirs was a common kind of enmeshment that allows us to polarize, and in so doing to disown aspects of ourselves which we project onto someone else, and which we then reject in them. When we criticize someone else for something we cannot accept in ourselves, we may believe that we ourselves are free of or have escaped that rejected aspect of ourselves. But then, day in and day out, we must confront the projected part of ourselves in our partner. For example, no matter how much Jerry wanted to disown his ambition, he experienced it all the time through his wife. Projection doesn't work because we never succeed in getting rid of that which we don't like; all we do is blame someone else for it.

So it was with Jerry and Jane. Their squabbling over this issue kept on escalating until it was just a matter of time before a show-down occurred. One day, Jane told Jerry point-blank, "You want to move to the country about as much as I want to live in the sub-way."

Taking her up on what he saw as a dare, he went on an inter-view for a job in a charming small town in Vermont. On the drive back to the city, however, something odd happened. At first, as he whizzed by the beautiful scenery, he gloated inwardly about "showing" his wife that he had been serious about his desire to move. But after a while, his thoughts started to wander back to the bright lights and action of the big city. "This really is isolated," he began to realize. "I'd miss my friends. The job does seem sort of dull compared to what I've been doing. And I hate to admit it, but I really do like the fast pace of the city."

Sobered by the reality of what moving to the country would actually mean, at the next therapy session Jerry was able to own up to his inner drive to achieve. Given this opening by Jerry, Jane then felt comfortable enough with her own doubts to confess her ambivalent feelings about work and success, and further admit that she had concerns about raising a child in such a competitive environment.

I tried to reframe the arguments between them as arguments within themselves. Both were ambivalent, and both acted out their mixed feelings with their spouse. Marriage provides fertile ground for this kind of inside-out polarization, since partners know each other well enough to anticipate accurately each other's attitudes. As often happens, once Jerry and Jane began to see that their ambivalent attitudes about success and ambition came from within both of them, their squabbling diminished considerably.

As with Jerry and Jane, when we split off parts of ourselves and locate them in someone else, we do not own up to our own ambivalence. Ambivalence is tricky because we may be prone to only own up to one side of our feelings and project the other side onto our partner ("I'm laid back and relaxed, you're the competitive one"). This is what fuels polarization. But, as Jerry and Jane discovered, we can't run from ourselves.

Fortunately, as therapy progressed, Jerry and Jane were able to see that only by acknowledging ambivalence and reintegrating split-off ideas and attitudes can we reestablish a sense of partnership. It was a fairly short therapy, and before long, they realized that they actually shared similar feelings. Together, through therapy, Jerry and Jane were able to become partners in ambivalence, rather than isolating themselves from each other because of it.

Cultivating Our Garden

As we've seen, competition makes mutuality and compromise impossible. When we struggle against the experience of enmeshment and merging, we take on opposing positions vis-à-vis each other. We thrust ourselves and our partners into roles that play out our internal psychological dramas. And they do the same to us.

When we feel burdened by the roles we unwillingly or reluctantly play, we may claim that others are forcing us to do something or be somebody we don't want to be. Similarly, we may claim that when our partners don't play the roles we want them to play, they represent obstacles to our happiness. This is why so many of us experience our mates as not being on our side, as trying to thwart us or enviously trying to compete with us.

But we must cultivate our own garden and worry less about how much and how fast other gardens are growing. Here are the conditions that permit our own growth and development, and the mutual growth necessary for a relationship to thrive:

1. The stronger we feel inside, the easier it is to accept our partner's differentness. When we accept the fact that our partner is pursuing his or her own interests, it will be easier for the partner to accept our separate interests. We need to become comfortable retaining our independent sense of self while remaining involved in an enmeshed and merged relationship.
2. We must look within and focus on our own goals, not blame our failures and frustrations on our partner. Personal growth is for ourselves, not others; our struggles are usually within us, not between us and others.
3. We must do our best to resist getting swept up in the destructive opposition of polarized positions. Even as others project certain roles or ideas onto us, disown facets of their own personality, or blame us for their ambivalence, we must try not to feel burdened by these qualities. We can be ourselves regardless of how our partner views us.
4. We need to see we're on the same side, that what benefits you also benefits me. Mutuality, not envy, is the key to a successful relationship.

10
Separation Pains
Moving Beyond the Scorched-Earth Divorce

We saw in the last chapter how marriage can turn into an envious competition in which we tear each other down rather than build each other up. Relationships can deteriorate to such a degree that no sense of connection or hope of reconciliation remains.

Breaking up is the final, logical extension of the inside-out dynamic: If I believe you're the reason I feel so bad, then I also believe that in leaving you, I will feel better. If we see our spouse as the source of our unhappiness, the key to renewed happiness is to get as far away as possible. Divorce becomes the magic bullet that will deliver us from pain and free us from constraints.

Even if we don't blame our spouse for all our unhappiness, we may still view him or her as the main source of the marriage's destructive patterns. And if we do, we'll also believe that in leaving the marriage, we will be magically liberated from these destructive patterns. We think we'll unburden ourselves of our spouse (and, more important, our spouse's projections), and we will finally have the opportunity to make our own identity—a new beginning without expectations and preconceptions. This is the appeal of separation: It symbolizes relief from bitterness, anger, and hurt feelings.

Life is rarely so simple, though. Divorce does not result merely from falling out of love, or growing distant and disaffected. It is the culmination of the blaming dynamic, the result of our simplistic belief that we can rid ourselves of unwanted parts of ourselves when we rid ourselves of our spouses.

This does not mean divorce is always bad. Acknowledging irreconcilable differences and getting out of a bad, destructive relationship may be a wise choice, one that is in both partners' best interests. When it becomes obvious that a relationship isn't working, I do advise my patients to separate—but only if I am convinced they understand why they are doing what they are doing, appreciate what they are leaving behind, and, finally, know what they are looking for and can realistically expect in the future.

Sifting through the debris of a marriage to gain that insight can be difficult. During a marriage crisis we're especially inclined to blame our partner for our anger and hurt feelings. But to take such a black-and-white perspective is to fail to acknowledge the complexity of our feelings for our spouse, and to refuse to accept responsibility for our own contribution to the relationship's problems. Although we rarely own up to it, divorce is associated with much more ambivalence than most people appreciate. At the time of separation and divorce, people feel too vulnerable to acknowledge this. When they do, it is usually retrospectively, once they are comfortable and secure in their postdivorce life.

If the inside-out way of thinking has fueled our decision to divorce, then we are likely to repeat similar patterns in the next relationship and make the same mistakes again and again. It is misguided to believe that we can shed our skin when we rid ourselves of our spouse. We may be able to escape the constraints of our marriage, but we can't escape ourselves and what we think of ourselves. And it's not our spouse's view of us that makes us the way we are.

Sometimes divorce does signal a new beginning, but the reason is not that our spouse won't be there to hinder us or provoke us or make us crazy. *A new beginning is only achieved when we change the way we think about ourselves.* Divorce may enable us to tap into internal psychological resources that had lain dormant. But that can only happen when we acknowledge our contribution to the problems in the marriage, understand our own ambivalence, and recognize why we have made the choices we have. Most important of all, we must let go of our intense anger and our mutually destructive tactics. Instead of blaming and demonizing our partner, we must look within and we must look beyond what I call the scorched-earth divorce.

From Angel to Demon: Robert and Sally

Whenever I treat a couple in the throes of divorce I am struck anew by the disparity between what they once felt for each other, and how they feel now. I ask myself: How can two people who loved and idealized each other so much at one point in their lives despise each other at another point? How can a once-beloved partner be transformed, over the course of a marriage and divorce, from angel to demon? How and why do our perceptions get turned both topsy-turvy and inside out? Finally, how and why do we come to blame the partner who we once thought was the key to our happiness for now holding us back?

As we'll see in the story of Robert and Sally, the answers often have more to do with us than with our partner.

When I first saw Robert and Sally, he was in his early forties and she was ten years younger; by this time their marriage was long past salvaging. Bickering and mistrust were pervasive; even their body language bespoke hostility and division. Yet they both told me that when they first married they had been passionately in love. Robert had been swept away by Sally's beauty and was obsessed with her. "I needed to touch her, be by her side, literally attached," Robert told me. "I had never wanted to be with anyone so much in my whole life."

For her part, Sally had been attracted to Robert's handsome dark looks and cynical sense of humor. "He understood me. Whenever I had a problem, Robert made me laugh, but at the same time he would offer a perceptive analysis of the situation. He was my protector, my confidant, my best friend back in those early days. I counted on him and trusted him."

They both agreed that for the first months of their affair, neither one could do wrong in the eyes of the other. They married in a whirlwind and quickly had a son. And then after two years, the whirlwind passed, leaving their marriage airless and dry. Now they were at a crossroads. Robert was thinking about splitting up, and Sally had begged him to see me for a consultation in order to give the marriage one last chance. Sadly, it was obvious to me right away that reconciliation was unlikely. Robert already had one foot out the door, only neither of them realized it. From my standpoint, they needed to understand what had happened to their love and come to terms with it.

According to Robert, Sally had become a ball and chain. "She's focused solely on our son and wants to move to the suburbs. That would be the death of me. It isn't at all like when we were dating."

When Robert said this, Sally frowned. "What bull. You know what's really bugging him? He can't stand the idea of having sex with one woman the rest of his life. He wants to run around, and I won't stand for it."

"Talk about bull!" Robert shot back. "All you want is my charge cards."

From what I could tell, Robert thought he could buy Sally off with his money. For her part, Sally took his money and kept her complaints to a minimum (a silent agreement they had come to), but she also wanted more from him: for him to be faithful, to spend time with her, and yes, to become a responsible family man.

"She's not attractive anymore," Robert told me privately. "Ever since our son was born, she hasn't been able to keep her weight down. Her stretch marks turn me off. When I touch her, I picture us years from now with her turned into an old hag."

To Robert, neither Sally's size 6 beauty nor the fact that she was ten years his junior seemed to filter through anymore. He changed the subject quickly when I mentioned that we all age; and though I diplomatically resisted pointing this out, I took note of his thinning hair and the beginnings of a paunch.

I tried to work with him, but Robert would not accept that the angst he felt at getting older resided in him, not in his wife's barely perceptible wrinkles. "These feelings of revulsion at the aging process are inside you and are inescapable," I told him. "Leaving Sally won't make you any younger. Whether or not you divorce, this issue will still be something you'll have to deal with."

As I saw it, Robert was experiencing a midlife crisis, precipitated by the birth of his son. Like many perennial bachelors, Robert had married late after flitting from woman to woman, trying to keep his options open. At first, Robert was faithful to Sally, but during her pregnancy, he had initiated a series of extramarital affairs. Although I was not terribly familiar with Robert's psychological makeup, it was my impression that having had a controlling mother, he imagined that Sally would begin to control him in a similar fashion once she became a mother herself. So he aggressively flaunted his freedom. Nevertheless, after the birth he felt supplanted by his newborn son, with whom he now had to share the limelight, and fell into a low-grade depression.

To make matters worse, at the time of his son's birth, Robert suffered a number of business setbacks, which further disturbed him. He had held grandiose hopes of building a clothing empire, but despite his investment of time and money, his design line went nowhere. For the first time in his life, he had begun to doubt himself, losing the self-confidence that had buoyed him along for years. Robert was a self-confessed dreamer, but unfortunately, reality was falling well short of his long-held dreams. As middle age approached, he had not acquired the money and power he had hoped for, and it didn't look as though he would anytime soon. With the birth of his son, he was saddled with the kinds of responsibilities that he had always run away from and that he now resented. And he couldn't come to grips with the notion that his beautiful wife could also be a mother.

Robert's wish to leave his marriage reflected his perception that Sally was holding him back from achieving his dreams. Yes, she was somewhat needy and dependent, and that much more so since their son was born. But she was the same person he had been head over heels for when they married. It was easier for him to blame her for his sense of being trapped than to acknowledge his own choices and mistakes. He thought that in divorcing Sally, he would be able to regain his youth and fulfill his dreams. In fact, Robert was not moving in the direction of self-fulfillment, nor was he escaping the frustrations posed by his marriage. Robert was running away from himself. He felt like an aging failure, and he could not tolerate it.

During this limbo period, prior to Robert's final decision to divorce, Sally kept trying to reach out to him. She wanted to make the marriage work. But the more she reached out, the more he fought her and pushed her away. He experienced her entreaties not as an attempt to salvage a marriage she valued, but as her continued efforts to trap him. A polarization developed wherein Sally became the spokesperson of their love and marriage, and Robert the spokesperson for all that was wrong with their lives together. She tried to save the relationship, and he tried to break things off. Because Robert and Sally were so polarized, Robert had never to come to terms with his own feelings of ambivalence about splitting up.

For Robert the appeal of life without Sally may have been a

mirage, but it held enormous sway over him, and nothing I did or said over the next few months had much effect on him. I tried to get Robert to articulate what he did like about their life together, what had attracted him to Sally, what he would miss. But to no avail. He showed no interest in trying to make the marriage work, and kept reiterating that Sally was the problem.

At this point Robert started to escalate his acting out. He abandoned Sally for days at a time, making it perfectly clear that he was conducting an affair. It was as if he was trying to offend her intentionally.

And yet, no matter how much Robert claimed he wanted to leave, something stopped him from leaving altogether. To me, his insulting behavior proved how ambivalent he was and how difficult it was for him to let go. He was halfway out the door, but he needed her to shove him all the way out and close the door behind him in order to overcome his own misgivings about leaving. As long as Sally articulated the wish to keep the marriage going, he denied sharing any such feelings—but part of him did share this wish. If he could get Sally so angry that she closed off any opportunity for reconciliation, then he wouldn't have to face his ambivalence.

It was at about this time that Robert dropped out of couples therapy. Their marriage quickly disintegrated, and soon Robert moved out of their apartment as well. I continued to see Sally individually.

When she heard from Robert's lawyer, Sally was distraught. It turned out that Robert had moved in with a younger woman in his office with whom he had carried on an affair during Sally's pregnancy. Although this affair had hurt her deeply, Sally had forgiven him because Robert had sworn the woman meant nothing to him. Now Sally felt completely betrayed. That revelation seemed to signal the lifting of all constraints for both of them.

The very language they now used to describe each other dra-

matized how their images of each other had been wholly transformed in the course of two years. In his eyes; she became a
"clawing witch" trying to hold him back from happiness, and in
hers he was "an exploitative S.O.B." In both partners' view, the
transformation had run full circle, from angel to demon.

Anger Is the Fuel

This cycle is not uncommon for couples in the throes of separation.

The intensity of this kind of mutual anger can only be compared in its intensity to the original idealization. But only when
our spouse is transformed from angel to demon do we feel justified in breaking off with him or her. Our anger fuels our resolve to
separate, while demonizing our spouse serves to justify behaving
toward him or her in the most horrendous ways in our efforts to
exit the relationship. My office walls echo with the laments and
recriminations of broken marriages. In the short run, anger and
hatred are simpler to deal with than the more complex feelings
that characterize most marriages and divorces. But what is the
psychological function of this level of hatred and animosity?

At the simplest level, demonizing our partner helps us explain
why the relationship failed. It's easier to blame our spouse for
why the marriage didn't work than to deal with the guilt or
shame surrounding its failure. It's an odd paradox, but true
nonetheless, that we feel unloved and rejected even if breaking
up was our decision. We then turn these feelings into anger and
hatred at our former spouse, declaring, "I can't love you because
you don't love me," or "I reject you just as I feel you reject me." In
this way, whether we're doing the rejecting or being rejected, we
turn our feelings inside out, transforming our discomfort into
intense anger at our former beloved.

On a deeper level, anger propels us out of the relationship, undoing the bonds of mutual dependency and merging. Remember, the level of our hatred for our spouse is a measure of its exact opposite: our earlier attachment and love. Psychologically speaking, divorce is the reverse of the process of falling in love. In marriage we fuse our individual psychological selves; when the union goes sour, we must disentangle our psychological selves and extract our individual identities from the complex mixture of mutual identifications and enmeshment.

Anger serves as the fuel that incites us to wrench ourselves away from this powerful attachment. But giving up a former identity as part of a couple is no easy task. It is an emotional upheaval, and our hatred reflects our attempt to define ourselves in opposition to (rather than merely separate from) our ex-spouse.

Robert and Sally were far from alone in the mutual and remarkably destructive anger that led to their ugly, scorched-earth divorce proceeding.

The Scorched-Earth Divorce

Fueled by such intense anger, we may feel entitled to take advantage of our intimate knowledge of our partner's weak spots. But nothing is gained by a bitter, prolonged divorce. Such acrimony merely perpetuates the relationship we claim we want to leave. Our anger—and our willingness to continually act on that anger through escalating demands and court orders—keeps us tied to our spouse. We remain entrenched in a destructive relationship, unable to move forward with our lives.

Instead of giving in to these destructive urges, we must keep our focus on the real psychological task of divorce: to separate and move on. Wanton destruction and revenge fantasies prevent us from working toward this goal. Acting on our anger may be tempting and satisfying in the short run, but, as we've seen again and again, venting and blaming is not the answer. The challenge lies in acknowledging the complexity of our feelings toward our spouse, without making ourselves vulnerable or letting ourselves be taken advantage of.

Robert and Sally needed to learn these lessons—badly. From the day he moved out, Robert treated the breakup as if he were preparing to do battle. First he spread rumors about Sally's "exploits" with a former boyfriend; then he initiated a suit for custody of their son, claiming she was an "unfit mother." And, to further increase the pressure, Robert cut off Sally's credit cards and refused to provide money for living expenses or child support.

Robert's "take no prisoners" posture cut Sally to the very core. His actions also confused her because she knew that Robert did not really want the responsibility of caring for their son. To her, it made no difference that this was clearly a preemptive legal maneuver to pressure her to settle quickly, on financial terms favorable to Robert. She still asked, in as much bewilderment as anger and pain, "Why is he being so nasty?"

Moreover, as is typical during a divorce, in addition to feeling hurt and angry, Sally felt a wide range of other emotions. For example, she was afraid of what life would be like on her own. Yet her anxiety also confused her, and made her that much angrier at Robert for leaving her. At the same time, from the moment Robert walked out, Sally had felt a tremendous sense of failure. "I'm a zero, just like my mother," she said plaintively, referring to the fact that her father had walked out on her mother. She felt "like the air has been kicked out of me." His abandonment had recapitulated strong childhood hurts and "proved" that she was both unlovable and unable to bestow love.

Sally was further unprepared to deal with Robert's aggressive tactics because her attitude was completely different from his. She was the one who at first had tried to reconcile, and she now continued to be more conciliatory and more willing to compromise. In fact, she tried several times to call Robert to discuss one or another issue in a reasonable fashion, but he had ordered his secretary to not put through her calls.

Robert's provocations became so egregious that even Sally began to realize she was locked in a struggle, and she belatedly prepared herself for all-out warfare. Whereas earlier she had been too naive and hadn't protected herself sufficiently, now that she had wised up, she was fired by the desire for revenge. She was determined to take Robert for every penny he was worth.

Fueled by the terrible pain of rejection, Sally came to see Robert as the devil incarnate. Her anger was so great that she could not keep herself from lashing out, regardless of how destructive she might become. Her motto now was "Why protect a relationship that's going nowhere? Let it crash, let it burn, it's dead already." For instance, when Robert came to pick up their son for a visit one day, a slight sarcastic inflection in his voice provoked her to such an emotional frenzy that she threw an expensive china plate at his head. On another occasion, she tried to break into his new home to steal his financial records in anticipation of a court hearing. Unlike any other person in her life, Robert could strike a chord of vulnerability in Sally that caused her to behave in irrational and uncontrollable ways. Sally was appalled by her own behavior in retrospect. But such is the power of the intense anger generated by a scorched-earth divorce.

Although the stated purpose of divorce battles of this sort is to inflict hurt upon the other, they damage the partner who lashes out just as much, if not more, than the person who is the object of the wrath. Whether it's a house that's at stake, a car, financial holdings, or that most precious asset of all—the children—a tragic rage takes over: *I'd rather destroy something precious to me than give it to you.*

When I see couples caught in this trap, I think of the most terrifying myth Greek tragedy has given us, that of the princess Medea. After helping her husband Jason achieve innumerable triumphs, Medea found herself cast aside in favor of a younger wife. Her revenge was swift and horrible: rather than see him enjoy his new marriage, she killed his bride. Worse, rather than allow him even the comfort of his children, she murdered their two beloved young sons. She hurt Jason—but in murdering her own children, she also irrevocably damaged herself.

With this terrible myth in mind, the more angry I saw Sally become, the more I feared the psychological damage her attempts at revenge might end up causing her. Her bitterness toward Robert had served its purpose: to change her view of him and help her recognize the destructive effects of her masochistic marriage. In addition, her hostility had protected her from further suffering by forcing her to mobilize for the battle to come. But she had gone too far. The challenge now was for Sally to learn how to stand firm and be on guard in her negotiations with Robert, but to refrain from escalating their battle to ever more mutually destructive heights.

The damage done by uncontrolled rage and vindictive actions is not only manifested in financial or material terms. Uncontrolled, uncontained anger directed at our ex-spouse has ramifications for how we think about and feel toward *ourselves*. As discussed in Chapter 3, when our emotions are out of control, we ourselves feel less safe. I cannot emphasize how important it is to take a more moderate and modulated approach—not merely for the sake of the children (who inevitably get caught in the crossfire), but for our own psychological stability.

Sally's priorities were to find a job, set up a stable home life for her son, and understand what mistakes she had made with Robert so she wouldn't repeat them in the next relationship. Her child's needs were quite different: Children need to idealize their parents, and when the message is communicated that one parent is the enemy, the child will be terribly confused and insecure. The longer and more hostile the divorce, the more harmful the psychological effects would be for the child and for the parent-child relationship. Many parents in the throes of a divorce mistakenly think that their ex is the devil incarnate and therefore a terrible parent; we're so angry because of the emotional damage they've caused us that we believe they'll be just as damaging to our children. This is not so.

Although many people are ultimately able to achieve better insight and emotional equanimity about their former spouses, during the divorce itself we tend to be too emotional and embattled to see clearly. Divorce represents a loss not just of our marriage but also of our hopes and dreams. If we find it difficult to tolerate such loss, we are likely to transform it into anger. In our blaming mode, whom better than our ex-spouse to hold responsible for these feelings?

That attitude, however, is like looking to the judge for vindication in the same way that two young siblings look to their parent to adjudicate a dispute. In our competition over who's right and who's wrong, we will be sorely disappointed if we expect a judge to give a final verdict. We must give up the attempt to win that competition, and move on.

To think of our ex-spouse as the enemy does a disservice to the complexity of our feelings. Of course there are negative feelings, or we would not want to end the marriage. But even after so much hurt, positive feelings and memories also remain. Because human relationships are characterized by ambivalence, however certain we may be about our decision to divorce, some amount of reluctance and hesitation is inevitable. It's natural to struggle with those aspects of the marriage that we'll miss, and features of our ex-spouse that we still love. For example, Sally remained attracted to Robert's incisive analytical ability, and there were times when she wished she could still rely on him. And she still had to stop herself from being seduced by his intelligence and sense of humor. Accepting the loss of these positive parts to her relationship with Robert were crucial. They helped Sally begin to gain awareness of her own part in the breakup, and allowed her to realize that placing one hundred percent of the blame on Robert was wrong.

To deny our ambivalence is a major psychological mistake because it means disowning parts of ourselves. This is as true for our ambivalence about a bad marriage as it is for the ambivalence inherent in a more fulfilling, ongoing romantic relationship. When patients ask my advice about whether or not to leave a marriage, I always urge caution. Not because I think it's a mistake to get out of a bad relationship, but because we always need to be aware of the manifold psychological issues that we're playing out. Once we understand what we're responding to, then we can make a more psychologically informed decision.

Separation and Our Sense of Self

As divorce proceedings dragged on, Sally and Robert bickered about everything. Sally did not want Robert to get their dining-room corner cabinet, not because of its monetary value, but because she was so strongly identified with it (it represented her notion of what a beautiful home should look like). Even more important, she could not abide the thought of her ex-husband keeping any part of her, proving to me that she was still emotionally involved with him. Robert took a similarly stubborn, uncompromising attitude toward a financial settlement. His attitude was summed up in a simple statement: "She'll never get her hands on my money."

Back and forth they and their lawyers went, fighting over the most minor points. But what they were really fighting over was an important psychological issue: how to reclaim, redefine, and get back what each had given up to the other in the course of the relationship.

This process of becoming "unmerged" is also a common—and often bitter—part of divorce, but psychologically it is completely understandable. To the extent that we merge with our spouses when we become romatically involved and then marry, when we break up we also must separate our psyches and emotional lives: We need to get back the part of ourselves that resided in our spouse and that we shared with him or her. This is why divorcing couples fight so much about their possessions and money. Couples go through their music collection, divvying up which CD belongs to whom; fight about who gets the season tickets to the Knicks game, and so on. I've even seen couples divide up which restaurants they can go to so they don't have to see each other.

This is another way in which divorce is the flip side of marriage: Instead of a merger and intermingling of selves, it's a reclaiming and redefinition of our self in the opposite direction, an attempt to revert from "we" to a new "I." Continuing divorce battles only serve to underscore the fact that forging a new, postdivorce identity can be particularly hard, especially since the "self" that predated the marriage may be outdated or difficult to reclaim.

Yet such aggressive attempts to establish independence reflect the fact that inside we feel as enmeshed as ever, and not prepared to be separate and autonomous. It is our inner uncertainty, desperation, and doubt ("How in the world will I ever get through this?") that leads to hostile acting out and acrimony. The more confident we are that we can make it on our own, the less likely we will be to fight over trivial issues during the separation and divorce proceedings.

If we have difficulty with boundary setting, we may try to take a psychological shortcut and oversimplify the relationship, painting

everything in stark black and white: We despise everything associated with our ex-spouse and blame her or him for all the failures in
the marriage. There is no acknowledgment of mixed feelings, no
common ground, and thus no way to compromise. And though we
may pay lip service to mutual responsibility for the problems, we
inwardly continue to blame the other for the pain we feel (as manifested in continued legal battles). But it's a kind of brittle boundary
setting that fails to appreciate the continued ways in which we
remain psychologically intertwined with our ex-spouses. (In many
cases, we will maintain a continuing relationship of one sort or
another, if only because of the children.)

Too often we believe that divorce is so wrenching because of
the obstacles our ex-spouse places on our path toward self-definition. We feel as if we're trying to take back our self, and our ex-
spouse resists us. But we don't need our ex-spouse to approve our
self-definition. What's difficult is not the obstacles others place in
our path, but our inner uncertainties and vulnerabilities.

For all these reasons, even though hostility, conflict, and the
demonization of our ex-partner may seem like a way of breaking
free, it is far better to struggle with our ambivalence and work
toward the recognition that the bad outweighed the good.
Revenge can appear to be satisfying, but it does not help us
progress toward independence, self-definition, and a new life
with the possibility of new romantic relationships. Revenge is a
backward-looking focus; but separation and divorce is a time
when we need to look forward.

We Divorce the Way We Marry

It's fascinating to observe that people divorce in the same way
that they marry. We hope that in divorcing we will break free of
the familiar angry, competitive patterns that marked our marriages, but alas, the bitter, vicious cycle of the relationship actu-

ally continues. The ex-partners-to-be become as intensely divided and contentious over how to divorce as they ever were over how to live together. What a grim paradox!

We've all seen it:

- The ex-husband who had withheld financial support during the marriage still won't pay child support or alimony later on.

- The ex-wife who constantly criticized her husband during the marriage snipes at him even more sharply now through mutual friends, family, and the ever-present lawyers.

- The failed businessman who blamed his domineering, take-charge wife for his low self-esteem still lets her take all responsibility for the children's needs, even to arranging play dates during his custody time. She had hoped that in getting out of the marriage, she wouldn't have to shoulder all the responsibility, but she continues to do so willingly. He discovers that he's still unhappy with his career, and she learns that it isn't so easy for her to let others take control.

Stories such as these demonstrate that prolonged divorce battles are really about how we don't uncouple, not about how we do. Instead of breaking off relations, we hold on to the very relationship we claim to want to end. Most startling is the contradiction between the stated aim of the parties—to get out of the unsatisfactory relationship—and their uncompromising, mutually hostile behavior, which only perpetuates the connection. As long as two people can't reach a divorce settlement, each remains a primary psychological figure in the other's life. There's only one difference: This all-important other figure is hated rather than loved.

Moving Beyond the Scorched-Earth Divorce

Not surprisingly, as Sally's therapy continued, the main thrust became helping her get "unstuck." She needed to contain her anger and change her simplistic view of Robert, examine her contribution to the downfall of their marriage, and understand the complex feelings she experienced in the aftermath of this devastating hurt (including how it related to her childhood templates). I pointed out to Sally that in pursuing her scorched-earth divorce, she was continuing the barter game she and Robert had played during their marriage, forcing him to "pay up" for his transgressions. "You need to change your role," I told her, "because until you give up fighting tit-for-tat with him, you won't be free to move forward and do something new with your life."

Gradually, as Sally stopped blaming herself for her "failure" to make Robert continue to love her and slowly began to feel more confident about life on her own, she was able to let go of her anger. After the final divorce papers were signed, she went to work for a home-decorating firm and became quite successful at it. By keeping an eye on the budget she was spending for other people, she learned how to be less extravagant in her own purchases and made do quite well without Robert's credit cards. By her own admission, this "new" Sally was different from the "old" Sally: less materialistic, less angry, and less vulnerable during Robert's weekly custody visits to their son. At our last session, when I reminded Sally of the "scorched earth" she had threatened to leave behind her in the wake of her divorce, she let out an embarrassed laugh and said, "I'm glad I left some greenery, after all."

As I told Sally, when we start to consider divorce, and then after we decide to divorce, we need to remember the following points:

1. It's a mistake to see our spouse as the obstacle to our self-fulfillment, or believe that the key to changing our lives is to get rid of our mate. We must look within for the solution to our frustrations and disappointments.

2. If we're considering divorce, we must make certain we understand why we are unhappy—what we're leaving and what we're going toward.
3. We must ask hard questions about why our marriage didn't work: What was our own contribution, and what was our spouse's contribution to the failures (and successes)? Have we made all efforts to make it work?
4. We need to squarely face our ambivalence about our marriage: What happened to our positive feelings for our spouse? Can we acknowledge our love, attachment, and associated feelings of loss, as well as our anger and bitterness? Can we face our fears about life on our own, as well as our hopes and dreams for this new start?
5. Once we've reached a decision to divorce, we must focus on the psychological process of separation, postdivorce "what's-me-and-what's-you" boundaries.
6. Even though we may feel hurt and vulnerable, we need to control and contain our anger and maintain a multifaceted view of our spouse. Acting out is no solution; a scorched-earth divorce just perpetuates the relationship's destructive, competitive patterns.
7. Letting go of our marriage means letting go of our anger. It is the only way to move forward. We must stop blaming, stop raging, and stop projecting. Even though the marriage may be over, the way we feel about ourselves will continue.
8. Getting unstuck from the past can be quite scary. How many times have I heard someone say, "I can't get involved with anyone because I'm in the midst of a divorce." But to me, this is actually a way of saying, "I'm afraid to get involved with someone new and be hurt again."

Finally, escaping the scorched-earth divorce cycle is difficult, but necessary, in order to move forward with our lives.

11
Reconciling the Past
Healing Ourselves, Forgiving Others

By and large, forgiveness is an ignored topic in psychology. It is more often discussed by religious writers, whose focus tends to be on unburdening the sinner of his guilt: By making an apology, a person who misbehaves (or worse) formally accepts responsibility for the deed, is forgiven, then feels relieved of the burden of guilt.

But what about the *victim's* side of the story? There are many psychological implications of forgiveness for the injured party as well. Our capacity to forgive the transgressor reflects our inner strength and maturity. Conversely, the inability to forgive reflects a need to hold on to anger and bitterness that stems from an inner fragility and negative attitude about ourselves.

In my conceptualization of forgiveness, I am much more interested in the person who does the forgiving than I am in the person who begs forgiveness. As I see it, the one who benefits the most from the act of forgiveness is not the perpetrator but the victim. For when we forgive our partner, we unburden *ourselves* of anger, mistrust, and hurt. We mend relationships that have been damaged, and in repairing our relationships, we heal ourselves.

This is the positive side of the inside-out dynamic: As we learn to forgive others, we also learn to forgive ourselves. Because the object of our anger exists within us, in holding on to that anger, all we do is perpetuate the enemy within. Regardless of the legitimacy of our sense of hurt, our unwillingness to forgive others reflects more about ourselves than it does about others and their actions.

The capacity and willingness to forgive represents a level of personal growth that supersedes anger and the damage to which it can lead. In forgiving, we do not deny the pain or injury others have caused us; we realize that we have enough resilience to absorb it, and to move on. We acknowledge others' hostility toward us, but are not threatened by it.

Others' hostility toward us? Yes, others feel ambivalently toward us, even those who claim to love us dearly. They can harm us, and they often do. Aggression, anger, and competition are facts of life; they pervade all relationships, personal as well as professional. But just because others are aggressive toward us (or competitive and ambitious) does not mean that we must feel aggrieved. When we forgive others, we acknowledge their anger and the pain they caused. But by letting go of our hurt, we can stop the vicious cycle of mistrust; we remain trusting and safe, despite all. As I made clear in Chapter 1, I'm not saying that we should naively and masochistically allow ourselves to be repeatedly hurt, but we do need to let go of our anger.

It is crucial that we forgive others—not merely those we remain actively involved with and continue to love, but also our ex-spouses and former romantic partners whom we no longer see, as well as long-dead—or living—family members who may have harmed us terribly in childhood. We must let go of our anger in order to reconnect with our partners and reestablish trust. Anger tears lovers apart and creates an isolating emotional distance, but forgiveness helps us to move close once again and allow our relationships to flourish. Anger at figures in our past serves no useful purpose, either, since it burdens us with a legacy of bitterness and mistrust that keeps us from moving forward with our lives. Ultimately, the only way to relinquish a view of ourselves as aggrieved victims is to change our perception of others as enemies. That is why I say that in letting go of our hurt, we change the way we think of ourselves; consequently, in forgiving others, we heal ourselves.

Throughout this book we ask the question "Is it you or is it me?" In the face of a clear-cut act of hostility, the answer would seem to be obvious. If you've harmed me, then of course it's "you." You're the one who's at fault. You're the one who's in the wrong. I'm the innocent victim.

We don't change this basic view when we forgive another, but we enrich the answer "It's you" with the further realization that we are strong enough to absorb another's anger and aggression, and that we have a comparable capacity to inflict harm on others. We recognize that "you" may be the one at fault, but I'm not threatened by it (which is why it is crucial that we feel safe in our relationships). We also acknowledge that next time the one to blame could just as easily be "me." This spirit allows forgiveness to heal our relationships and ultimately ourselves.

In forgiving others, we don't deny others' aggression toward us, but we demonstrate to ourselves that we are safe enough to absorb it. This is why it is so difficult to forgive people when we ourselves feel weak, unsafe, and embattled. But once we can handle others' blows with equanimity, then we can break the cycle of retaliation and, more important, change our internal sense of fragility and vulnerability.

Once we come to understand that aggression is an inevitable component of human nature—ours as well as others'—it is easier to forgive others for the damage they cause. *The reluctance to forgive others generally reflects an unwillingness to acknowledge our own aggression.* Rather than pretend that we are wholly innocent, if we see that we have a comparable capacity to inflict pain, we can accept that capability more easily in others. Having done that, we can forgive others for their anger and hostility—and we can forgive ourselves as well.

Letting Go of Anger: Andrea

These were the points I emphasized to Andrea, a public relations executive in her early thirties who came to see me nearly six months after the breakup of her three-year affair with Derek, a successful entertainment lawyer whose suave manner provided cover for a self-centered nature.

When she first came to see me, Andrea was furious with Derek. Their relationship had "gone down in flames," Andrea told me, when Derek's philandering, which she had always suspected, became too flagrant to ignore. That had been six months ago. Yet Andrea talked as if the breakup had occurred only the day before. She felt "aggrieved, injured, completely victimized." Derek had "abused" her trust by his callous treatment, and she blamed him for the pain she felt. "He's the reason I feel so bad," she said more than once, adding that she thought she would never be able to forgive him for what he had done to her.

This breakup, more than any previous ones, had struck a nerve in her. Unable to let go of her anger, she remained preoccupied by Derek, replaying in her head scene after scene of their relationship, wishing that she had told him off, even just once.

Why was she mired in such pain, she asked, while Derek seemed to have gotten away scot-free? She fantasized about having the opportunity to treat him as insensitively as she perceived him to have treated her. She kept waiting, hoping that he might see the error of his ways and apologize for—or at least acknowledge—his actions. But in the six months since their breakup, he had shown not a hint of remorse. On the one occasion when

Derek did call to "see what would happen if we got together one night," she felt no sense of vindication in her rejection of his interest. All this incident did was prove once again what a philandering "S.O.B." he was, since by this time he had a new steady girlfriend.

The more she talked the more it struck me that Andrea's was a brooding anger that she nursed with exceptional care. Being angry at Derek gave her a certain strength; it enabled her to make it to work every day and helped her to pass the time during the evening as she plotted revenge. Without this anger, she was afraid she'd fall apart. Anger gave Andrea a purpose in life, something and somebody to focus on.

Andrea was in no way ready to get involved with someone new, although she met many men who were interested in her. When they called her, she put them off. On the rare occasion when she agreed to go on a date, her prickly temper and irritability let the men know right off the bat that she was, as she herself admitted, a "handful."

Why was Andrea holding on to her anger and bitterness at Derek with such fervor? Why wasn't she moving forward with her life, allowing herself to get involved with one or another of these new men? The answer was that her breakup was only the proximate cause of her hurt feelings. The reason it had the power to wound her so deeply was because it had resonated with a series of unsatisfying prior relationships and a toxic childhood history that had taught her that men were not to be trusted.

As we examined Andrea's feelings more carefully, I discerned that underlying her anger at Derek was a feeling of being completely unlovable. She had held on to her relationship with Derek, against her better judgment, because she thought that it was the most she could expect from a man. Her father had been an unreliable alcoholic who had had numerous extramarital affairs himself, and her mother had been extremely bitter about it. Andrea's mother had been so needy that she felt she had no choice but to put up with her husband's behavior. Like her mother, Andrea felt victimized and bitter, but also confused and uncertain, wondering whether she had done something to turn Derek off.

By holding on to her anger at Derek and keeping him as the central psychological figure in her life, Andrea was actually holding on to that relationship. Letting go of her anger would mean having to let go of Derek and deal with the emptiness she felt within. Andrea thought she lacked the strength to deal with the failure she felt herself to be. I told Andrea she had psychological resources and real-life options to pick up the pieces and move on that her mother never had. The mistake her mother made, and the one Andrea was in danger of making, was to perpetuate herself in the role of victim: She saw herself as someone without options, who was unlovable and deserved nothing better, who didn't have the strength to bounce back from the trials and tribulations of life.

As long as Derek remained the central focus of her life, Andrea was in essence tied to a demoralizing and unsatisfying relationship. The fact that she had put off the men who expressed interest in her suggested that she thought herself so emotionally frail that she could not afford to make herself vulnerable. She believed her distance protected her, but from what I could tell, all it did was perpetuate her self-image as fragile and unable to be loved.

"As paradoxical as it sounds," I told her, "your anger at Derek is really anger at yourself. You wasted years in a dead-end relationship. You feel ripped off by him, but your own poor judgment is responsible for how you feel." The only way Andrea would be able to let go of her anger at Derek was to let herself off the hook: Acknowledge her mistakes, accept them, learn from them, and move on. I continued, "When you can let go of your anger at yourself, you'll be able to let go of your anger toward Derek, and then you'll be ready to meet someone new."

Gradually, over the course of many weekly sessions, Andrea began to understand that her feelings of fragility long predated her relationship with Derek, and that his mistreatment of her merely confirmed what she thought about herself, which itself derived from her childhood template. That's why he had struck such a powerful chord in her. In coming to terms with herself and her own history, Andrea began the process of forgiving herself for being weak and unlovable, and that in turn led to her forgiving Derek. It was only by reaching a peace with the enemy within that she could come to terms with her apparent enemy outside.

Forgiveness is about letting go of anger, yet moving beyond anger is admittedly difficult to achieve. Once we've demonized somebody, how do we transform that image and begin to see the person differently?

Let me make an analogy. In a successful psychotherapy, an interesting change occurs, which signals it's time to terminate the therapy: The patient's harsh judgments of people begin to soften and become more nuanced. Whereas before they saw only the negative sides of people's personalities, now they begin to see some positive sides as well. How does this relate to forgiveness? As we've seen, the fact that people are multifaceted explains why our feelings about them are characterized by so much ambivalence: We like the good sides, dislike the bad sides, and are not so certain about the gray in-between. We recognize that one and the same person can call forth both our like and our dislike. Forgiveness represents the fundamental acceptance of this ambivalence. Forgiving others does not mean ignoring the negative, it means perceiving people in all their complexity. They may have done something bad to us, but they're not all bad.

Forgiveness is a by-product of any successful therapy. We come to see that others are not all that different from us. They have their hopes and fears, anger and love, wounds and struggles, just as we do. They may do us harm, but we may do harm to them. They are not the devil, and we are not so righteous. There's a huge, gray, confusing middle ground that most of us live in, where there are no clear-cut enemies, nor any clear-cut saviors.

And so I knew the therapy with Andrea had taken hold when her preoccupation with Derek began to lessen. She talked more about her parents, who in different ways had left her feeling terrible about herself. With this shift in focus, Andrea tacitly acknowledged that the way she felt had less to do with Derek than with herself and her childhood history.

At first, the story Andrea told about her parents was uniformly negative. She spoke of the many times her father disappointed her and described him in the most malevolent terms. She recounted incident after incident in which her mother exhibited an embittered self-pity that her father had used as the excuse to explain his escape into alcohol and extramarital affairs. But eventually, Andrea's negative preoccupation gave way to some happy memories: of her mother reading *Little Women* and other books aloud to her, and of taking long weekend walks in the country with her father. Her parents may not have been the greatest, but there had been some bright spots. Without saying as much, Andrea learned to forgive her parents for their shortcomings; she even showed a fair amount of sympathy once she was able to understand them in terms of the choices they faced at that time.

Therapy interweaves past and present. In coming to terms with her past, Andrea learned to come to terms with her present. She learned to differentiate between her toxic parental memories and the men she encountered now. Some of these men were just as problematic as her parents had been (although she was not in a position to be harmed by them as she had been by her parents), but others were much healthier and the relationships had potential. More important, Andrea was learning to tell the difference. Having forgiven her parents, Andrea no longer needed to play out the legacy of her anger in her current relationships. By letting go of the past, she had become unstuck in time. In doing so, she opened herself to the possibility of a different kind of relationship, which she soon found with Michael, a responsible, caring man.

Near the end of Andrea's treatment, I asked her what had been the most meaningful aspect of the therapy for her. She said, "Looking back, I can now see what a bitch I was to a whole string of men, including Michael, even Derek, although he sort of deserved it. But most of all, I was a pain in the ass to you since you saw the uncensored version of me. Still, I always knew that you wouldn't give up on me, and would stand by me through thick and thin. I knew that you liked me, no matter how I behaved. You always had more confidence that a man would love me than I did. But once I let Michael in, I came to see that you were right. Sometimes, I look at him and I'm amazed that he has stayed with me."

What Andrea finally learned was to forgive herself for how she behaved with Derek, with Michael, and also with me. As always, if we can forgive ourselves, we can forgive others.

Forgiveness Is Not a Sign of Weakness

It is a common misconception that forgiveness is a sign of weakness. In our cynical world, where too many of us look for every advantage, if someone feels guilty, we are advised to use it as leverage to get what we want. It's payback time; even if we don't retaliate, we believe that we should seek retribution. In this view, having been injured gives us the upper hand, and if we don't exact some kind of penance, we'd be a "jerk," as one patient said about her relationship with her husband. (This patient went on a buying spree every time her husband "misbehaved.") But this kind of quid pro quo has nothing to do with true forgiveness; it's merely a way of gaining a tactical advantage.

Retribution works, my patients tell me. If their romantic partners thought they wouldn't have to pay for their transgressions, they would have free license to do whatever they wanted. They engage in complex calculations of perceived strength and weakness within relationships, and if they have an advantage, they feel compelled to use it. In this scenario, their partner's guilt puts them in a position of strength that should not be ceded without getting something in return. No wonder they view forgiveness as giving up a tactical advantage.

I'm often shocked when patients offer this cynical rationale; to buy in to it is to reduce romantic relationships to a mere jockeying for position. How can they believe this works? Using such a strategy may get them something they want—a spouse who walks on eggshells around them for a few days, or an empty apology—but it leaves unchanged the cycle of guilt and retribution. Once the partners have paid for their "crimes," the slate is wiped clean and they are once again free to misbehave.

Is this forgiveness? Is this letting go of anger? By no means. Far from working through feelings of guilt and responsibility, far from forgiveness, this approach serves to reinforce antagonistic feelings and mistrustful preconceptions. It continues the sense of mutual mistrust.

True forgiveness is much different. It reshapes our view of others—no longer are we enemies who take advantage of each other's weakness—and may also reshape our partner's view of us.

It is impossible to consider forgiveness without also addressing the issue of apologies. Apologies represent the perpetrator's effort to reconnect with his or her partner and repair the relationship. Sincere apologies are crucial, but not mandatory, in helping us decide that we are safe enough to trust our partner once again. We need this evidence because we will make ourselves vulnerable only if we are convinced that it is safe to do so. Apologies help us to make that determination. But how do we determine whether an apology is sincere or insincere, and whether a relationship is safe or is likely to hurt us again and again?

Needless to say, there are no hard and fast rules for evaluating someone's sincerity. Each situation and each relationship is different. How much is the right amount of wariness, and when have we gone overboard, into a mind-set of mistrust? This is the problem we face when we are asked to accept our partner's apology. When should we reestablish trust and when would it be masochistic to do so?

The reason I endorse a "forgive and remember" approach is that it strikes a balance between trust and self-protection. When we keep in mind the prior misdeed, we are unlikely to be harmed over and over. Isolated, out-of-character incidents of hostility are of much less concern to me than continued, repeated patterns. Over time, we know from another's behavior whether or not they were sincere, and so it makes little difference whether or not we're fooled by someone's empty apology. By contrast, we're never fooled by patterns of behavior, which is all that matters anyway. Despite people's promises to turn over a new leaf, the real issue is whether they do, in fact, change the way they behave.

Finding the Capacity to Forgive

Forgiveness is like therapy in that it does not come in an instantaneous epiphany. It is a process occurring over time. As with many psychological processes, there is no single way to achieve forgiveness. Some of us process it consciously by talking it through with the person who harmed us, or thinking about it from many different angles; others process it unconsciously through dreams; still others are able to turn the other cheek and not give the hurt another thought.

In fact, we should not presuppose that forgiveness is the goal we seek. When forgiveness is a stated goal—which is often the case with certain religious and pacifistic types—it very well may represent a denial of anger and aggression. Rather, forgiveness is a by-product of realistic trust and openness. I liken it to a state of mind, a feeling of connectedness that acknowledges the harm people do to one another.

In many ways, forgiveness resembles the psychological process of mourning and grief. In grieving, we come to terms with the fact that someone we love is lost to us forever. Forgiveness means accepting another kind of loss—that someone has disappointed or damaged us. What has been lost is our idealized relationship, as we are forced to give up the belief that someone can and will care for us exactly as we require. Just as holding on to anger (often unconsciously directed at the person who died) can prolong grief, holding on to our anger at the person who harmed us prevents us from forgiving him or her. Viewed this way, both grieving and forgiveness are psychological processes of accepting loss, and in both cases the process of accepting loss can be delayed or prevented by the continued presence of anger. If we can hold the loss within us without blaming or acting out, then we can grieve successfully as well as forgive successfully.

Forgiveness bespeaks a more textured experience of the world, a mature attitude that seeks to repair relationships and renew connections. It is neither appeasement nor emotional blackmail; nor is it denying that damage has been done. Forgiveness is being fully aware of pain, and feeling resilient enough to move on. In forgiving, we discover that anger (whether ours or others') is not so destructive as we fear, and we learn that we as well as others are fairly resilient. We may think that forgiveness is about letting others off the hook. More important, forgiving others is about forgiving ourselves.

12
Going Forward
Insight, Mastery, Tolerance

I have written this book to help you on a journey that takes place inside yourself.

I began this book with the observation that all too often we turn our emotions and attitudes inside out and blame others for feeling the way we do. We may fall prey to any number of distorted perceptions that derail our relationships: We hold others responsible for our own vulnerability; find others untrustworthy because we ourselves have difficulty trusting; see enemies and adversaries among our closest loved ones; become angry at others because of our own disappointments; or feel we're not well taken care of but won't let others take care of us.

Perhaps most destructive of all, we become caught up in a cycle of mistrust and anger that leads us continually to escalate our quarrels, with increasingly destructive results. I've shown how men and women have somewhat different flashpoints in relationships, and that sex makes all of us particularly vulnerable. And I've described how, when relationships deteriorate beyond salvation, they can ignite a firestorm of hostility that destroys everything in its path.

But most important of all, I've also demonstrated that change is possible, with three important tools: insight, mastery, and tolerance. First, we need to change the way we think. Then, we must change the way we behave. And finally, if that still doesn't make us feel better, we just need to learn how to live with uncomfortable feelings.

Insight

Psychological insight provides us with the understanding that even though intimate relationships inevitably evoke uncomfortable feelings, other people are not responsible for these feelings; they come from within us.

We ask the question "Is it you or is it me?" Insight is what provides us with an exceptional clarity about who's doing what to whom. Insight offers a lucid vision that helps us make our way in life.

- Insight helps us identify our mind-sets, our propensity to view life through our own filter and thus to distort and misinterpret events and relationships. The mind-set of mistrust is one of the most dangerous of these emotional slide projectors because it is so circular and self-fulfilling. But with insight, we are able to compensate for our perceptual biases and see others and ourselves more accurately and realistically.

- Insight helps us discern repetitive patterns in our relationships, which by definition mean that "it" can't all be someone else's fault, since we play out these same patterns in vastly different situations and with a range of different people from childhood through adulthood. Thus, it is insight that helps us to apportion responsibility appropriately in relationships: how much is it me and my emotional baggage, and how much is you and your emotional baggage? What are my projections and what are your projections?

- Insight allows us to set good psychological boundaries, a clear but flexible sense of who I am and who you are. The more emotionally involved we get with someone, the more merged we feel. Insight is the understanding that we can be simultaneously enmeshed and yet separate. Insight teaches us that we cannot control others (although we can influence them) and shows us how to accept their autonomy without being threatened by it (or made jealous by it).

- Insight is the recognition that all personal relationships engender uncomfortable emotions, especially anxiety (that others may not reciprocate our feelings), anger (when they hurt our feelings), frustration (when they don't live up to our expectations or when the reality of daily life sets in), disappointment (when our idealizations prove unrealistic), and sadness (when we face inevitable losses). Insight explains to us that just because these emotions are ignited by our relationships is no reason for us to hold others accountable.

- Insight helps us to understand that when we're not getting what we want, maybe we're not putting ourselves in a position to get what we want. Others cannot and will never do a perfect job of caring for us.

- Insight allows us to accept the fact that anger and competition are a part of human nature and will pervade all relationships, even with those who love us the most.

- Insight is what helps us to see that our partner is not our enemy. Bad things may happen, and we and others certainly have faults, but the gift of insight lets us develop a more nuanced, textured vision whereby we can take into account our ambivalent feelings without splitting them off or projecting them onto others. If we're able to see that people are multifaceted—not just one thing or the other—we will have come a long way toward gaining insight.

Mastery

Mastery of our uncomfortable emotions means, first and foremost, owning up to them rather than turning them inside out. But mastery goes beyond an awareness that our emotions emanate from within. In my view, the only way to feel in control of our lives is to control our emotions. That is why acting out, denial, deflection, and avoidance are not effective solutions. Although others may provoke and stimulate our feelings, emotional control always resides inside.

- Mastery means being able to modulate our emotions in order to express ourselves effectively. Emotions that merely spew out or are regurgitated are not useful. We need to contain and give shape to our emotions rather than diffuse them or act on them.

- Mastery means finding constructive solutions to the situations and relationships evoking negative emotions. To do that, we first must understand what we are reacting to (the connection between interpersonal causes and emotional effects). We must then consider possible strategies (how various means will lead to different ends)— and only then, after we've weighed these possibilities, choose the best solution.

- Mastery involves figuring out how to get what we want when we're not getting it. Venting, blaming, and complaining get us nothing.

- Mastery protects our relationships from the destructive consequences of our anger. It keeps us from escalating when we're tempted to do so. Mastery thus creates a safety net which allows trust to flourish.

- Finally, mastery means learning how to assert ourselves without being angry; knowing how to fight for our own interests while others fight for theirs; and becoming comfortable negotiating solutions and compromises that are mutually satisfactory.

Tolerance

When there's nothing more we can do about our uncomfortable emotions—when insight and mastery have taken us as far as they can—then we must develop the capacity to tolerate those emotions. Tolerance means learning how to sit with uncomfortable emotions (such as depression, disappointment, frustration, anxiety, or anger) when there is nothing we can do about them. Feelings abate despite our belief that they won't. Tolerance and patience thus become our fallbacks when all else fails.

- Tolerance means developing a thicker skin, so we're less emotionally sensitive to the touch, and feel less vulnerable and easily bruised. We need to appreciate our own inner strength, which in turn gives us the confidence to face possible hurt and harm with the knowledge that we have the resilience to bounce back. Tolerance is the security that comes from knowing that even though others may be hostile, competitive, or merely apathetic, we can handle it.

- Tolerance helps us to accept loss.

- As we develop this capacity for tolerance, we realize that others possess a similar capacity. That means that they can also handle our anger, our competition, and the frustrations and hurts that we may mete out.

- Tolerance is what gives us the capacity to accept people's shortcomings, and to forgive others and ourselves.

- Tolerance gives us the freedom to experience a full range of emotions without escaping them. Ultimately, tolerance means holding on to our ambivalence, for only by sitting with that ambivalence will we find ways to resolve it. It may sound like a Confucian proverb, but it's true: We have to sit with our confusion to find clarity in our lives.

Soothing Ourselves

One of the ways we learn to tolerate life's blows is by knowing how to soothe ourselves. Once we have the ability to soothe ourselves, we're in a much better position to show others how to soothe us. Whether it's taking a warm bath after a hard day, reading a novel, listening to music, strolling through the park, or going on vacation, we need to know how to treat ourselves well. When we have the confidence that we can soothe and care for ourselves, we find it easier to trust in others as well as in ourselves.

Beyond these concrete steps there are other strategies, psychological ones. When bad things happen, we must remind ourselves that all is not lost. We can counteract our uncomfortable negative emotions with more positive ideas. Sometimes this means doing things that we know will make us feel good. At other times it means understanding what it is that is making us feel bad and doing something about it. And we must recognize that the key to our happiness lies within us, not in others.

In learning to soothe ourselves, we cultivate an inner emotional barometer that helps us measure what feels good and what doesn't. When we deny, dissociate, and project our emotions, this emotional barometer cannot function properly and gives false readings. Once we reclaim our own emotions, however, we can begin to correct and fine-tune that barometer. The better we understand our emotions and give weight to our own perceptions about relationships, the better able we will be to calibrate and regulate that emotional barometer, and the more we'll be able to trust it.

The ability realistically to read and then effectively to adjust this internal emotional barometer will buoy us through life's ups and downs. Our internal barometer reflects and gauges our stable self-concept and stable self-esteem. This stable self-concept is like money in the bank; we're able to draw on it whenever it's needed: It's that reassuring sense that we're still standing when everything is going down around us. It's the feelings of worthiness regardless of what rejections or frustrations we may experience, regardless of what losses or traumas come our way.

Being able to soothe ourselves also means being able to adjust and regulate our moods. In contrast to a weather barometer, which is wholly dependent on the outside atmosphere, a well-tuned emotional barometer is independent of external events. We can't let our sense of ourselves be wholly contingent on external events and relationships or what people expect of us. We can't experience ourselves through other people, and we need to know that we exist and will survive despite what goes on outside us. The ability to soothe ourselves thus provides us with perspective: the knowledge that we have had good experiences in the past and that we will have more good experiences in the future. The ability to care for ourselves lies within us.

The Process of Change

When thinking about how people change in life, it may be useful to examine how people change in therapy, which is what we have been doing in the case histories described throughout this book. Unfortunately, all too many men and women don't make it into therapy because they don't perceive the "problem" as residing within them but see other people as the problem. These edgy, angry, and mistrustful individuals are poor candidates for psychotherapy, even when they do show up in my office.

As we saw in many of the case histories, when patients do come to see me it's usually with the implicit request that I change their partner. Such patients may come into couples therapy with their partners or may even be patients in individual therapy who spend the whole time complaining about their partners. In either case, the message is clear at the outset: "Change my partner, and I'll feel better." There is no acknowledgment of their own contribution to their bad feelings or the role they may play in a bad situation.

As therapy progresses, many of these individuals become uncomfortable with the whole process: They don't trust me, they suspect my motives, they accuse me of being there not to help them but because what I really want is money, power, or some form of ego gratification. They play out their suspicion and mistrust in the arena of the therapy. They're uncomfortable with the openness of therapy, the submissiveness of it, and the one-sidedness of it (since I don't make parallel disclosures or make myself vulnerable to them as they do with me). If and when the therapy does overcome these initial obstacles, these patients inevitably enact the same anger and hostility in therapy that they do in their romantic or family lives.

"Is that good or bad?" you may ask. In my view, when therapy works it's in large part because my patients discover that when they do enact these aggressive patterns, I can tolerate their anger and survive their ruthlessness. Seeing and experiencing that interaction changes their basic assumptions about themselves and others.

Hostility unfolds progressively in psychotherapy. At first patients may try to protect me from their anger. Then, when their anger inevitably does emerge, they can't believe that I don't retaliate. They may even read in signs of retaliation when none exist. Gradually, over time, they come to see that I'm on their side, that I'm not hurt by their anger, and that I'm more resilient than they imagined. As they watch me digest and metabolize their anger, they learn to metabolize it themselves.

This realization spills over into life outside therapy: They find that other people in their lives (whether a new boyfriend or a spouse of many years with whom a new pattern develops) can also tolerate their anger. With this insight in hand, they gain more control over their emotions and feel less compelled to enact the old counterproductive patterns over and over. They thus change their preconceptions and expectations of others as they change their ideas about themselves.

At the outset of therapy, patients often feel a good deal of relief that there is a sympathetic person who will help them with their pain and struggles. It's in the middle phase of therapy that patients often begin to feel somewhat sad and depressed. This happens once they've begun to develop enough insight to see that they contribute to their own problems. Insight keeps them from turning to their former negative strategies like venting and blaming as a solution. Instead, they're forced to do the hard work of therapy from within.

I've had patients at this stage of therapy dream of being trapped in quicksand, an image I interpret as the regressive mud and muck of their neurotic patterns. In these quicksand dreams, as in their relationships prior to beginning therapy, their inclination is to act out immediately (which only gets them stuck further) or to helplessly scream for help (which does no good). As therapy progresses, they begin to see that only by thinking through the problem and taking small but effective actions will they be able to pull themselves out of the quicksand.

The recognition that blaming, externalizing, and acting out do no good can be quite sobering. For this reason, it is particularly important to develop the capacity to bear and tolerate depression. There are no major breakthroughs in therapy, no magical light bulbs going off that illuminate and solve the problem permanently and completely. Rather, therapeutic success comes through the gradual accumulation of effort and experience: trying and failing, and trying again.

Over time, after repeatedly working through their particular issues, my patients gain enough insight to recognize the dysfunctional patterns they have fallen into without my having to point these out to them. Eventually they become impatient with themselves, worried that they will screw up another relationship or another opportunity yet again. This impatience with their old neurotic ways and awareness of what those patterns have cost them in terms of their life and happiness gives them the motivation to take the difficult steps to move forward.

One of the key issues of the final phase of therapy is the patient's belief that I am responsible for the positive changes in their lives, and that once they terminate, they will lose all the progress they have gained. My job is to show them that the changes exist within them, and will remain with them, and that they will continue to reap ever greater dividends long after we've stopped meeting. I tell them the door is always open to them, but that at this point I see myself as superfluous.

One patient's dream illustrates this awareness. Although problems still remained even at the termination of a long therapy, he came to see that he had the ability to cope with them. In his dream, Nick was lost in a building with no electricity. Fortunately, he was carrying a flashlight. Nonetheless, he was waiting for someone to rescue him, at which point I showed up with my arm in a sling. Without my help, Nick found his way out of the building using his flashlight. He then discovered that he had to dig a mass grave for dozens of corpses and skeletons lying outside the building. Since my arm was in a sling, I was useless; but it turned out that not everyone was dead, and he got help from those who were still alive.

To me, this is not an unusual end-of-therapy dream. Nick was concerned that he would not find his way in life, when in fact he possessed the resources (a flashlight) to do so on his own. Cleaning up the mess he had made of his life and past relationships—the skeletons in his closet—was represented in the dream by his having to dig a mass grave. The figure of the one-armed therapist showed Nick's dawning recognition that he didn't need me to make his happiness. There was more work for Nick to do in his life, but he didn't have to be in therapy. He had gained the insight, mastery, and tolerance to go forward on his own.

In attempting to answer the question "Is it you or is it me?," I've tried to provide an appreciation of the complex, intermingled ways in which we contribute to the problems in our relationships. Above all we need to remember that our relationships are reflections of our inner lives, not of other people's influence;

whether or not others change is largely irrelevant to our own process of change. It is always futile to wait for others to change in order to move forward ourselves. Each person needs to start now to change from within and become the true master of his or her fate.

Index